Praise for *Love M.*

"In *Love Me True*, Jason Whiting boldly tackles the most important component of successful romantic relationships: truth.

I was amazed by how many angles were covered and by all of the ways we can distort, avoid, or rationalize relationship interactions. But these concepts do not overwhelm the reader. The book is clear, well-organized and full of stories which bring academic concepts to life for everyone. It is full of suggestions on how to think differently about tough relationship issues, and it provides helpful tools to have difficult but kind conversations."

—Ty Tashiro, PhD, author of *The Science of Happily Ever After* and *Awkward: The Science of Why We're Socially Awkward and Why That's Awesome*

"What a gem! I really loved *Love Me True* and was impressed at the research made usable for all couples. Whether you are trying to improve your relationship, understand why your past relationships have fallen short, or work with couples trying to find true love, Jason Whiting's book has much to offer. It is engaging and includes many examples from Dr. Whiting's marriage, clinical work, and research. It is hard to put down!"

—Sandra M. Stith, PhD, author of *Couples Therapy for Domestic Violence: Finding Safe Solutions*

"Reading this book is like taking your favorite class from a smart and engaging teacher. You'll get access to the author's wide experiences with real couples, along with the fruits of contemporary research. You'll have a better shot at getting an 'A' in being honest, open, and healthy in your own relationships!"

—William J. Doherty, PhD, author of *Take Back Your Marriage: Sticking Together in a World that Pulls Us Apart*

"*Love Me True* pulled me in right away—it's compelling, expertly written, and will take couples on a journey to help them understand what they need, why they need it, and how to communicate to achieve it. This book helps us see ourselves honestly and build a close, enriching relationship."

—Kathrine Hertline, PhD, author of *Systemic Sex Therapy* and *The Couple and Family Technology Framework: Intimate Relationships in a Digital Age*

"In *Love Me True*, Whiting advocates honesty with kindness and describes virtuous behaviors that build safety, trust, compassion, and passion. He shows the reader how to create the kind of relationship that heals and calls out the best in us, often through engaging stories and compelling science. The result is a book both helpful and hopeful."

—Fred P. Piercy, PhD, author of *Research Methods in Family Therapy* and editor, *Journal of Marital and Family Therapy*

"A rare author that keeps us laughing while gently looking inward, Whiting inspires greater authenticity in ourselves and each other. Through true-to-life experience, solid content, and Monty Python references, Whiting provides practical steps toward compassionate honesty. The summary content and discussion questions make it all the more user-friendly. *Love Me True* is savvy and personal."
—Kay Bradford, PhD, professor of Family, Consumer, and Human Development, Utah State University

"This engaging book will lead readers on a path of insight and relationship growth. Written in an easy-to-follow, easy-to-apply style, the chapters are filled with techniques to help couples overcome bad habits and create authentic connection. It is a must-read for those interested in healthy, vibrant relationships."
—Stephen T. Fife, PhD, author of *Couples in Treatment* and *Techniques for the Couple Therapist*

"Relationships don't come with a manual, but this book gives couples tools to build a strong bond. It is a fascinating look at how relationships get confused, and how they can find clarity."
—Lee Johnson, PhD, author of *Advanced Methods of Family Therapy Research*

"With a blend of research and storytelling, Jason Whiting shows how we deceive ourselves and others in large and small ways. With a strong emphasis on kindness as well as self-care, Whiting explains how you can obtain deeper intimacy through authenticity."
—Scott Stanley, PhD, author of *The Power of Commitment*

"Wow! I expected to read *Love Me True* from a professional perspective, but I became fully engaged and was personally inspired by the many entertaining examples and insights. With a humorous and humble approach, Dr. Whiting presents a compelling appeal for the truth. He inspires us to enjoy real love through integrity and backs up his insights with experience. It is an awesome book!"
—Lenore McWey, PhD, professor of Marriage and Family Therapy, Florida State University

"Written by one of the field's sharpest thinkers and compassionate clinicians, *Love Me True* draws you into yourself in such a sensitive, convincing way that you almost can't help but change for the better. You need to read this book—you'll be surprised at the subtle ways you're sabotaging connection in your relationships and how easy and freeing it is to get out of your own way and allow the relationship you've always wanted to emerge."
—Sean Davis, PhD, author of *Common Factors in Couple and Family Therapy* and *Family Therapy: Concepts and Methods*

Love Me True

Overcoming the Surprising Ways We Deceive in Relationships

JASON B. WHITING, PhD, LMFT

PLAIN SIGHT
PUBLISHING

An imprint of Cedar Fort, Inc.
Springville, Utah

ISBN 13: 978-1-4621-1861-8

Published by Plain Sight Publishing, an imprint of Cedar Fort, Inc.
2373 W. 700 S., Springville, UT 84663
Distributed by Cedar Fort, Inc., www.cedarfort.com

LIBRARY OF CONGRESS CATALOGING-IN-PUBLICATION DATA

Names: Whiting, Jason B., author.
Title: Love me true : overcoming the surprising ways we deceive in relationships / Jason B. Whiting, PhD, LMFT.
Description: Springville, Utah : Plain Sight Publishing, [2016]
Identifiers: LCCN 2016030604 (print) | LCCN 2016038300 (ebook) | ISBN 9781462118618 (perfect bound : alk. paper) | ISBN 9781462126538 (epub, pdf, mobi)
Subjects: LCSH: Interpersonal relations. | Deception. | Self-deception.
Classification: LCC HM1106 .W4585 2016 (print) | LCC HM1106 (ebook) | DDC 001.9/5--dc 3
LC record available at https://lccn.loc.gov/2016030604

Cover design by M. Shaun McMurdie
Cover design © 2016 by Cedar Fort, Inc.
Edited and typeset by Jennifer Johnson

Printed in the United States of America

10 9 8 7 6 5 4 3 2 1

Printed on acid-free paper

For April, of course.

Contents

Introduction
Connection and Confusion

The meeting of two personalities is like the contact of two chemical substances:
If there is any reaction, both are transformed.

Carl Jung

It was the night before his wedding, and Neil McArdle knew he was forgetting something. His fiancée Amy had asked him to reserve St. George's Hall in Liverpool for the ceremony, and as he was heading for bed, he realized what was nagging at him. He never booked the hall. So, he did what any desperate man in love would do. He called in a bomb threat.

It seemed logical at the time. He figured his party could slip in and have the wedding while the other groups evacuated. On the morning of the big day he went out early, telling Amy he was going to see his mum. Amy became suspicious: "I remember asking him why, because we would be seeing her very soon." She was right to worry. He went to a corner pay phone and called the hall. In his best fake voice, he said, "This is not a hoax call. There's a bomb in St. George's Hall, and it will go off in 45 minutes."

When Neil returned, things were heating up. He was supposed to have reserved a car but had forgotten that too, so he told Amy there were none available. Amy became agitated as Neil called a taxi, and they sped off.

When they arrived, Amy was stunned to see the chaos of police sirens blaring and bomb experts combing the hall. She tried to talk to the staff, but Neil held her off. "His mannerisms were odd and he seemed nervous and edgy," she recalled. "But I put it down to wedding jitters so I carried on." Things escalated when she pushed through to the concierge and asked what would happen with her wedding, and was told there had never been a reservation.

Amy exploded. She said, "Neil and I had a proper row in front of everyone, as you would do in that situation. I was screaming at him, asking him why he is so stupid."

Amy's sister started to suspect that Neil was behind the fake bomb threat. She joined the attack, and Neil ran for his life. Amy said, "It was a total disaster, and one-by-one, I watched my family and guests leave before I was left standing outside, in my dress and on my own."[1]

We sympathize with Neil and Amy. Many couples fall in love, then fall apart. Otherwise mature partners get flustered, make excuses, and even betray each other. Neil ended up rethinking his relationship skills in jail, and Amy moved on. "I don't think I'll ever marry now," she said. "I don't ever want to see him again." How did they go from crazy in love to just plain crazy?

Neil and Amy may be an extreme example, but all couples experience deception. *Love Me True* shows how easy it is to become deceptive in relationships, and how this plays a role in almost every problem couples experience. Deception happens in what partners say and in what they see.

Deception in What We Say

Subtle fibs are surprisingly common. Take Neil and Amy. He falsely assured her he would take care of wedding details and said things were under control when they weren't. Neil's dodging was for supposed "good" reasons, like reassuring Amy and keeping the peace. But these small fabrications led to big problems. When his lies caught up with him he didn't come clean, because he didn't want to let Amy down. His barrister friend recalled, "She looked amazing. He just could not get out the words to . . . tell her what he had not done." *Love Me True* will discuss little lies and rationalizations, as well as more serious betrayals and accusations. Stories of real couples and findings from research will give guidance on how to be more honest and strengthen trust.

Deception in What We See

In relationship wars, truth is the first casualty. When Neil panicked, he lost touch with reality and his judgment went from bad to worse. Instead of honestly trying to make things better, he covered his tracks. His denial led to irrational plans of disguised voices and bomb threats, but these actions exploded in his face. When Amy figured out what was going on, she became enraged and saw Neil as the enemy. She attacked, and he retreated. They went from a happy couple on the verge of marriage to angry foes. Emotions are drugs that alter what people see, and these chapters discuss proven ways to soothe emotions and increase understanding.

Authentic Connection

Perhaps if Neil and Amy had been more honest they might still be together. Maybe if he had admitted his mistake on his wedding day he might have reinforced openness and authenticity in their relationship, and they could have worked through those early bumps with some straight talk. Being authentic takes commitment, and *Love Me True* is here to help. Couples can learn how to see more clearly, have important conversations that bind them together, and stoke fires of passion.

The Journey to the Truth

Most people want to find love, but after they do, it can contain unpleasant surprises. Why do lovers like Neil and Amy attract and repel each other like crazed, subatomic particles? What causes these operatic swings in emotion, from ecstasy one minute to misery the next? To get answers, I have spent my career interviewing and observing lovers about their perceptions and actions and reading piles of studies on the mysteries of love. From this I have learned that partners are highly reactive to each other. They connect and transform, sometimes building each other up and sometimes tearing each other down. These interactions often include confusing and deceptive elements. However, I found that even the crankiest couples could identify and admit their deceptive practices. They didn't usually see it during conflict, but they could when they were calm and reflective. Awareness often led to insights and improvement, and this is why *Love Me True* was written. It provides credible information to help partners step back, see differently, and grow closer.

Regardless of the state of your relationship, you will identify with the stories in *Love Me True*. Have you ever had an argument with your mate that left you frustrated? Did your partner misrepresent you or say something that wasn't accurate? Have you ever exaggerated something or tried to sound innocent? If so, you are in good company. Read on and learn how to clear out the clutter and connect in true love.

Part I
Deception in What We Say

Chapter 1
Dishonesty and Deception

The secret of life is honesty and fair dealing. If you can fake that, you've got it made.

Groucho Marx

Love and Lying

[From a text message posted online]:

Hi babe, what are you doing?

Nothing much, I'm really tired. Just going to sleep now babe. And you?

In the club standing behind you.

Most people consider themselves to be pretty darn honest, but ironically, this is not honest. People deceive themselves and their partners with alarming frequency, which may be why so many stories about love are dripping with deception and betrayal. Here are just a few Lifetime movie titles that should be said in a dramatic announcer's voice: *Seduced by Lies. Cyber Seduction: His Secret Life.* And best of all, *Stranger in My Bed.*

Before you become too convinced of your own honesty, consider these questions: Do you ever do something and not tell your partner? Have you used excuses to avoid responsibilities, like, "I am really busy this afternoon," or, "I didn't understand what you meant when you asked me to . . ." Have you pretended to not hear your spouse when they are calling from the other room? Said you were too tired to help with the dishes or be intimate? Some act like they are listening, then say, "I know exactly what you mean," when they really don't. Others get annoyed but say, "I'm fine!" In this chapter, we will discuss why deception is so common, the effect it has on relationships, and whether lies are ever acceptable. We will start with a love story that could be made into a Lifetime movie.

Eddie was a dentist in his mid-thirties with commitment issues.[a] He destroyed a relationship with a former fiancée when he backed out on the marriage. He then pursued Denise, whom he met online. He volunteered to fly her out, put her through dental hygienist school, and lavish her with money and bling. She came, but it didn't go well. When they visited with me, they both were entrenched in patterns of pretense. Eddie liked to exaggerate how hard his job was and often claimed to be working when he was at friends' houses playing *World of Warcraft*. He also claimed incompetence when she would get frustrated and want to converse, saying he "didn't know how to talk about feelings." When he forgot her birthday, he said that he didn't get her anything because she was hard to buy for.

Denise would say she was ugly to get Eddie to compliment her and would make hollow threats to leave so he would take her shopping. Each made countless promises and follow-up excuses. Not surprisingly, they didn't have a lot of trust and were constantly suspicious of each other.

Eddie and Denise didn't feel close even though they were strongly drawn to each other. Their distance was a result of a cycle, where the lying caused distance and the distance led to more lying. Research has shown that when people feel less invested in a relationship, they are more likely to lie to each other.[2] However, this downward spiral can be reversed. As Eddie and Denise realized what they were doing, they became more open about their true motives and concerns, and they spoke directly, instead of dropping hints or threats. This helped them feel closer, which led to an important conversation about what they really wanted from each other in their relationship.

Most agree that it is good to be honest and authentic. We are drawn to those who are "down to earth," and don't put on a front or act phony. One reason we appreciate this quality is because it isn't all that common. People frequently put on a face to fit their situation and don't realize they are being deceptive. In one study, strangers talked to each other for ten minutes. The participants were simply asked to get to know each other. Then, upon review of these recorded interactions, the researchers asked participants what they said that wasn't exactly accurate. Most could identify several things, including insincere compliments or embellished statements like, "Oh, I totally agree," or "Wow, that is interesting!" About 60 percent of the subjects lied at least once during the ten minutes, and the average number of lies was close to three.[3]

---

a. All of the clinical and research examples in the book have had identifying information removed or altered. Also, in this book terms such as "partner" or "spouse" are used interchangeably to reflect committed romantic relationships (dating, engaged, married, etc.).

When presented with evidence like this, people concede that they might lie about once or twice a day, but some research estimates that it is closer to ten times.[4] College roommates are false with each other in about 38 percent of their interactions, with claims like, "Hey man, I don't know whose dishes those are!" However, even in marriage, which should be the most intimate of relationships, about 10 percent of communication contains some kind of deception.[5] Why do we do this?

Why Lie?

Mel was a foreman for a big box store, where he oversaw shipping and unloading. He was a husky blonde who was addicted to Juicy Fruit gum. He told me that he had a "little gaming issue." He didn't want his wife to know, because he felt like she wouldn't understand or would give him grief. Our conversation began with me asking him what, exactly, he was referring to.

"I sometimes play online poker or other gambling."

"For money?"

"Yes, but I often win, and I think I will make it all back soon."

"How much are you in the hole?"

"About $130,000."

[Pause] "Say again?"

"But I am paying it down. Do you think I should tell my wife?"

Avoiding Conflict or Protecting Feelings

Mel's claim that he didn't want to upset his wife is one of the most common reasons for lying.[6] He said he didn't think his wife "would understand," or that she would be angry "over nothing," but these were excuses. It was easy for Mel to claim he was protecting his wife by keeping her in the dark, but do you think she would want to know about his house-sized debt? I bet she would. The reason he didn't tell her was because he didn't want to stop gambling, and he didn't want the fight that was going to erupt when his wife learned the truth. Most don't like conflict, and it is sometimes easier to sweep things under the rug than confront reality.[7]

Lying for Love

Humans also lie because they love. Our raging desire to find a mate leads to schmoozing, preening, and pretending. In the earlier study that examined strangers' interactions, the highest rates of lying were from those who were instructed before the task to try and "be likable."[8] Imagine a situation where Jack and Jeanie are starting to date and are feeling the love. He may not be as excited to see *Mamma Mia!* as she is, but he will happily go to appear sensitive. She doesn't really care about his carburetor collection but will nod and listen to his stories about them, saying nonsense like, "Wow, that is really cool!" They will each watch for signs that their efforts are paying off, and adjust their words and bodies accordingly in order to woo the other. Like Jerry Seinfeld said about his twenty years of dating, "That's a lot of acting fascinated."

The irony of course, is that the foundation of a relationship is trust. If you impress a future mate with bogus tales of adventure and fake interests, it won't bring closeness.[9] The bigger the deception, the more likely it is to backfire. It is one thing to discover that your flirty friend isn't into the TV show he claimed to love, and it is another to find out he is married with triplets and didn't mention it.

The worse the motive for the deception, the more damage will be done to the relationship. If your date is flattering you because they are genuinely excited about the relationship, it is of less concern than if they are trying to manipulate or control. As one example, Mel the gambler liked to take trips to Las Vegas to play poker. Dealers would tell him he was skilled and cool, which are minor lies to keep him playing. But a mysterious woman had more sinister motives. She sidled up to him, smiled, told him how amazing he was and asked him to share his advice over a drink. He felt manly as she breathlessly gushed over his stories. However, at one point she excused herself to powder her nose, leaving Mel to bask in the glow, but he soon realized she had been gone a while, and something else was gone as well: his wallet with the fourteen thousand bucks he had won.

Facebunk: Misrepresentation on Social Media

The social media network is a vast relationship minefield where people try to impress others and troll for feedback. It's a virtual world, but it has real impact on relationships. This is partially because the phoniness and distance of being online makes it easy to lie. One survey found about 25 percent of women post things on Facebook that are exaggerated or completely untrue. These usually involve trying to make their lives sound more interesting, like saying they are "Chillin with some friends at a restaurant" when they are home watching reality TV, or, "Just had an intense meeting with the VP ☺" when they were actually snoozing at their cubicle. Some lies were about alcohol use, holidays, or relationship status.[10] Being online tempts people to share exaggerated details about their life, emphasizing cool details like, "Totally surprised to get an award at work!" (this is the *humble brag*). They are less likely to share unflattering things, like, "Just ate four Krispy Kremes." Researchers looking at online deception concluded that the pressure to present a front is strong, but doing so ultimately leaves people feeling more disconnected and alone. It isn't particularly fulfilling to get "likes" for fake behavior. Smart technology can also tattle on users. It doesn't impress friends if your post says you are at a hip concert but your location setting says you are in your apartment.

It is worse on online dating profiles, where as many as 81 percent of people misrepresent themselves. It's not that people hate long walks on the beach, but many pretend they are thinner or richer than they actually are. Women in their twenties claim to be about five pounds lighter; in their thirties about seventeen pounds lighter; and in their forties about nineteen pounds lighter. Men exaggerate their income and education, and they Photoshop out their bald spots. Some fudge their relationship status and others claim to love kids when they really just think they are sticky and annoying.[11] This type of deception is so common that many experts suggest it is acceptable or even expected. Putting one's best face forward, it seems, often involves digital enhancements.

There is a motivated reason for this deception. It works. A flattering picture will get more interest than a lousy one (so it may be a good idea to stop by the glamour shots booth at the mall), and women without pictures will get only half the responses of those with photos. Men who say they earn over $250,000 a year will attract 156 percent more interest than those who say they earn less than $50,000. Interestingly, only 20 percent of people admit they lie on their dating profile, but when those 20 percent were asked how often others lie, they assumed that about 90 percent do. So those who were honest about their lying were accurate about everyone else.[12]

While questionably effective, online deception can be dangerous. One client found that two of the guys recommended to her had the exact same dating profile. "It was pretty impressive," she said. Both included, "Engineer, lost his wife to cancer, loved snuggling . . ." We couldn't figure out if one ripped off the other or if they both bought a bogus profile from the same source. Another guy who was eagerly chatting with a babe with the nickname "Luscious Lipz" found out that she was actually a thirteen-year-old punk named Josh.[b] It may be tempting to lie in the online meet market, but it isn't the best path to an honest relationship.

A Culture of Fake Smiles

Another reason people put on a front is because they feel like they should. How often do you ask someone, "How ya doin'?" when you really don't care? It's about as honest as the "Great!" response you get in return. In the US, we value cheer and a can-do attitude so much that it can pressure people to put on a happy face. This can leave depressed people feeling guilty for feeling bad and non-depressed people feeling bad for having typical ups and downs. Of all age

---

b. This is called "Catfishing," after a documentary movie from 2010 (and subsequent MTV show) where online relationships turn into real life encounters. This often involves completely fake identities and deception, as in the case of Manti Teo, a Heisman candidate football player for Notre Dame in 2012, who was in an online relationship with a woman who apparently died and later was found to be a man leading him on. He was catfished.

groups, teenage girls have the highest rates of lying, and this is attributed to the pressure to be totally rad and conform to social expectations and appearances.[13] After a rousing class discussion about this, I ran into a friend and asked him how he was. "Never better!" he said. Taking him at his word, I responded, "Wow, you are peaking right now! This is the best you have ever been and I am here to witness it!" He laughed and admitted that things actually "kind of sucked."

Social pressure is also why conversations often end with, "Well, I had better let you go. I am sure you are busy!" This is more acceptable than the more honest, "I really want to stop talking to you." In intimate relationships, a partner says, "I miss you," and the other responds, "I miss you too," because it sounds better than, "I am having a great time and haven't thought about you for one second." It also sounds better to claim to understand something ("Yeah, sure, I got it") instead of responding honestly ("I have no idea what you want; I was thinking about lunch"). It is hard to be fully present all the time, and sometimes partners are caught off guard: "And I was like . . . [blah, blah, blah]. Can you believe that?" *I haven't been listening, just nodding and looking concerned—wait they just stopped. I'll respond with,* "Wow, that's intense!" (Therapists might also use this skill occasionally.) Maybe it is unrealistic to expect total transparency in conversations, but there is a subtle cost if misunderstandings occur. If it is important that I hear you, it is better to admit that I was checked out: "Wait, I got distracted; could you repeat that last part?" This has a better result than feigning a connection that doesn't exist.

Late night TV host Jimmy Kimmel exploits this pressure to lie for appearances. Interviewers ask questions of random people on the street, but the questions are a setup. For instance, they will ask people what they thought of last night's political debate when there was no debate. People will weigh in on it anyway, saying "I thought [my candidate] looked calm, had a lot of good points; the other one looked nervous, pandered a lot." In other editions of his "Lie Witness News" people are asked what they thought of nonexistent earthquakes, "Oh yeah, it was a doozy" or fake bands at the Coachella music festival: "What did you think about *Dr. Slo Mo and the GI Clinics,* or the *Obesity Epidemic*?" People happily offer opinions of these bands that are "so obscure they don't exist." "I just like their whole style, their genre, they are very innovative." *Regis and the Philbins*? "Yeah, I had a radio station up in Canada and I used to spin them all the time." Social pressure is powerful, and if an interviewer with a video camera asks someone a question, a truthful answer ("Never heard of 'em") likely won't get them on TV. Our world reinforces lies, and people obligingly put their best fake face forward.

Ducking Responsibility

In addition to saving face, some lie to avoid responsibility. When he claims he is busy and can't come to the kid's preschool concert, or she says she doesn't feel well enough to help clean, they may be avoiding natural obligations that come in a relationship. This happens when partners make excuses to avoid important conversations, help when it is reasonable, or just be there for each other. Some deception is opportunistic, created in the moment of pressure. This not only shows up in business decisions, but also in relationships.[14] When caught off guard, like when a date asks, "Is my perfume bothering you?" it is easier to deny ("No, no [cough]") than admit uncomfortable truths ("Smells like a scratch-n-sniff poster of Willie Nelson"). In college, I was a classical radio announcer and once found myself on live air needing to give a weather report. However, I got distracted and realized too late the report wasn't there, so I made up a fake forecast. This seemed more reasonable at the time than telling listeners I was a numbskull.

Even with small things like weather reports, lying is a subtle betrayal of a commitment. In an intimate relationship, there is an understood obligation to be responsible and open, and lying prevents this. This is why honesty is universally valued and always has been. In the Old Testament, liars could be stoned to death, and in colonial America, people could be flogged or have their faces branded for lying.[15]

Although most agree lying is bad in principle, in practice, people are morally flexible about their deceit. Partners say they want honesty from their spouse but admit that in some situations, their own lies are acceptable.[16] This leaves a door open for interpretation, depending on the situation. What one decides not to share ("Surely he wouldn't want to know that I bought three dresses") might be considered important by the other ("Hey, why didn't you tell me you spent $350?"). When things are hazy or complicated, people often present events in a way that favors them.

In one survey, only 6 percent of people said it is better to lie if it prevents conflict, but when asked if there was ever a time that honesty was not the best option, about two-thirds could think of times they would lie.[17] In other words, people are saying something like, "It is *not* okay to lie to me, even to avoid conflict. But sometimes I need to fudge things just to keep the peace." Huh? We clearly struggle with this double standard. Should we be strictly honest about everything we think and feel? Should we always be blunt? What does it mean to be honest in a relationship?

Reactivity and Honesty

Being honest does not mean spouting off the first thing that comes into your head, especially when you are tense. A key point we will explore in this book is that responses in escalating situations are often distorted. When a fight starts and someone claims they are "brutally honest," they are probably being more brutal than honest. An angry statement like, "I am just telling you the truth; you are acting like a selfish idiot," is not usually true. It may *feel* honest to be harsh, but it is probably spite. This is why we don't say everything that pops into our heads. Can you imagine a relationship where both partners said everything they thought?[18] Angry thoughts about your partner, their behavior—or their mom— are usually biased and inappropriate. Even if they *are* truly being selfish, this can be expressed in a way that is both honest and constructive.

Before speaking, take a hard look at your motives and emotions. Are you blaming someone else for your own actions? Are you letting anger and defensiveness distort your view? After stirring things up, couples often need time for the sediment to settle and the water to become clear. It's likely that strong feelings are clouding the truth, making things seem worse than they are. Testy companions need to hold their tongue and think carefully when they are tempted to let loose with what feels like a true accusation. People need to edit their words, not to hide the truth, but to take the time to find it.

I discussed this with Ron, a chef at a local restaurant. He was in the midst of a nasty divorce, and his wife had been uncooperative about co-parenting. One day, she was being difficult when he came to pick up their kids. He snapped and yelled at her in front of everyone, "Well, you've gotten fat. You let yourself go, and good luck finding someone who will want to snuggle up to your big ole' body." He lamely attempted to defend himself later: "She has gained a lot of weight, after all." But what was accurate here? He was being cruel and juvenile and eventually admitted it: "I shouldn't have done it. The kids were upset, and I felt like a jerk." The truth of his *intent* was that he was trying to hurt her by lashing out. The truth about her size wasn't relevant.

Sweet Little Lies

One night, my wife, April, and I were getting ready to leave to teach a marriage enrichment class. "How do I look?" she asked. "You look nice," I said, and then realized that I hadn't looked at her. Pretty harmless, but an honest answer would have been more meaningful. She did look nice, but I hadn't bothered to check.

A white lie is usually a trivial falsehood said in a tactful way. Sometimes white lies are offered to avoid hurting feelings: "You are such a Romeo" or "This tastes delicious." These are the subtle things, the 10 percent things. Other white lies consist of things unsaid, like allowing a partner to believe something that isn't true. Back when I was getting to know April, I had gone on a campout with friends, including girls who were our dates. She heard that I had gone, and asked what guys talked about on camping trips. Since I was becoming interested in her, I didn't really want to mention that we had dates, especially since she knew mine. I dodged and said, "Um, guys just talk about sports." She later found out what happened and was hurt that I hadn't told her the whole story. I rationalized: "I never claimed that I didn't have a date . . . er, exactly." But she was right. I was skipping a detail that was fair for her to know, since our relationship was progressing. It would have been awkward, but not as awkward as the conversation we had later when the truth came out.

Distance and Deception

Small lies can have big consequences. Mary Kaplar created the awesomely named Lying in Amorous Relationship Scale (LIARS), which assesses attitudes about lying. Kaplar assumed that lies for altruistic reasons, like avoiding conflict, would not harm a relationship. However, she was surprised to find that even nice lies hurt relationship satisfaction. Kaplar concluded that people should be direct, even when the truth isn't fun, rather than telling soothing white lies.[19]

This is because lies cause distance. False accusations and exaggerations are clearly harmful, but even lies to flatter or get close can backfire. One study asked participants to keep written records of their social interactions for a week. They rated these on how meaningful the relationship was, the type of interaction, whether there was any deception, and what the other's reaction was if there was deception. Lies were usually nice, like, "You look great!" and for emotional reasons like keeping the peace. Most journal keepers told one to two lies per day. (Of course it is possible they were lying about how often they were lying.) However, the truthful exchanges were rated as more enjoyable than the deceptive ones.

The researchers concluded that, "everyday lies violate the nature of close relationships. If people's presentations of themselves to another person are so distorted as to be deliberately misleading, and if they hide and fake their feelings and opinions . . . then their relationship with that person may no longer be a close one."[20] Deception puts a person in a different mindset. It's fake and weakens the threads of the intimate bond. It doesn't leave the liar feeling good either. If you tell your spouse you worked really hard when you didn't, you might get thanked, but it isn't validating to be praised for a put-on.

It is not hard to lie to those we don't care about. We can easily tell the salesman at the door that we are in the middle of dinner when we aren't, but we have a harder time looking our spouse in the eye and lying.[c] People are most honest with spouses and children, and less honest with friends, acquaintances, and especially strangers.[21] Distance makes it easier to lie, which is why more lies happen on the phone or in texts than in face-to-face conversations.[22] If your date cancels via text, you might be more suspicious than if he talks to you about it. It is harder to lie with the whole body.[23, 24] If lies are easy in a relationship, then the relationship is not doing well.

Relationships move forward and become more intimate through honesty. I do a role-play in classes where I invite people to come up and pretend they are on a blind date. It is funny and awkward as they ask each other questions. The point is that strangers start with basic information and go deeper only as they feel comfortable and connected. It would be weird if a new acquaintance immediately started sharing their deepest secrets. Two people become one pair through honesty, and an intimate partnership requires integrity.[25]

Honesty and Kindness

Are all white lies damaging? Isn't it kind to protect each other from painful truths? It may depend on the motive. Dan Ariely is a professor of behavioral economics at MIT who studies irrationality and dishonesty, but his experience in hospitals after a burn recovery led him to wonder if white lies could be protective. His found that, "This will sting a bit" was better than, "Brace yourself, because you are going to feel horrendous pain."[26] If the pretense is from a desire to help, it is different than if it is a selfish dodge. Also, some half-truths occur because words have many meanings. When one says, "How are you?" They likely mean: "I am acknowledging you with a generic greeting we both understand." Clearly, most of us get these unspoken social rules. Exact truth may not particularly matter if the intent is harmless. And it may not always be a great idea to share everything, like my client who told his wife a certain lifeguard was looking good, for which he was immediately busted. So, what happens when you feel like you should tell the truth but wonder if it is going to be harmful?

This is a dilemma for many, and most of us just go forward with our mix of candor and hedging based on what seems reasonable at the time. We recognize that some truths to our spouse are harmless, but others need finessing. "You have a button undone" is acceptable. "I hate the framed photo of your parents you got me for my birthday," maybe not so much. In some situations, the truth is awkward. Here are examples of questions that may be asked in a relationship, followed by two possible answers. Both responses are honest, but one is kinder.

---

c. Unfortunately for moms, college students report lying a lot when they call home. It is easier to say "You didn't give me enough grocery money" than "I spent it all on Cheetos and Xbox games." Or, "I would have totally been ready for that test, but like, the professor didn't prepare us at all!"

Question: "Do you think that woman is beautiful?"
Less Effective: "Ohhhhhhh, yeahhhh."
Better: "She is nice looking; what do you think?"

Question: "Why are you so paranoid about me going out with friends?"
Less Effective: "Because your friends are idiots and you have no self-control and might do something stupid."
Better: "I am having a hard time with your drinking. I know there are lonely people out there and you are attractive, and I worry you will be tempted to do things you wouldn't normally."

Question: "How do you feel about getting married?"
Less Effective: "It may be great for other people."
Better: "I am afraid of that level of commitment, even though I am excited about where our relationship is going."

Question: "Were you mad when I wasn't in the mood last night?"
Less Effective: "Yes, and I thought you were a selfish brat."
Better: "I was frustrated, which is why I pouted for a while."

And the classic question: "Do these lime-green spandex shorts make my butt look big?"
Less Effective: "No. Your butt makes your butt look big."
Better: "I think that your jeans look nicer."

There are many ways to be honest and still be kind, even if that means to honestly defer a question or take time to think about it. This happens when you are put on the spot with a question like, "Do you love me?" A glib or fake answer in this instance isn't good. If the issue is an important one, it is better to be frank. If you are faking or evading, then you need to ask yourself why and probably discuss it with your partner.

The takeaway on white lies is that it is best to be honest, but there may be times when an omission is irrelevant. For instance, you might not need to tell your lover they smell funny when you are cuddling, and it may not be necessary to address every concern that arises. But consider carefully what is happening when you find yourself ducking the truth. What is the underlying intent of what you are saying, and what is the effect of it? Are you trying to deceive? To avoid something that should be dealt with? To punish? To be lazy? Can you be honest and still be kind? Are you protecting your spouse or yourself? Being thoughtful about these questions takes good judgment. And judgment becomes impaired with high emotion, so step back and get to a good place before speaking.

Flattery

Oh, love's best habit is in seeming trust,
Therefore I lie with her and she with me,
And in our faults by lies we flattered be.
—Shakespeare, "When my love swears that she is made of truth"

Flattery is a type of white lie, but why would it be a problem? Doesn't everyone like to be told good things about themselves? Sure, but false praise is not the same as a thoughtful, honest compliment. Often, we see through flimsy flattery. For instance, students who apply to our graduate programs have professors write recommendation letters. One professor has sent many letters, but frequently says he is recommending the "best student he has ever worked with." When everyone is "the best," the recommendation doesn't mean much. When every performance gets a standing ovation, it doesn't reflect the quality of the show.

Flattery can also be dangerous. Joanna learned firsthand about the power of a manipulative flatterer. In middle school, she was cruelly teased by friends for being an early bloomer, and this left her anxious and insecure. When she began her freshman year at college, she met Brad, who sensed her vulnerability. He began calling her relentlessly, texting her about how he couldn't stop thinking about her eyes or her voice. She was blown away. She felt deeply desired, and this was a rush. He pressured her for sex, even though she told him she wanted to wait. She eventually gave in and kept this from her friends, who were becoming concerned, and her mother, who she knew would disapprove of the whole relationship.

Things moved quickly, and Brad continued the flattery but also became jealous, asking her to stop hanging out with friends and wearing certain clothes. She found out he had a son from a previous relationship, but he had excuses and complained about how awful his ex was, convincing Joanna that she was the only person who understood him. Things turned abusive when he would make fun of her looks and take her phone as punishment. She was entrapped by this point and would believe him and blame herself for their problems. He would hit her and then buy her gifts, promise to change, and threaten suicide. He used flattery like many manipulators do—to control. As is often the case, the kindness mostly stopped after Joanna was too beaten down to leave.

Another instance of flattery involved a fresh-off-the-farm kid named Roy. He was nineteen and had left his rural home to take a job in a neighboring city. A single mother co-worker took an interest in him and would drop by his cubicle, smile, flirt, and invite him to lunch. He felt funny about it and made some weak efforts to push back, but it was fun, so he often went along. She soon pressured him to spend time at her house and talked about marriage. He was distressed and confused, because he had a long-distance girlfriend. When we discussed her flattery, he protested, "Are you saying I am not a good-looking guy, or nice? I like to be appreciated!" But as we looked closer, he saw the truth was a bit more complicated. He *was* a nice, good-looking guy. However, the lie was *why* she was telling him these things. It wasn't because she genuinely thought about his happiness and fulfillment. She was flattering him for her purposes—he came from family with money, and she liked the thrill of leading him along. If she really had his best interests at heart, she would have accepted his first protests and stepped back instead of pushing.

Flattery is dishonest when used to gain or control. It is effective because everyone has insecurities. Flattery is particularly common in dating and new relationships, but it usually wears off as relationships settle into commitment and reality. Established couples are kind and supportive but have usually given up the fawning. Flattery is like an artificial sweetener that seems good at first but leaves an unpleasant aftertaste. Someone starving for affection may eat it up, but it isn't as nourishing as the sweetness that comes from true compliments.

Moving Up and Down the Lie Ladder

Some lies are small and others huge, and there is a difference in their impact. To illustrate this, let's create a lie ladder. Imagine each deception is on a rung from zero to one hundred, with the worst lies near the bottom. A perfectly honest and open interaction is at the top of the ladder, and a blatant lie is at the bottom in the dark, at zero. Small lies and omissions are higher up than calculated lies. For example, if you exaggerate details in a story to make it funnier, you might be on rung ninety-one, and a minor evasion like, "I forgot to take the trash out," is on eighty-two. Mel's gambling addiction and lies hover around the thirties, and an ongoing affair with all of the accompanying lies and secrecy are down in the single digits and teens. This metaphorical ladder suggests the lower the number, the more damage done to the relationship. It also suggests that the more distant the relationship is, the more likely that lower lies will occur. And finally, when someone starts down the ladder at any level, they tend to continue sliding down. Small lies always precede larger ones.

Take Anna, who was committed to her husband, Chet, but frustrated with his demands. He didn't like her family, especially her younger brother who had been in and out of alcohol rehab. Because Chet was harsh, Anna didn't tell him she sent her brother money. She also minimized her past struggles with an eating disorder. After they had a premature child, their lives became nerve-racking, with doctor's visits, poor sleep, and worry over the baby's progress. Anna coped by binge eating and obsessive exercise. She carefully kept this from Chet, and as he asked further questions, her lies became more calculated and blatant. Her thoughts and actions crawled down the ladder. *He doesn't need to know that I had that gallon of ice cream; he would go crazy. I will use cash instead of a debit card for this bag of snacks. If Chet was more helpful with the baby, then I wouldn't be hurting so much. If I told him that I occasionally cut my arm to cope, he would leave me. I need to stop, but I will do it on my own.*

She became an expert at hiding evidence and putting on a front. Ironically, she was always an advocate for her younger brother in getting professional help, but convinced herself that she didn't deserve it. Her lies piled up and became more extreme and dangerous. Like pebbles that dislodge an avalanche, her small lies had big consequences. Her cover-ups to Chet changed their relationship and her own self-perception. She felt like a terrible person, and this continued to send her down the scale, as if she had a reputation to live down to.

Dan Ariely and colleagues confirmed the power that small falsehoods have to influence bigger lies. They asked female volunteers to try on sunglasses for the supposed purpose of evaluating them. The women were divided into three groups: One was told the sunglasses were an imitation of a luxury brand, and another group was told the sunglasses were the authentic brand, and the third group was not told any details. After the women wore the shades, they were asked to solve a series of problems, but given the opportunity to cheat. Of the women who wore the authentic brand, 30 percent cheated on the test. Those without information about what they wore had a 42 percent cheating rate. But 73 percent of the women who thought they were wearing fake glasses chose to cheat on the test. Even when the choice to be phony wasn't that of the participant, it loosened their normal moral constraints.[27]

Something that seemed like a small lie changed their view about right and wrong and sent participants down the ladder. The researchers called this the "counterfeit self," because when people rationalize and lie in small ways, it affects their whole identity. This is why lying has been called the "gateway drug" to bigger assaults, because if you are going to do bad things, you need to lie to yourself and others to get there.[28]

The good news is that the reverse is true as well. When partners choose to be honest, they are heading back up the ladder, and this direction is significant. It feels different. When someone acts upon their impulse to be honest, whether in a compliment or a confession, good things happen. When a spouse resists saying something distorted, they are choosing integrity, and this sends a message to their psyche. They are choosing to move toward the light.

Anna had many opportunities to stop her deception and come clean. She finally became so isolated and unhappy that she took the difficult step of admitting what was going on. She approached Chet and tearfully told him of her pain and struggles and expressed her concerns about their relationship. He was upset, but he surprised her by being open to her story and concerned about her well-being. He admitted he had not been there for her or their baby. They began a series of important conversations with each other and a professional. Although there were hard truths to face, the result was closeness in the relationship that hadn't existed for years. In the next chapter, we will learn more about severe lies and betrayals but also the kind of liberation that comes from moving back up the ladder into total honesty.

MAIN POINTS

- Deception in intimate relationships is very common but often hidden. It occurs out of a desire to avoid conflict, impress others, or avoid responsibility.

- Being reactive is not the same as being honest. Honesty requires attention to motives and feelings.

- Deception creates distance between people, and distance makes it easier to be deceptive.

- Greater intimacy in your relationship comes from being honest while still being kind.

- Even minor deceptions, like white lies and flattery, usually damage relationships.

- Dishonesty moves a person down the lie ladder. This direction has consequences and makes it more likely that a partner will commit further lies.

- Major deceptions and betrayals are always preceded by smaller lies.

- The commitment to be honest pervades the whole relationship in good ways.

DISCUSSION QUESTIONS

- What areas of your relationship would improve through more honesty?

- What are some of the ways you have used white lies or deception with your spouse?

- What would help you to be more honest and authentic with yourself?

Chapter 2
Betrayals and Accountability

Love all, trust a few, do wrong to none.

Shakespeare

Big Lies

Bruce and Sandi had been together for about six years but had grown distant. He was immersed in a graduate program, and she was working at a fast-growing startup company. Bruce had a colleague, Angie, who he tutored. As Bruce and Angie spent more time together, their interactions began to change. Bruce would joke with her about how she needed his guidance, and Angie would tease him with nicknames ("see you later, doc"). Sandi grew concerned as she picked up on this, and one evening she saw Bruce stifle a laugh as he read a text from Angie. Sandi asked about it and was surprised by his quick brush off of her question: "Nothing. Just a dumb picture." He changed the topic and was annoyed at her inquiry, and she grew more alarmed. When Angie invited Bruce to her apartment for a study session, he was flattered and told himself that Sandi didn't need to know. Down the ladder he went, justifying his actions and deceiving Sandi, until he landed at the bottom in a full-fledged affair.

Sexual infidelity is a classic example of how small seeds of dishonesty take root and bloom into betrayal. Affairs are fueled by many deceptive factors: the thrill of flattering and being flattered, keeping secrets, and the headiness of lust. When sex occurs, it is a culmination of ongoing betrayal that includes lies, misdirected thoughts and energy, and commitment breaking.[29] The sex is just concrete evidence of the deception. One partner is now giving him- or herself to a third party, while the betrayed partner is in the dark. Affairs can be extreme, including long-term hidden relationships, repeat philandering, or blatant cheating. One memorable client had lost several boyfriends before realizing that her own mother was seducing them away. Others affairs are subtle, short term, nonsexual, or emotional, and this is why cheating is difficult to define. It can include anything that is secretive and violates trust with a partner. Sex is an obvious form of treachery, but even without it, there can be many disloyal emotions and actions.[30]

"We Just Clicked"—Social Networking as Betrayal

A colleague of mine, Jaclyn Cravens, studies the interaction of technology and relationships. I collaborated with her on a study of infidelity that occurred through Facebook. We analyzed stories where betrayed partners described shock, pain, and damage that resulted from cheating behaviors that happened on the social network.[31] One man recalled, "I noticed she was spending a lot of time late at night hiding her chats, [and then] removed me, her husband, from her friends."[d] Another got suspicious from vague answers and went looking for evidence: "Sure enough, in her trash folder was over a month's worth of emails between her and a man that was my friend for over twenty years. These were not friendly emails. There was talk of being naked with each other in bed . . . I was completely destroyed."

One of the findings of this study was that the damage of social-network cheating was comparable to in-the-flesh affairs, even though the actions were sometimes only virtual. Pain was significant, with vivid descriptions like "My heart exploded" and "I am heartbroken. I hate Facebook now." Revenge and anger was also common. One man said, "I pasted the [evidence] into a message and sent it to people . . . she worked with that knew very little about her." Social network affairs may be more damaging than other kinds of online cheating such as pornography use or chat rooms, because there is already a relationship with the Facebook friend beyond the computer.[32]

Because intimate partners know each other well, they often recognize when the other is being sketchy. When someone is sneaking around physically or virtually, it leaves tracks, which was the case in the Facebook study. Often an affair came to light when the suspicious partner followed these signs. One lesson from this project is that partners shouldn't ignore their gut when it is giving warning signs.[33]

This happened with Bruce and Sandi. She grew concerned about Bruce's long hours at the lab and his cageyness in their discussions. She followed her suspicion by figuring out his phone password and opened up a scorching string of texts to Angie. He was upset by her breaking into his phone, but this forced a confession. At first, he admitted to an emotional affair with Angie and said they had feelings for one another. This was painful to Sandi, and she was angry but not satisfied with his explanations.

Coming Clean

The problem worsened as Bruce admitted to additional actions he had already denied. He said that he had kissed Angie but nothing else, but later admitted to a sexual relationship. This partial honesty backfired and infuriated Sandi. Bruce was frustrated, because he felt like he was being punished for his honesty, but half-truths are not honest. Each new revelation destroyed the small trust that was growing back, and Sandi felt re-victimized each time he admitted he hadn't told the whole story. Even when he swore there were no more details

---

d. The posts were found on the website facebookcheating.com, which was created as a forum for people to share stories of betrayal.

to share, she didn't trust him. To their credit, however, they both committed to total honesty about their feelings and what happened. This led to a painful but productive time in their relationship, where Bruce realized the extent of the hurt he had caused, and he willingly answered questions from Sandi and didn't become defensive. This was important, because it is common for the betrayed party to want details, and this can help them not obsess about what did or didn't happen. It is a legitimate request and is part of coming clean.

If you want to prevent big lies, there must be honesty in small things. If you want to recover after betrayals, there must be confession and apology. If you want to repair damage, there must also be honesty going forward. It is painful but essential to admit mistakes. I have seen many couples bravely admit affairs, addictions, and embarrassing lapses. This removing of masks gets people back to reality, and it is easier to navigate reality than a mirage.

The Damage of Betrayals

A family therapy colleague of mine, Fred Piercy, lived for a time in Indonesia, doing research and clinical training. While he was there, his friend Irwanto told him an unusual story of a marriage with serious trust issues. It stemmed from an incident when the wife left for work, and the husband snuck off to visit a prostitute. Upon arrival at the bordello, he was given a room, but the woman that came to provide services was his wife. Both were shocked, and some interesting conversations began.

Deception changes relationships, because it hurts, and once burned, partners are more sensitive. Sandi still loved Bruce but now had many fears about him and their future, and she continued to wonder about Bruce's mental fidelity, even though he stayed true in his behavior. One of the consequences of unfaithfulness is that both sides become oversensitive to things that used to be no big deal. Sandi would overreact to any hint of Bruce being distant or late, and he would become frustrated by her monitoring of his coming and going. Even when he was being completely honest, she would sometimes be skeptical. But it was like the boy who cried wolf. It was hard for Sandi to open herself up to trust when she had been hurt for believing Bruce in the past.

Lying also clutters relationships because lies tend to multiply, and deceivers become defensive about their carefully constructed stories. In a related Facebook study of ours, one woman claimed persecution when caught cheating. "When I confronted her about the call, she lied," her boyfriend said. "Then she became upset and accused me of spying on her." This counter-accusation of "spying" is common in betrayals, since the guilty person wants to divert attention from their behavior by complaining that the other is being nosy.[34]

Lying destroys credibility. Once I asked a graduate student to revise a paper and add some additional content to it. She made the font bigger and gave it back to me without changing anything else. This changed my perception of her integrity. A former student, Carlos Perez, found a surprising credibility gap as he was interviewing married partners about their recovery from affairs. One couple had gone to their minister for advice after the wife had cheated on the husband, but they were puzzled that the minister seemed detached and non-sympathetic. "He took us to get coffee, but we never had counseling; we were just hanging out," the husband recalled. They then discovered the pastor was sleeping with the secretary of the church, who was married to the man with whom the originally unfaithful wife had cheated. I guess it wasn't surprising that this minister was not helping them heal from infidelity while he was practicing his own.[35]

Pathological Liars

I met with a chronic liar in therapy because he could not maintain an intimate relationship. His girlfriend left him after catching on to his deception. His lies didn't always benefit him. They just happened as a matter of course in his conversations. He admitted his problem, framing it as an addiction, but after about two sessions it was clear that he wasn't always being honest with me. He also promised to send a check for our last session, which didn't happen.

People shun chronic liars. We want to trust others, and getting burned feels personal and upsetting. I once had a boss who would flatter, make promises, and use vague descriptions in his claims about experiences and accomplishments. He always "knew someone" important and made big plans. He was good at flattery and slippery in his details, so he was hard to pin down. But he didn't have close friends or credibility with colleagues.

Pathological lying obviously is incompatible with intimacy. Some put up with it, because they are used to poor treatment or they hope that the promises will come true. Regardless, the lied-to partner knows they can't count on anything they hear. Repeated lies show contempt for the person being lied to, because lies are condescending, placating, or manipulating.[36] As Anton Chekov said in a letter to his brother, "[Cultured people] are sincere, and dread lying like fire. They don't lie even in small things. A lie is insulting to the listener and puts him in a lower position in the eyes of the speaker."

Some partners tease or play tricks because they think it is funny to see the other look gullible or get duped. Maybe this is harmless when the teasing is gentle, but it can also veer toward cruel when one laughs at the other's expense. Like the dad who told his kid the ice cream truck was out of treats when it was playing music, it is funnier for the dad than the kid who feels foolish or tricked.

Habitual liars become skilled at convincing themselves. One study showed that even when someone cheats on a test to get a higher score, they still think they deserved the higher grade. They knew they faked their answers but still thought the inflated score reflected their abilities.[37] Another study tested this tendency by giving participants questions that had no correct answer, like "What is the last name of the only woman to sign the Declaration of Independence?" Even though there was no answer, about 20 percent of the test takers claimed they knew one ("It is on the tip of my tongue!").[38]

One client, Wendy, was getting out of an abusive marriage where her husband was a chronic manipulator and liar. During the divorce proceedings, he easily lied under oath about his finances and the things he said to her or the kids, as well as some details that were completely irrelevant. Despite the perjury, she said, "I swear he was totally convinced of his delusions and was able to look me and the judge in the eye and believe his B.S. as if it were reality."

The Importance of Trust

John Gottman may know more about marriage than anyone alive. He looks more like a kindly rabbi than a rock star, but researchers swoon and doctoral students ask him to sign their dissertations when he wanders by. For over forty-five years he has observed and coded couple interactions. Much of this has been done in his "love lab," which is an apartment at the University of Washington where couples live while being observed, measured, and monitored. He has described the most minute interactions of couples, learning what helps them succeed or fail, and I will cite many of his findings in these chapters. After decades of poring through data and squinting at statistics, what has he found? That most of the crucial accomplishments in a successful relationship "have to do with establishing trust."[39] Trust is at the heart of a healthy partnership, and nurturing it and repairing it when it gets damaged is a must. As Stephen Covey said, "Trust is the glue of life. It's the most essential ingredient in effective communication. It's the foundational principle that holds all relationships." Many studies back this up. Trust is one of the most sought-after traits in a partner, and most relationships will not progress without it.[40]

In one of my projects we asked low-income urban women about their attitudes toward marriage. These women valued many things, but trust and faithfulness were at the top. Ironically, this prevented many of them from getting married because they had bad experiences getting hurt in the past. One had what she called a "baseball policy" which was, "three strikes, you're out."[41] Trust is highly valued, because if you aren't sure whether your partner will hurt or abandon you, then your brain is literally on high alert all the time. This is a tense and miserable way to live.

Trust and Security

I will also cite many of Sue Johnson's findings. She researches couples and change, arguing that the need for safe connection is wired into our biology. Babies' lives literally depend on having a responsive caregiver that will meet their needs, and as people grow up, they still want someone to be there, respond to their signals, and show them they are important.[42] Johnson suggests this is why people react in dramatic ways when their lover lets them down. A betrayal feels like a blade, cutting ties of security. People panic when they feel abandoned, and this is particularly true for those who have been badly hurt. For many, growing trust takes time and responsiveness. When emotions go off like alarms, it is time to reassure, not back away. If your partner becomes agitated, resist the temptation to flee or fight back. Instead, try to stay calm and empathetic, and this will help solidify trust.

A secure relationship has less stress than one without trust. As Gottman says, partners who trust each other can operate with incomplete information. Spouses who have each other's back are as content as well-loved children, secure in the cocoon of a relationship that isn't going to disappear or cause deliberate pain.[43] There may be fights or hurt feelings, but energy is not drained by worry and suspicion. There is an old saying that it is better to be trusted than to be loved. Even when people don't feel in love, they need to know that their relationship is safe and secure.

Honesty and Change

Honesty changes people, and it includes admitting your false actions. This "meta-honesty" (honesty about your level of honesty) includes an ongoing evaluation of your motives.[44] When a partner admits that they overreacted or misrepresented something, it prevents issues from being swept under the rug, which keeps the relationship from growing distant.[45] Honesty also brings concerns to light, where they can be addressed. This happened with Raji, who was a striking and driven manager climbing the corporate ladder. She struggled with prescription medication abuse and the shame that accompanied it. She described herself as a "genius" at hiding evidence and getting more meds. It took months of therapy before she admitted that it was her main reason for coming in. When she finally revealed her struggle, real change began.

Honesty and Accountability

People are more honest when they are accountable to another.[46] You are less likely to give a lousy tip at the café when you are together and more likely to make better choices with personal habits when someone is there to encourage you. Children are an accountability factor as well. A while ago, the phone rang and my son picked it up. I heard him say, "You want Dr. Whiting?" I saw this and cringed, because when someone calls for Dr. Whiting at dinner, it is usually a chipper undergraduate student looking for an alumni donation. He saw my expression and said, "Uh, he isn't available right now." Dang. I didn't want to take the call, but I didn't want him to lie either. So we had a good conversation about morality and telemarketing.

When people think about the importance of the other person, they are more likely to be honest. Take Eli and Molly. Eli slept with Molly's best friend during a tumultuous early period of their relationship. There had been substance abuse on both sides and a lot of lying. Nevertheless, they came through this stretch determined to work things out. But little things kept derailing them. Eli came in one day, defeated. "I told Molly I had paid the cell phone bill, but I hadn't gotten to it yet," he said. "She went insane when she found out! This was no big deal!" What Eli didn't realize was that her reaction wasn't about the phone bill. His willingness to evade was an indicator of whether he would put her first. Each small indiscretion reverberated loudly, because she was still recovering from his affair. Once he understood this, he was more honest, even with minor issues. When he thought about his love for Molly, he put her reassurance higher than his need to put on a front.

Honesty with Tact and Right Motivation

Each time Eli and Molly bumped up against something in their relationship, they had an opportunity to reflect upon their motives, slow things down, and have a conversation. Once Eli promised Molly that he would make dinner for the family before she came home, but he forgot until the last minute and quickly made waffles, but they were so hard they would gag a goat. Molly was mad, but to her credit she sorted through her emotions and came to a better place. Her first thoughts were: "He only cares about his own stuff, not the family." However, she then realized that she was stressed and was interpreting events personally, as if Eli burnt the waffles just to stick it to her. Upon further reflection, she realized he had been working on some other things that she had asked him to do and had genuinely tried to come up with food as promised. Although Eli picked up on her annoyance at dinner, when they talked about it afterward she admitted that she was out of line, and they ended up laughing about it, much to Eli's relief.

Molly's motivation changed from wanting to blame to wanting to find the truth about her feelings. This takes a willingness to step back and diagnose what is causing strong emotions. One woman admitted to our research team that she would throw her husband under the bus in therapy: "If a situation gets brought up in counseling, I will blow it out of proportion sometimes, or say things that I'm pretty sure aren't even true . . . to make [him] angry or feel bad about the things he did."[47] Once my teenage son cooked himself a plate of bacon. I was irritated and told him he had taken too much and needed to be more considerate of his younger siblings, because they wouldn't get any. He was annoyed, but as I thought about our interaction, I realized that my accusation wasn't really true. I saw his bacon and wanted some myself.[e]

Scrupulous self-honesty reveals who you really are and helps you know your strengths and limitations. Doing this helps you live with more integrity in all aspects of life. I sometimes see clients who are caustic or unethical in their profession, and not surprisingly, they are having trouble at home. It is hard to be ruthless and dishonest in the office and kind and decent at home. It is better to live congruent with your internal moral compass than it is to go against values or project a fake image. Being untrue and fake leaves you feeling worse. Brené Brown said, "Trying to co-opt or win over someone . . . is always a mistake, because it means trading in your authenticity for approval. You stop believing in your worthiness and start hustling for it."[48] When you are honest you find peace of mind and closeness with others. This is how character is formed, through thousands of small decisions that occur with loved ones.[49] It is better to authentically live the life you have than create a phony one.

Main Points

- Small deceptions precede bigger betrayals such as emotional and physical infidelity. Online and other non-sexual betrayals can cause as much hurt to your spouse and relationship as do physical affairs.
- Lying destroys credibility, erodes trust in relationships, and often invites deception in return. It is an act of arrogance and disrespect.
- Relationship intimacy occurs with honesty and congruence between inner motivations and observable behavior. Honesty also leads to positive change in self and relationships.
- A life of honesty is part of being happy at home as well as in other areas. Small efforts can pay off in big ways.

Discussion Questions

- Can you think of a time when you dodged, exaggerated, or otherwise evaded something with your spouse? What consequences did you experience?
- What is it like to be lied to by a friend? By an intimate partner?
- When have you benefited from being honest in your relationship, even when it was hard to do?
- What are your strengths, weaknesses, personality traits, and tendencies? Where do you find it easier to be honest and where do you find it to be more difficult?
- What can you imagine needs to happen to help you live more authentically in every area of your life?
- If you find yourself creating excuses or being false, how do you turn it around? Do you need help to do this?

---

e. My microwave has a setting for a "bacon slice." Who eats only one slice of bacon? Someone was minimizing or self-deceived when they set that up.

Chapter 3
Rationalization and Reality

Man is not a rational animal but a rationalizing one.

Robert Heinlein

"We got pregnant the day we met." Brittany was telling me a tale of passion, anger, and chocolate. She met Joel at Denny's, where they were with other dates. Joel suggested going to an ice cream place that had a challenge: if you ate the whole frozen pile, it was free. His date was unenthusiastic, but Brittany loved the idea. She and Joel abandoned their dates and headed off together to see if he could eat one. He did.

"I like dessert," he said. He was a thin thirty-five-year-old cop who was fidgety and intense. His goatee was closely cropped, as was his hair, and he agreed that their relationship was highly charged. "I like her zest for life, and she is a great country line dancer," he said, "but she is driving me nuts." Joel complained about her messes, forgetfulness, and how she kept bouncing checks. He said, "Our son, Sean, needs help with his school stuff, but she is always forgetting things he needs or is making him late."

"I work part-time," Brittany said. "I have a lot on my plate and I am the one that takes care of Sean and the baby, and you just criticize. You stress me out so I forget things."

Joel was quick to respond, "I am just trying to help you. You need reminders, and I tell you to chill because you get so mad at Sean that he gets upset. You are a bad influence."

"You're the bad influence," she countered. "You are critical and always think you know the best way to parent." She turned to me. "Just because he had kids in his first marriage he thinks he is a parenting genius. He never even sees them."

"Well I know things you don't," Joel said. "If you would calm down and try my suggestions, it might help." Back and forth they went. Brittany accused Joel of drinking too much, and he said it was because of her nagging. At this point they were glaring at each other and beyond the help of ice cream. They were demonstrating something they were both proficient in: rationalization.

Excuse Me—Rationalizing in Relationships

To rationalize is to excuse behavior. Rationalizing is deceptive, because it is false to argue that actions are reasonable when they are actually selfish. When Joel said that he was trying to teach Brittany how to parent but was really criticizing her, he was rationalizing. When Brittany yelled at Sean but blamed Joel, she was rationalizing, because Joel didn't make her yell. They excused themselves in many ways. Once Joel cut Brittany off when she was telling me about a fight. He said, "You are rambling. He doesn't want to hear all that." He wasn't protecting me, however; he just didn't like being told on. In another session, Joel became irked when he discovered that Brittany had treated her friends to an expensive lunch and hidden it from him. Her excuse for not telling was that she forgot. But her actual reason was that she knew it was a bad use of their money. She liked impressing her friends and felt like she deserved to do what she wanted.

Joel's default excuse for his criticism was Brittany's housekeeping. It was an all-purpose justification for anger, drinking, and distancing. However, his accusations did not inspire her to do some spring cleaning. They just created new problems of resentment and anger. She hated being snapped at, so would ignore messes as a way to stick it to him. Rationalizing fuels conflict and solves nothing, but everybody does it, especially when things get tense.

Have you ever hurt someone's feelings? Did you claim that your behavior was reasonable given the circumstances? Have you made excuses for not doing something you committed to? Minimized your faults or exaggerated your partner's? We all have.

A Rash of Rationalizing

Rationalization is so common, we often don't notice it. We are especially blind to our own, because it feels better to believe excuses than admit we cause problems. There are plenty of reasons to rationalize. Maybe you didn't follow through on a commitment, so instead you pointed out what you did do: "I didn't get to the dishes, but I worked hard to mow the lawn." Some claim their behavior could have been worse: "I don't babysit our daughter, but I am better than my dad, who never even changed diapers or cooked." Others rationalize bad relationship decisions. "I know I shouldn't get serious with him, but I am really lonely right now, and it probably won't go anywhere."

I studied rationalization with fighting couples. I separated them to keep them from reacting to each other and then presented short vignettes of a bickering and excusing couple. I invited each person to reflect on how these stories applied to his or her (not their partner's) behavior. Nearly everyone was able to admit rationalizing. One guy recalled bellowing at his girlfriend. He said, "I'll try to make up excuses . . . I'll say, 'Well I had to do that because you were talking to me that way [in front of friends].'" He said that it was to "try to hype myself up, make myself look better." Another man would leave when his girlfriend tried to discuss concerns. This made her irate, but his justification was that he no longer "hit her." He said, "There's no way else to release my anger so . . . I'll go talk to some woman or go out to some bar."[50] Since he had stopped being violent, he could claim that any other behavior was an improvement.

In one marriage seminar I taught, a wife talked about her husband's frustrating tendency to rationalize when he would apologize. She called this his "sorry, but" tendency, because he would admit he was wrong, *but* then give reasons why he did it. He would say, "Sorry, but I was stressed because of the baby's screaming." Or, "Sorry, but you really shouldn't be that upset." I agreed that it must be difficult to deal with his sorry butt, because when someone apologizes in a way that deflects personal responsibility, it is not an apology. Have you ever had someone say "I am sorry you feel that way" or "Sorry, but you deserved it"? It doesn't exactly feel great. Sincere apologies and responsible actions bring couples together, but excuses push them apart.

The Reasons We Rationalize

If rationalizing hurts relationships, why do we do it? We excuse because we hate to think bad of ourselves. Feeling good becomes more important than being honest. If I have two ideas that contradict each other ("I just acted like an idiot, but I want to think that I am a good person") then I will shuffle the facts around to support the second idea. This illustrates the well-researched concept of *cognitive dissonance*: negative beliefs about ourselves are painful, so we modify them.[51] This is a quick process that happens almost outside of awareness. Like glasses that darken in the sun, rationalization activates in response to an uncomfortable idea. The bright glare from a partner because of a forgotten anniversary leads to excuses: "I was under a lot of pressure from this project and was totally planning on doing something for you later . . ."

This shows an interesting disconnect: we are *able* to be reflective and responsible, but when we're being reactive, we don't use these skills. The participants in my project could reflect on and admit their excuses, but only after they had calmed down. For example, the light bulb went on for one man as he realized that he had been minimizing his violence. He realized how out of line he was when he told his wife, "I just pushed you to the ground. It didn't hurt you. . . . That's nothing compared to what I can do." When he was in the argument, his strong emotion convinced him that he was justified.[52]

Jacob and Rosa illustrate how rationalizing can be hidden. They reported violence, but Jacob wasn't the stereotypical batterer. He was a scrawny computer tech with thick glasses and a nervous laugh. His girlfriend Rosa was a strong Latina woman who didn't like backing down. They would nitpick and make sarcastic comments to each other. She would mock his job, and he would ridicule her family, and they would blow up and sometimes hurt each other. On the surface, it appeared Rosa was the aggressor. She would lose her temper, throw books, and push and slap Jacob. My interview with Jacob, however, revealed how he provoked her to excuse his violence. He said,

> I would start off small, grabbing her arm as she's trying to walk away—not put too much force behind my actions—to instigate her to go even further so that I could justify going a little bit further myself. When she pushes me too hard, in my mind I say, 'Thank you for giving me what I wanted, pushing me. You hit me hard so I'm gonna come back and hit you just as hard or even harder.' . . . It's like the sting of the slap is making me grin. . . . Now I can take it a step further myself and I'll lash out on her [with] all the anger, frustration, I'm feeling at the moment.[53]

On the surface, Jacob and Rosa's story seems to be about violence or anger. But the gasoline fueling the fire was deception. Jacob *wanted* Rosa to slap him because he benefited from it. It gave him an excuse to "lash out on her." He rationalized his behavior by saying that he only "start[ed] off small"—just a little grabbing of an arm. But he knew this would provoke her and give him a reason to hit. Rosa had plenty of excuses to behave badly as well. Jacob was getting in her face and harassing her. They both needed excuses, and they each used the other's behavior for this purpose.

The Blame Game

Instead of claiming that your immaturity made you lose your cool, why not blame your spouse? He or she is close by and helpfully does annoying things that you can complain about. Jacob and Rosa blamed each other, and they each had plenty of material to draw on.

One of their fights began when Jacob invited a down-on-his-luck friend, Eric, to stay in a trailer on their property. He didn't tell Rosa and when she complained, Jacob went on the offensive: "He is struggling, and we can help. I would have told you but I knew you would refuse." Jacob's generosity to Eric included loaning him Rosa's pickup and borrowing money to bail him out of jail after he was stopped with marijuana. Rosa told Jacob his priorities were screwed up, and he told her she was selfish. The tension spilled over one night as they were putting up a shelf and Rosa dropped her end. "You always mess stuff up!" Jacob said. "You are as useless as an ejector seat on a helicopter!" Their son saw this and was upset, which angered Rosa further, and they both remained unapologetic.

Blame is self-perpetuating. Spouses become defensive when blamed and often blame right back. Ironically, when people blame their spouses, they often cause the exact problem they are complaining about. When Rosa attacked Jacob for helping Eric, he became more entrenched in his virtuous battle to save him and prove her wrong. They became more aggressive in their boxing match of blame. The unfortunate thing is that they were complaining about concerns that needed to be addressed, but they were doing it in a way that added more problems to the existing ones.

This is like injecting flu viruses into a sick patient. Instead of working together to heal, these two would poke at sensitive areas and rip off scabs. This mode of blame and attack is different than mutual problem-solving. The first approach is destructive, where partners try to pin the other to the wall, and the second is constructive, where people are sincerely trying to figure out what the problem is. James W. Pennebaker at the University of Texas studies how the words couples use reflect the health of the interaction. He has found that the most damaging word in a relationship is "you" because it is often a blaming statement.[54]

We feel better when we can blame something else for our troubles. One study found that people feel worse about accidents that happen to them as a result of dumb luck as compared to an accident from human negligence. The reason? They like having someone—the negligent guy—to blame.[55] Sometimes an accusation in a relationship is the equivalent of, "I didn't say it was your fault. I only said I was blaming you." We like to blame, even when it isn't logical. How do we get out of this trap of blaming?

Seeing Yourself Honestly

We are good at trying to present ourselves in the best light. What if we tried to do the same for our spouse? It is easy to be generous when first in love, but it's hard during a disagreement. Consider whether you are applying the same judgments to your partner that you give yourself when angry. For example, in a heated argument you wouldn't usually say, "I am just being mean, irrational, passive-aggressive, and petty." But you might say (or think) that about your spouse. If you cut her the same slack, you might think something like, "She must be stressed out or frustrated, and it wasn't a good time for my sarcasm." Or you might see his grumpiness but choose not to take it personally.

Successful couples acknowledge each other's efforts and give credit. They say, "You were very patient with me while I was sick," as opposed to, "You are only being nice because you want sex." Partners deal with a lot in life, including from each other. You would extend compassion to friends who were struggling, and if they said something off kilter, you wouldn't attack them and call the whole relationship off. We don't say to friends, "You always come home from work mad at the world." We might call them on being cross but would do it respectfully.

Unfortunately, the closed nature of rationalization renders couples deaf to the answers to their problems. The solutions will be found as both look at what they are contributing and hear the other's suggestions. When one partner considers his or her own flaws, rationalization stops in its tracks. The tone changes, and the other frequently softens in response.[56] Teamwork is needed, because both created the problem and it will take both to fix it.

Rationalizing our Rationalizing

> Jughead: "I feel guilty about that money I've owed you! Here!"
> Reggie: "Two dollars? You owe me ten!"
> Jughead: "But this brings the guilt down to a level I'm comfortable with!"

It is easy to rationalize, and some excuses are very handy. For example, people do things online that hurt their relationship, such as flirt or sext with strangers. Why do they do it virtually when they wouldn't physically? Because it is easier to rationalize, as they can say, "It was just for a minute. It wasn't real, and I don't even know them."[57] Few would steal cash from their job, but many take pens and paper, use the company copier for personal purposes, or spend work hours surfing Pinterest. Dan Ariely put Cokes in some dorm room refrigerators and plates of dollar bills in others. Within a few days the soda was gone, but the money was not. No one grabbed a buck and went to the vending machine to get a Coke.[58] Why not? It was easier to rationalize swiping the drink than the dollar. Did you ever steal cash from a roommate? No? Did you ever eat their food in the refrigerator? I did too (but it was only stuff they had a lot of, or didn't really want—plus, they ate mine sometimes . . . I'm pretty sure).

Ariely has also shown that people will cheat on tests when given the opportunity to do so, but they will keep their deceit within a limit. Even when given the answers, participants will bump their grades up only a certain percentage. Like Jughead, we keep excuses at a level we can comfortably justify.[59] In your relationship, you might not lie about cleaning the basement, but you might fail to mention that you also caught some reality TV for a while ("a deserved break") in the middle of it. You might not cheat on your spouse, but you might flirt with the nice-looking server at lunch.

The more convenient an excuse is, the more it will be used. Some partners blame their parents ("My mom was a screamer, so that is just how I respond"), work ("I am too busy with this project to come home on time"), and other people ("They were all doing it") because these excuses are convenient. The famous Milgram experiment showed that participants were willing to administer what they thought were shocks to a stranger because they were told to by an authority figure.

If there is a person who can be easily blamed, he or she will be. This happens in companies as employees collude to reinforce sketchy behavior ("Everyone was lying about their hours, so I did too"), and it happens in intimate relationships. If she sneaks off to buy something for herself, then you have an easy reason to do it as well. If one is making outlandish excuses, then the other will often follow suit. It may be one of the reasons spouses tend to gain weight together.[60] She is having seconds on cheesecake? Don't mind if I do! Some partners engage in "revenge infidelity" where one is unfaithful because the other one was. Not exactly helpful to the relationship.

Rationalizing is also a key feature in addiction, because it oils the hinges on the door to relapse. Jacob knew it was a bad idea to go to the bar, but surely he *needed* the time away from Rosa's hysterical and demanding presence. Besides, he was only going to hang out with friends, and on and on.

Rationalizations fuel all kinds of addictive behavior, including drinking, drugs, or donuts. Relapse starts with subtle self-talk. One client lost his job for surfing porn at work. He promised that he wouldn't but convinced himself that he was just taking a news break, which led to celebrity news, which led to sports and swimsuits and then to porn. His thinking descended the usual path. *I won't do it. I will only do a little. Since I have done a little I might as well do more. I have blown it; I might as well keep going. Why try? I am just a loser.* Excuses are so ubiquitous in addiction that if you go to a twelve-step program and try to rationalize your behavior, you will be called out. Those who are serious about recovery know that rationalizing is the road to relapse. How can we avoid this tendency to excuse behaviors?

Drawing Portraits, Not Caricatures

I like drawing and always have been impressed by those who were good at caricatures. Once during a slow statistics class in graduate school, I was sketching the teaching assistant. His name was Orland and he had a Weird Al vibe: long curly hair, big glasses, and a mustache. I was happy with my progress, but then he came by to see why I wasn't paying attention. I thought he might enjoy his likeness, but his reaction was one of indignation. What was funny and harmless to me was obnoxious to him. Caricatures can amuse, and we recognize them because they portray someone by singling out a few features, like long hair or big teeth. But while they may entertain, they are distortions of the truth. Instead of drawing for accuracy, a caricature is an exaggeration for effect.

When we rationalize, we caricature a situation or person. We emphasize a few things that were said or done and neglect the rest. Have you ever had your partner repeat back what you said in an exaggerated or angry tone to make you sound worse? You have been caricatured. A few pencil strokes cannot capture the richness of a person's life, and accusations and select bits of evidence do not represent the wholeness of your partner. We mistake our simplistic cartoon for a realistic capture.

An artist can also look for the good. People pay big money to have their portraits done in a flattering way. Sometimes we see our spouse in the manner of a model photo, with filters and good lighting. This is when your biases can work for you. It is good to be crazy about your soul mate. One study found that nearly everyone (95 percent) thinks their partner is above average in appearance, intelligence, warmth, and sense of humor. Exaggerated and irrational? Sure, but there is a benefit. Those who think they have picked a jewel of a lover are more satisfied and committed in their relationship.[61] This ability to minimize faults and appreciate virtues is critical for relationship success.[62] She isn't the most organized, but she has a great laugh? Go with it. He isn't very romantic but is fun with the kids? Build upon that. Wouldn't you rather sit for an artist who carefully and kindly paints you in your best light than for a caricaturist who exaggerates your blemishes and gives you a huge nose? So would your partner. No one likes to be portrayed as goofy or ugly.

Take time to see the whole picture and acknowledge when your vision has become limited or biased. Jacob eventually saw that his desire to provoke Rosa was his excuse. "It makes me feel superior and in control," he said, and Rosa committed to stop yelling and slapping, "Even if he is being awful, I have to control my own temper and not set a bad example." They each tried to show appreciation for the other and give the benefit of the doubt. As they filled in the gaps of their relationship picture, it became more accurate and suitable for framing.

Main Points
- Everyone rationalizes their behavior in relationships. This is usually for self-protective reasons or because it is easy.
- Rationalizing often goes unnoticed, because it is subtle, frequent, and convenient.
- To counter excuses, try and see your spouse's behavior in the same light as your own. Give the benefit of the doubt, and try to see both sides.
- The more convenient an excuse is, the more it will be used. Excuses and blame lead to poor outcomes.
- Don't exaggerate or caricature your partner's behavior or motives.

Discussion Questions
- Can you think of times when you intentionally rationalized your behavior to avoid feeling guilt?
- When have you blamed your spouse for something that wasn't fair?
- What happens when you try and give credit to your spouse for his or her efforts?
- Recall a time when you may have caricatured your spouse during an argument. Now, reconsider that argument and give your spouse the benefit of the doubt.

Chapter 4
Smugness and Self-Pity

Nothing is easier than self-deceit. For what each man wishes, that he also believes to be true.

Demosthenes

Moralizing in Marriage

Markie was squirming. She did not want to tell her husband she was chatting online with men. "I know it isn't right," she told me. "But nothing will come of it. They all live far away, and it is fun. It is hardly ever inappropriate. He wouldn't understand because he is the jealous type and kind of hyper. Plus, he never even takes me on a date." She argued that not telling him was for his benefit. "It would upset him. He is having a crappy time at work and would take this the wrong way and be trippin'. This helps him because it gives me something to do without bothering him." This illustrates a new kind of deluxe excuse: a false reason that claims to be a moral one. Markie's favorite excuses were those where she convinced herself that she was being helpful to the person she was actually hurting.

It is, of course, ironic that we excuse bad behavior by saying we are doing good. However, if I need a rationalization, why not go with one that makes me sound like a swell fellow? It feels better if I claim that I snapped at the kids because I am such a hardworking provider. Harvard psychologist Steven Pinker calls this the moralization gap, where people who behave badly assert that they are, in fact, doing a very good thing.[63]

People give many magnanimous reasons for their behavior. One violent man told me he threw ice water on his wife to teach her: "It was for her own good. It was a lesson about consequences." As previously discussed, partners lie to each other to "protect." Like Markie, they say they wouldn't want to hurt their spouse's feelings by telling the truth. Researchers suggest that "people feel that deceiving their partners is not merely acceptable under some circumstances, but is in fact the proper and—perhaps from some ethical standpoints—the moral thing to do." Not surprisingly, these partners who claimed they were lying to protect their spouse didn't want to be lied to. They suggested their reasons for lying were better than any their partner had.[64] As Leo Tolstoy said, "For the justification of sins there exist false arguments, according to which there would appear to be exceptional circumstances, rendering the sins not only excusable, but even necessary."

Luke demonstrated this moralizing skill. We asked him to discuss a medium-level relationship concern with his girlfriend, Iris.[65] We left them alone and recorded their conversation for later analysis. They were rehashing an argument about a date.

Luke: "You think I am always mad at something. And every time I say something you always snap back at me . . . and that makes me upset. Sometimes I might snap back, but I don't mean anything by it."

Iris: "Well you've been coming across real irritable and real snippy, so I snip back."

Luke: "See, I don't see how. I guess I am not seeing it. All I ever do is I try to help you and say, 'let me help you with this and that.' And all you ever say is nothing, or, 'I'll do this, fine.' . . . I don't feel like I deserve that because I am just trying to be helpful."

It is convenient for Luke to suggest his "snapping" is innocent (he doesn't *mean* anything by it) and Iris's is aggressive. He shows typical moralization gap reasoning as he claims the only reason he does anything is to "be helpful." He used exaggerations like "*all* I ever do" and "*all* you ever do." If spouses are using words like *always* and *never*, they are likely (maybe always) exaggerating. It would be an unusual partner who *always* was a certain way. When someone is in a moralizing mode, they see themselves as always right and others always wrong.

Self-Righteousness and Self-Pity

Smug explanations can morph into strong excuses, because everyone assumes that their views and preferences are the best. Your opinions about how clean to keep the bathroom are "right" to you, but preferences lead to judgmental comments: "Didn't your mother teach you to unfurl the toilet paper with the new sheets on the front?" When partners moralize, normal differences lead to snootiness ("You shouldn't blow your money on that"), and idiosyncrasies get harped on ("Why would anyone collect *Lord of the Rings* action figures?").

Do you like being judged for your preferences? Not likely. It usually causes resentment and distance. One blended family I know is made up of two committed spouses and fourteen total children from the previous marriages. Although the wife and husband were generous and devoted to the new marriage, the challenge of blending was head-spinning. As the husband told me, "We were arguing over habits, like what to do for Christmas, but we were acting like our tradition was best and the other's was worst. We realized many issues are not *right* or *wrong*; they are just matters of style."

Everyone wants what they want, and when you merge with another, not all of your wishes will be granted. Can you allow your significant other to have his or her own morning routine or spend free time free of judgment? Do you get annoyed when the dishes are not put away in the "correct" way? Do you condescend and sigh about your partner's driving? Do you claim that your job is harder, or your sore throat is sorer? Moralizing explanations are annoying, but they have appeal because it feels good to be superior. As author and scientist David Brin has said, "Self-righteousness can also be heady, seductive, and even . . . addictive. Any truly honest person will admit that the state *feels good*. The pleasure of knowing, with subjective certainty, that you are *right* and your opponents are deeply, despicably *wrong*."[f]

If I Make You Angry I Am Right, and If You Make Me Angry You Are Wrong

Think about a time you made your partner mad. What did you do? Why did you do it? Now, think about a time your partner made you mad. What did he or she do? Why? Go ahead, ponder. Now, consider the differences between the two explanations you came up with. If you are like most people, both of your stories favor you and your motives. A series of studies by Roy Baumeister at Florida State University have examined this curious phenomenon. People were asked to describe times they upset someone, as well as a time they had been provoked to anger.[66] Participants shared fervent tales of broken promises and fury. But almost without exception, the perpetrator story and the victim story were different in quality.

The perpetrator story (when they made *someone else* mad) sounded like this: "I did it because I had a good reason, and it was only fair. Plus, it wasn't that bad, it was easily fixed, and it is time for them to get over it!" But victim stories (when someone made *them* mad) were like this: "This was another hurtful thing out of many. It was intentional, senseless, and cruel. I have been badly harmed and won't forget what happened. It has caused long-term injury to the relationship." The same participants gave different kinds of stories, depending on their perspective. When they perpetrated harm it was excusable, but when they received harm it was not. Baumeister summarized, "Our results do not indicate that victims and perpetrators are different kinds of people; rather, the same people see things differently depending on whether they participate as victims or perpetrators. The biases are in the roles."[67] No wonder things escalate. When partners

---

f. Brin has explored this theme in some of his fiction (see *Existence*) and this quote is taken from davidbrin.com, where he has posted the following: "An Open Letter to Researchers of Addiction, Brain Chemistry, and Social Psychology" where he suggests that self-righteousness needs to be taken as seriously as other common addictions.

become adversaries, the deception switch is flipped, and two separate stories of the same event start changing in different directions.

The researchers were now curious. Would people still distort when telling a story they didn't have a stake in? They did a follow-up study telling participants a tale of two roommates. The first (named Harold or Harriet), bailed out on an offer to help the other one (Arthur or Amanda) with an important math assignment. The participants in the study were asked to either identify with one of the story characters ("Pretend that you are Harold") or just be a neutral observer.[68] After they heard the story, the participants did some busy work for five minutes, crossing out vowels in paragraphs. This was to prevent them from rehearsing the details of the story they just heard. Then they were asked to assume the role they were assigned, and write down what happened in the story. As in the first study, people told a tale that emphasized the details that supported their side. The Harolds/Harriets downplayed the harm that was done by backing out, pointing out that they had generously offered help in the first place and had sincerely apologized. The Arthurs/Amandas recalled the details that made the victimization more severe: they were left hanging, it was an important paper for their major, and their poor grade damaged their GPA. Both sides minimized the pieces that didn't fit their preferred explanation.

So even where there was no personal connection to the story, it was psychologically important for these participants to look good in the roles *they were pretending to be*. Participants didn't like admitting that their avatars caused harm. Only those who were asked to keep a neutral perspective wrote an unbiased recollection of the events. Research has replicated this moralizing and victim-playing tendency with intimate partners. However, when the relationship quality is higher, victim stories are less likely to exaggerate the impact of the offense. In other words, when people are getting along they see these spats more clearly. Happy couples are inclined to give each other the benefit of the doubt, saying things like, "She was having a bad day. She didn't mean it."[69]

Be a Scientist, Not a Lawyer

Let's look at ways to be more accurate and less self-centered. In the roommate study, the participants who were told to recall the interaction from a *neutral* perspective had different recollections than the Harolds or Harriets. The neutral observers told stories that were more correct and more reflective of the whole picture.[70] If partners are willing to step back and look at the situation from both perspectives, the tone becomes curiosity instead of animosity.

To be curious is to be open and seek truth—like a scientist. Scientists gather evidence from all angles and see what it suggests before making conclusions. To argue one side is more like a lawyer. Lawyers *start* with a conclusion and then sift through evidence to support it. A scientist tries to understand, a lawyer to persuade. The problem, as physicist Leonard Mlodinow argues, is "the brain is a decent scientist but an absolutely outstanding lawyer."[71] We are neurally wired to defend ourselves and create a preferred "truth" based on fragmentary data. Like a courtroom attorney, we naturally minimize evidence that works against us and dramatically unveil smoking guns and evidence in our favor. Social psychologist Jonathan Haidt said it this way: "Although many lawyers won't tell a direct lie, most will do what they can to hide inconvenient facts while weaving a plausible alternative story for the judge. . . . Our inner lawyer works in the same way, but, somehow, we actually believe the stories he makes up."[72]

Not to disrespect the legal profession, but it is this aspect of flesh-and-blood attorneys that can contribute to the nastiness of divorce. Angry partners go to lawyers whose job is to attack and demean their ex. It is no wonder, then, that mediation, which is more of a neutral, fact-oriented process, is a better way to keep tensions from boiling over into war.

When couples come for therapy, they are often in lawyer mode and see the therapist as the judge, before whom they present their cases. To succeed, they must shift into a constructive, curious team. If willing, they become like anthropologists, exploring the richness of their life together. They look for strengths, root out misconceptions, and try to see the relationship accurately, with each considering their contribution to the problems. Did you overreact when she took your car without asking? Did you claim that his comment was intended to hurt you, even though you know he didn't mean it? Can you admit that you shouldn't have said her mom was batty? Haidt suggests a three-step process to try to shift into a curious attitude. First, think of a recent conflict with your partner. Second, identify one way in which your behavior was not that great. And third, extend an apology for your role in the conflict.[73]

This doesn't always come naturally. We all get frustrated, illogical, and off base. Is it really possible to be neutral? One study looked directly at this question and found out how beneficial trying to be a scientist can be in a relationship. Social psychologist Eli Finkel of Northwestern University recruited 120 married couples for a two-year project. For the first year, the couples checked in every four months and reported how satisfied, how intimate, and how trusting they were. They also told of their "most significant disagreement." In year two, the researchers randomly assigned half the couples a task to step back and reflect. These spouses were asked to reconsider the disagreement and write about it "from the perspective of a neutral third party who wants the best for all involved." People took about seven minutes rewriting what happened after a disagreement, but the long-term effects were significant. They now viewed their conflicts in a more calm way and were less upset when remembering them.[74]

The startling thing about this study is how little time and effort it took to make a difference. Trying to be objective for about seven minutes *three times a year* changed the way that couples perceived their whole relationship. The simple act of looking at the disagreement fairly did something to the memory of what happened. Agitated partners softened as they thought through their part of the fight, and this made them more fair. To be open and curious takes some effort, but a little goes a long way. This is also why therapy can help—it sets up a structure to slow down and hear both sides. Do you spend time stewing on how you have been treated? Do you exaggerate your partner's aggression and your own innocence? It may be worth twenty-one minutes a year for you to imitate Einstein and scientifically consider all angles of the relationship.

Be Open to Change

Being willing to consider the evidence must include a willingness to do something about it. If a scientist has a preset agenda and won't change her theories in the face of contradictory evidence, then science fails. If you are not willing to change your perception when your partner shares information, you are butting heads and damaging the relationship. The first couple I ever saw in therapy illustrated this. I was a new graduate student, and the intensity of Brett and Natalie caused me to reconsider my career choice. He had dark hair and piercing light blue eyes like a wolf. He would glare aggressively at Natalie when he thought she was off base, and at me when I asked something he didn't like. Natalie fit the stereotype of the poetry student: dreamy, romantic, and scattered. Brett was rigid and opinionated, and it was excruciating for him to deviate from his plans, because they were superior, in his estimation, to hers. He would often shut her down, shaking his head impatiently while she talked. At one point, I tried an active listening exercise, where his task was to reflect what she was saying without judgment. It sounds basic, but he couldn't do it. He would start to rebut her comments, and I would stop him, which led to his teeth clenching and his face flushing. I told him he didn't have to agree—just listen and summarize. He squirmed and thrashed and eventually fell on the floor writhing in agony at the pain of hearing her talk while keeping his mouth shut.

Being willing to listen, learn, and modify perceptions is what Gottman calls accepting influence. This means being open to your spouse's opinions and feelings and making a place for them in your brain. Accepting influence is a natural cure for smugness, because it implies an equal valuing of perspectives. If a functioning couple has different opinions on what furniture to buy, they hear each other and negotiate, eventually finding something they are both okay with. Unhealthy partners say things like, "I am buying this because you don't have good taste." Gottman found that women usually accept influence more easily than men. This is particularly true in violent and controlling partnerships, where abusers never accept influence. This is why couples therapy is a bad idea for relationships where one partner is controlling. This partner will use session information against the other, rather than learning and improving. When partners do not have freedom to express ideas and preferences, their relationships often fail or become abusive.[75]

Playing the Victim

In early studies of deception, researchers assumed that victims were honest about being treated badly. Perpetrators were obviously going to downplay their actions, but the hurt one should be believed. Who wants to challenge somebody's story when they have been through so much? But Baumeister found that victims changed just as many details in their stories as did perpetrators. To complicate this, in relationships, things aren't usually divided neatly into perpetrators and victims. There are exceptions to this, as in violent and controlling relationships where one is clearly abusing the other. But in most pairs, each person is sometimes hurtful and sometimes gets hurt. The question, "who started it?" will be answered differently depending on who you ask, and both will have a version of what happened. They both will be right. And wrong.

Your difficulties are hardest for you, and it is natural to focus on the way you are hurt. However, your partner's view might be that you caused them to be hurtful by being so difficult. This is why it is risky to unload relationship woes on friends or family, because it can reinforce self-pity. They listen to your story, show indignation, and call you "poor baby," and you now are more committed to your inaccurate view. This can happen when one spouse goes to a therapist to complain about their love life. If the therapist isn't savvy, she will get recruited into fortifying the victim narrative. It is nice to be validated for a story about living with a pathetic partner, but it probably won't help the relationship improve. This is one of the reasons the field of family therapy sprung up in the first place. Professionals found when they brought multiple family members into sessions, stories changed a great deal. When spouses and kids call each other out on their deceptive stories, it becomes clear that stories are incomplete and many members contribute to the problems.

Some become so attached to their victim role that it colors their whole life. I was supervising a case where a woman, Faye, was reporting abuse from a boyfriend. The stories were shocking and often bizarre. She said that he would wake her in the night to berate her, play loud music, or shine lights in her face. She said that he made fun of her and didn't want her to go to therapy. But her reports had an unusual, incongruent quality. Instead of being teary or desperate, she seemed overly sincere and even enthusiastic.

One day the therapist reported that she had come in that morning and was attacked by a stranger on the way. The therapist could not believe the bad luck Faye was having. She had grass on her clothes and scratches on her arms. However, I had heard this story before. Faye had seen another therapist in our clinic about six months earlier, and the exact same thing had happened then. She didn't mention this to her current therapist and obviously did not realize her situation was being discussed with the same supervisor over time. As we looked closer at this and other stories, it became clear that much of it had been made up. She was not only exaggerating, but also inventing stories to present herself as persecuted and abused. These victim narratives served her well, as they allowed her to seek sympathy and demonstrate how hard her life was.

Genuine Victims

One unfortunate aspect of this case is that because Faye was lying, we didn't know whether to believe any of her stories, and some were probably true. She likely had been mistreated, perhaps severely. Yet she was not seeking therapy to change her situation, but was performing stories of abuse to get validation. Of course, many are genuinely victimized, and I am not suggesting they want it or are unwilling to change. Many victims cope in ways that seem crazy to outsiders, like downplaying serious abuse.[76] In these cases, well-meaning friends might become shocked at the cruelty and become judgmental: "How can you put up with that?" Victim blaming oversimplifies a tricky situation and is done because it provides an excuse for outsiders ("If she won't leave, then I don't need to worry about helping her"), but it doesn't help the problem.

Once I was discussing my research with another domestic violence scholar, and she became upset. She told me I was being insensitive when I suggested that victims of violence downplay abuse. I told her I was not equating rationalizing with contributing to, or *causing* the abuse. I feel very strongly that victims of violence experience pain that demands justice and compassion. Often survivors of violence are so psychologically beaten down and traumatized that normal expectations aren't viable. However, finding and making choices is one of the keys in empowering victims to leave.[77] Getting out of an abusive situation is harder than outsiders realize, but an important step is seeing abusive behavior for what it is and refusing to downplay or excuse it.

Willing Victims

As you can tell, it is hard to disentangle genuine victimization from self-inflicted victimization. Faye's story illustrates how many play up their victimized status because it somehow benefits them. It may seem insensitive to suggest that people are responsible for their own troubles. However, only focusing on being victimized keeps a person stuck. When people focus on options they often find more of them.

Being a willing victim also provides an excuse to be mean. This is what we saw in one of our studies as we watched a blond, bearded art teacher named Justin berate his wife. He would cut her off and pout when she tried to make a point. He was angry because she had left him. Although she had come back, he was holding this over her head and telling her what she owed him because of it. At one point, she interrupted to defend herself and he jumped back: "You gonna let me finish? When you break trust it's hard to gain trust back. Now when anything comes up from the past, it seems peculiar or suspicious. It is automatically going to make me assume the worst." He admitted he used her separation to excuse his aggression. "Because of what has happened I am going to pick at every little thing, because I am being resentful and I am being ugly . . . you as my teammate should not be letting me push you away. You should be finding other methods to soothe me."[78] I am not suggesting that Justin wanted her to leave him so he could use it as a weapon. Most people don't "ask for it." But he was going to milk it to hurt her.

In some extreme cases, acting as a victim becomes tightly woven into one's identity. There are many fake accounts of victimhood including stories of fake illnesses, persecution by the government, or alien abduction. Typical relationships involve more subtle claims: "She spends all her time at karate class with other men and abandons me." "He only values me for my appearance, and I am getting older and more wrinkled." These are difficult clinical issues, because these claims often have truth mixed in with the deception. If a professional digs for accuracy, they may be seen as unsympathetic. Some do have pain and poor health, some have been run over by the system, and all have legitimate complaints about their partners (and heck, maybe some have had close encounters with E.T.). Where does the truth end and the deception begin?

Let's break this down with Julie, from one of our research interviews. She had a reasonable gripe about her husband's habit of being abrupt but admitted that she would exaggerate her emotions to prove how bad it was. Her recollection was funny: "I have purposefully cried . . . [and sometimes] cry a little bit louder so he hears me even if I'm in the other room." Her tears are part of showing him that he is victimizing her.

But isn't he being rude by interrupting her? Yes. Isn't she then exaggerating how bad it is by sobbing? It sounds like it. These are key questions a professional asks when working with a couple, but a bigger goal is to ask them yourself. What is your motivation when presenting your concerns? Are you willing to try to see where you might be moralizing or feeling sorry for yourself? Are you being fair in the way you represent your side and your partner's? If so, you are heading for success.

Main Points

- Some excuses involve moralizing, or claiming that one's bad behavior is actually good.

- People naturally tend to exaggerate stories to make themselves look better, especially during conflict.

- When things are going well, partners are more likely to see their spouse's strengths.

- In relationships, it is better to be a scientist than a lawyer. Lawyers start with a conclusion and try to gather evidence to support it. Scientists explore, are curious, and look at evidence from multiple angles before drawing conclusions.

- We see our own hurts and difficulties most clearly, and sometimes this leads to self-pity, or playing the victim.

- Genuine victimization does happen and should not be dismissed or downplayed. It is sometimes difficult to detangle true victimization from willing victims who make no efforts at changing their circumstances.

Discussion Questions

- When have you claimed superior or moral reasons for your behavior?

- Think of an argument or challenge in your relationship and try to approach it scientifically. Examine both sides from the perspective of one who wants things to work out. Maybe write this out. Do you notice any changes in how you feel about it?

- If you knew your relationship would improve if you made some changes without waiting for your spouse to change, would you do it? Are you willing to change even if your spouse is not?

- Have you played the victim in a disagreement or shifted to a self-pity mode?

- If you've played the victim willingly, what was your motivation?

$\mathcal{P}art$ II
Deception in What We See

$\mathcal{C}hapter$ 5
Anger and Safety

Anger is never without a reason, but seldom with a good one.
Benjamin Franklin

Rodney Dane Higginbotham was on the run, wanted for charges of domestic violence. In a report entitled, "Squeezes cheese, and flees," details of his crime were recorded: "Police said that Higginbotham argued with his wife because she had not cooked anything. When she began cooking, he began making spaghetti while eating crackers and squeeze cheese. They argued and he squeezed cheese on the kitchen floor. She squeezed the cheese on his truck, and he squeezed the cheese in her hair before fleeing in his truck. The wife said that she washed her hair before the police arrived to take her complaint."[79]

The Power of Anger

What is it about anger that turns otherwise reasonable people into red-faced, shrieking toddlers? How can a basic emotion lead to violence, war, and divorce? Lovers who would die for each other one minute would kill each other the next when angry. In fact, when someone is murdered, the police investigate the spouse first. This says a lot about the power anger has in a relationship.

Anger is one of our strongest emotions, and when it kicks in, we see things differently. When partners are under the influence of anger, specific sections of their brains light up and others shut down. They become like pilots navigating through a storm. Their vision becomes impaired, mental alarms buzz, and automatic guidance systems kick in. They see red and become tense and overreact. Instead of trying to understand the situation, angry partners try to control it. Anger is a whole-body experience that is strong, irrational, and may lead to misusing squeeze cheese. Actions that begin with anger often end with regret.

This chapter explores the primal power of anger and what sets it off. We will meet angry couples and see how this emotion has damaged their trust and closeness. We will discuss how partners can soothe themselves and each other and steer out of the storm of anger and return to safety.

The Roots of Rage

Anger is powerful because it is connected to basic survival mechanisms. If you are fighting for your life, all systems go on high alert. Has your spouse ever stomped into the room looking like he or she wanted to kill? Your body responded in milliseconds, before any thinking did. We are good at this, because if someone is coming at you in a fury, you need to react fast. However, these instant emotions often turn into unnecessary fear and anger.

One day my daughter was trying to get her pet rabbit into its cage, but it was tearing around the room and hiding underneath the bed. She became exasperated and yelled, "Get out here right now! What is the matter with you?" I doubted this would calm the rabbit down and invite him out. When someone is yelling at us, our first impulse is to run away, not approach. Bunnies and spouses jump back when threatened, even when they are being told not to. We almost can't help these reactions. Our physical responses override everything.

Charles Darwin was interested in this. He did an experiment with a snake to see if he could force himself to stay calm when his body felt threatened. He wrote, "I put my face close to the thick glass-plate in front of a puff-adder in the Zoological Gardens, with the firm determination of not starting back if the snake struck at me; but, as soon as the blow was struck, my resolution went for nothing and I jumped a yard or two backwards with astonishing rapidity. My will and reason were powerless against . . . [a fake] danger."[80]

Even partners who are good at staying calm have to work at it when provoked. The fear and anger that results from another's threat is designed to protect, but like a snake behind glass, most of our partner's actions are not life-threatening. This is why anger is deceptive. It distorts the person in front of you, painting your partner as an enemy. We want to hurt what we think is the source of our pain. A partner who can at other times be a fount of love and security now becomes an enemy to be dispatched. A man in one of my studies described this sensation: "I felt the rage starting up, the adrenaline, and I just didn't care . . . It was at that moment . . . I honestly just wanted to hurt her physically."[81]

This irrational hostility happens when part of the brain called the hippocampus goes inactive. The hippocampus usually takes notes, locating events accurately in the memory. But when angry, the brain shuts down this scribe. Facts become secondary, and emotion and attack become primary. This also makes it almost impossible for enraged couples to come to an accurate agreement of what happened.[82]

John Gottman says that anger makes "rational thought almost impossible," which is another reason this state is damaging.[83] Instead of making choices that will help you and your relationship, anger leads to destructive exchanges that Gottman compares to *The Roach Motel*, where couples get in but can't get out. Like cage fighters, they become trapped, flooded with adrenaline, and their pulse and blood pressure rise.[84] Have you had fights like this? If you are having a lot of them, your relationship is not doing well. The next time you start losing it, remember that "anger" is one letter short of "danger," and it is time to get out of the cage.

Anger Is Contagious

One reason that anger locks people in is because it spreads from one partner to another. Have you ever been in a foul mood then seen your partner become tense and irritable? Like many negative emotions, anger is a response to a problem that often expands and creates new problems. For example, have you said something like this?

> "Why are you upset?"
> "I'm not."
> "You look unhappy with me."
> "No, I am fine! Sheesh!"
> "I can tell you are *not* fine."
> "Dang it, I am!"
> "Anyone can see that you are mad!"
> "Aaahhhh!"

Partners infect each other with anger, but so do strangers. Researchers who studied the emotional content of social media demonstrated this. They found that anger is more likely to spread electronically than other emotions, such as joy, disgust, or sadness. These investigators looked at over seventy million tweets on the Chinese site Weibo (similar to Twitter). They labeled these posts according to their emotional content and mapped how each was retweeted and responded to. Anger was by far the most influential emotion and tended to rile up readers and get forwarded on with a similar emotion.[85] Even with body language removed, angry words have power to ignite and spread fire.

Anger and Rejection

Wayne was one mad cowboy. He was a small-town Texas rancher who drank heavily, wore his jeans ironed, and was nursing a broken heart. His ex-girlfriend, Lacy, was a friendly waitress who was pretty from a distance and wore perfume strong enough to make eyes water. Wayne was particularly hurt by this breakup, because he had just given her brand-spanking-new breast implants. With these new developments, she decided that she was out of his league and went looking for a man who "would treat her better and wasn't such a drunk." She agreed to join him for therapy, even though she told us that her mind was made up. These two used anger like experts and had a loud history of attacking and wounding.

Our sessions were a minefield. We would jump from topic to topic, and soon one would explode. These eruptions were astounding in their ferocity. Lacy would scream, calling him lazy, irresponsible, or stupid, and he would retaliate with words sharp as spurs. He criticized her fidelity, looks, and her family. She would seethe, abruptly widen her eyes, and give him a withering stare. Like Medusa's gaze, this would turn him to stone. He would freeze and clench his jaw, and his face would turn purple. I would try to calm them down and help them reflect, but soon another hair trigger would be tripped and we would all be ducking and shrieking again. Afterwards, I would go to the office next door and apologize for the noise.

Wayne and Lacy demonstrated the intense and contagious nature of anger. They had a hypersensitivity to each other related to their previous traumas. Both came from volatile and abusive backgrounds and had unhealed emotional injuries. Most bullies have been bullied, and these two fit this bill. Even though their old hurts were not physical, they left a psychic mark. The brain experiences criticism and rejection in the same place as physical pain (the anterior cingulate cortex).[86] Verbal attacks hurt. Just like we instinctively block our face from an incoming projectile, we flinch at cutting words. The brain registers verbal abuse as pain, as does the body. It floods with cortisol, becomes tense, and aches.[87] Couples who are verbally aggressive will have more anxiety, pain, and misery. As one wise spiritual leader (Yoda) said, "Fear leads to anger. Anger leads to hate. Hate leads to suffering." Anger is the path to the dark side.

The Deception of Anger

Anger as Accusation

Anger blinds, confuses, and leads to blame. One research participant, Marie, told us how anger led her to lie: "When I am feeling hurt, I take some of the things that he does personally as an attack toward me. And I am an insecure person, so as a defense mechanism I make jabs. I will cover it by saying, 'I am not attacking you, but I am telling you the truth, and I am sorry if you don't like to hear the truth.'"[88] Marie's story illustrates how anger is often an accusation because it is directed toward someone. Sometimes anger is an attempt to convince yourself and your partner that your cause is just, like the woman in the last chapter who purposely cried louder so her husband would hear in the other room. Anger also activates prejudice and stereotyping, like when someone blames a group for something when they are mad: "Conservatives [or liberals] are ruining the country!" or "men are such pigs!"[89]

Aziz was an accountant who had just come from an intensive treatment program for sex addiction. His doctor told him to seek regular therapy and abstain from any kind of sex for ninety days. He couldn't believe it and wanted to know my opinion. I told him this was a common recommendation to reboot his brain, which was warped from a barrage of pornography, masturbation, and being sexually demanding with his wife. He became livid, claimed that doctors were idiots, and said that no self-respecting professional would keep him from sex in his marriage. He went home, yelled, pouted, and threatened suicide. His family begged him to follow the treatment he needed and had paid a lot for. His anger sprayed out at whoever was near, but none of us were causing it.

Philosopher Terry Warner argues that anger is deceptive, not only because it has an accusation, but also because it claims victimization: "Since you are hurting me, I must be innocent." This is why anger at someone is different from anger at something, like when you hit your thumb with a hammer. If I am angry at someone, I am demonizing them, and this puts me in the wrong. When Aziz was lashing out at everyone, he gave weak explanations for it. He claimed others were persecuting him and being unreasonable, which distracted him from the real issues, which were his addiction and the suffering he had caused. Although his anger was real, it was falsely fueled by his rationalizing, and in his mind, others were now the problem. As Warner says, "When we're stuck in troubled feelings, we believe that all our feelings are true—that is to say, we believe that by our emotions at that moment we are making accurate judgments about what's happening. If I'm angry with you, I'm certain that you are making me angry. [However], though we truly have these feelings, they are not necessarily true feelings. More likely I'm angry because I'm misusing you, not because you are misusing me."[90]

Revenge and Rationalizing

Imagine watching a movie where the bad guy kidnapped children, sneered at victims, and was pure evil. Would you like it if he eventually got away and retired to a private island with his doting servants? Of course not. We all expect him to get justice, and we cheer when he is thrown off a building by the good guy. Our desire for revenge is so strong that we see death as an appropriate response to unjust situations.[91] We get chemical pleasure from revenge, which helps explain why partners get trapped in cage fights. Instead of lovers, they become dispensers of vigilante "justice," punishing each other because they both "deserve" it. It feels good in the moment, even though it feels bad later when the brain calms down.[g]

The revenge reaction helps explain why anger deceives. When you are annoyed, you feel free to hurt another person, because it is *payback*, not cruelty. In one study, researchers had an assistant leave money on a table to reimburse

---

g. [Steven Brin said, 2012] "Rage is obviously another of these harmful patterns, that clearly have a chemical-reinforcement component. Many angry people report deriving addictive pleasure from fury, and this is one reason why they return to the state, again and again."

participants after they completed a task. Volunteers were told to take the money they earned, but it was possible to sneak more. Then they signed a receipt and left. In half of the cases, the research assistant took a fake phone call in the middle of their short discussion with the participant. This call lasted about twelve seconds ("Pizza, tonight at 8:30. My place or yours?"). The participants who had to deal with this seemingly small interruption took extra money from the reimbursement pile 86 percent of the time, while those not interrupted by the call took extra money 55 percent of the time.[92] Even subtle aggravations in a relationship can lead to punishing the other person and excusing it.

Controlling Our Anger

How can we hope to control anger if we are naturally wired for it? One clue lies in the ability we have to keep our cool with our boss, or a police officer. We have control over all of our impulses, including anger. We just do. To pretend otherwise is an excuse. Imagine what life would look like if humans couldn't control their anger. There would be constant fights to the death at home and at work. There would be tantrums on the highway, assaults to customer service representatives, and things thrown through the TV during annoying commercials. The reason that these things are rare is because we can show restraint. This doesn't mean it is easy. We don't always have control of our initial physical reactions when provoked, but we have a lot of control over what is done next. First responses are powerful, but so are built-in restraints.

Our emotions are like cameras. When we prepare to take a picture, there is an auto-focusing mechanism that zeros in on what the camera deems most important. However, we can manually override this response and refocus on something else or add filters to make it look different. We do this emotionally when an aggressive driver cuts us off. The auto focus occurs as the amygdala flares up, the heartbeat skips, and we get tunnel vision in our thoughts ("That #@$%*!"). But we then override this impulse and manually focus on other things. This might happen as we grit our teeth and use the frontal cortex to restrain our impulse to mow him down. We might use self-talk ("It isn't worth it" or "Maybe that guy is having a terrible day") or refocus on something else ("I need to stay away from crazy drivers").

Unfortunately, many get into habits of always giving in to initial impulses. This becomes an excuse to turn off the brain and its ability to manually focus. The override becomes weaker and initial angry thoughts feel irresistible. Wayne once claimed this, shrugging, "Yeah, I got me this intermittent explosive disorder, so I just go off on Lacy sometimes. I can't help it." This excuse, that "the devil made me do it," is common. However, it is a false claim. It may be easy to "lose it," but it is possible to "control it." Bringing the brain back to sanity after it gets provoked is worth working on, because controlling one's anger always benefits relationships and the people in them. There are several ways to reduce anger.

Examining the Effects of Anger

Wayne and Lacy were surprised when they realized how severely anger was damaging their lives. Lacy pointed out that Wayne had lost many friendships over the years because of his temper. Wayne downplayed this at first, but then he mentioned his 1978 Camaro. He had been restoring this classic car, but after a fight with Lacy he had taken an ax and gone Tasmanian devil on it, demolishing it completely. Wayne was also an angry driver, which had not only driven Lacy away, but nearly killed him and others. He liked to swerve at cars that were too close to the center line, and he once got into a highway chase with another hothead, and they ended up brawling on the side of the road. Wayne was recovering from back surgery at the time, so the fight "tore him up pretty good." He often drank as a way to calm down his racing heart rate and angry emotions, which were taking a toll on his body. One study showed that an episode of intense anger made a heart attack eight-and-a-half times more likely in the next two hours.[93] Lacy had pointed this out, saying that Wayne looked twenty years older than he was, and she realized that this would sometimes make her angry as she got annoyed with his poor self-care. She also realized her attacks were juvenile and that she often started the fights she had with Wayne. They both realized that they felt terrible after losing it.

Hopefully, couples who examine their anger patterns don't find the extreme problems of Wayne and Lacy, but even small irritations and flares add up and take a toll. One of our research participants told us his temper almost caused a divorce: "I knew that somewhere down the line it was going to cost [the relationship]. . . . I was being an ass to her."[94] Other participants realized that their anger was unresolved resentment, self-pity, or an excuse.

Take a close look at your own anger style. Ask yourself these questions: What usually sets me off? What do I say or do when frustrated? What is my typical response to others? How do I react to my partner's anger? How severe does it get? Most couples can break this down and calm themselves down if they try.

Safety and Soothing the Self

Wayne had always anesthetized his tension with alcohol, so he had little tolerance for discomfort. When he felt rejected, irritated, or resentful, he would hit the bottle. Our early work focused on identifying his reactions to stress. Through relaxation exercises he found that he clenched his jaw a lot and obsessed about self-pity and resentment. He was also surprised to realize he had had a nasty headache for the last two weeks. He was so disconnected from his physical self that he was not aware what his body and mind were doing. He learned to observe his thoughts instead of getting trapped in them, and he got better at realizing when his shoulders and stomach tightened. He realized that his thoughts became mean and irrational when he was irate. He wrote down all of his favorite angry statements.

Lacy agreed with these, and said, "That's when he starts hatin' on me." She told Wayne how these words felt, and she worked on "talking herself back from the cliff" when she found her anger rising. She made her own lists and they discussed them. They did breathing exercises and body scans and wrote down their self-talk that fed their rage. They improved sleeping habits, ate better, and hit the gym.

Step Back from Angry Thoughts

Slowing down helped Wayne and Lacy become more aware of their extreme perceptions. We did cognitive therapy to highlight their thoughts during their arguments (*I am so sick of this whole thing; He/she is so stupid; I am never appreciated for all I do; This relationship is a disaster*). But since their irrational thoughts were a *product* of the anger as well as a *cause* of it, they also needed to defuse anger at its core. They listened to each other's concerns and would stop and breathe. They got less reactive and their habits changed. This is what Dan Siegel calls mindsight, which is the ability of the mind to rewire the brain.[95] Old habits are reworked into new ones, as the brain changes through new and repeated mental energy. This is neuroplasticity, where the "neurons that fire together wire together."[96]

Calling Time Out

When Wayne and Lacy could not stay calm or have a constructive conversation, they learned to step away. We practiced what Sandi Stith and Eric McCollum call a negotiated time out.[97] This is designed to help reactive couples take a break in a way that makes them both happy. We started by creating a time-out signal (I asked them to come up with a hand signal, but their first efforts were not appropriate). We established ground rules. When one signaled for a time-out, they would break for half an hour, then reconvene. At that point, they decided if they were ready to 1) continue their discussion; 2) postpone it further; or 3) let it go. They found it useful, especially when they used the break to calm themselves down and not fume. They were mostly successful at getting back to common sense. Gottman tries a similar approach, asking agitated couples to go read magazines for a while, and reports, "Taking a break can have a dramatic effect . . . partners return to the table looking and sounding as if they have had a brain transplant. Once more, they can be logical, neutral, empathic, and attentive. Their good humor also returns."[98] When partners calm themselves down, they will be more successful at calming each other.

Soothing Your Partner

In a healthy relationship a spouse is a healer. James Coan at the University of Virginia did an experiment where a married woman was placed inside an fMRI machine to monitor her brain while she received random shocks to her big toe. This wasn't exactly a trip to the spa. The pain lit up her limbic system, which is activated by threat and fear. However, when she held the hand of her husband, her brain stopped the danger signals and calmed down. This effect was stronger when the marriage was better. However, when a stranger held her hand there was no calming effect. She remained jumpy and fearful in the same way as though there was no helper. The effect isn't gender specific and is also found in other intimate relationships, including gay and lesbian couples.[99] A loving, present partner is powerful tonic and can help to soothe emotions when they are heating up.

Successful couples realize when they are setting each other off, and instead of fighting fire with fire, they use water. Cooling off has a good effect on both partners, and when people are in close proximity they influence each other's level of calmness.[100] The next time you or your partner is getting angry, put your own oxygen mask on first, take a deep breath, and then help your partner breathe.

Focus on Basic Needs

Wayne and Lacy learned to identify the pain feeding their anger. They looked at their history with new eyes and realized that Wayne was terrified when Lacy had left him. But he handled this by yelling at her, which obviously didn't help. He learned instead to express his fears and tearfully told her he needed her and asked her not to run away. This was a new experience for Lacy, and it softened her feelings and helped her discuss her concerns in a gentle way. She told Wayne it frightened her to see his drinking binges, which in times past had led to her angry demands to engage him. This caused him to feel like a loser who was causing her pain: "If she thinks I suck so much, then why even try? If she is going to be psycho and hate everything I do, [note the exaggerations and self-pity] then I will go to the bar." When he did this, Lacy went elsewhere for security.

Ironically, it was the strong connection that caused the intense friction. If they didn't care about each other, they wouldn't feel hurt. Adults who lose connections feel afraid and abandoned in the same way that a baby howls when he can't find his mom.[101] Although it was not helpful for Lacy to call Wayne a baby, it was good for both of them to realize their explosions were related to legitimate needs for closeness and safety. As we addressed these underlying emotions, they calmed down and were able to hear each other without erupting. They had what are called the A.R.E. dialogues, emphasizing *accessibility*, *responsiveness*, and *engagement*.[102] They stayed open to each other even when scared; tuned in to each other's signals, including their body language and emotions; and focused on the other's needs and respected them.

Use Soothing Speech

How do you soothe a crying baby? Yell at her? Tell her to calm the heck down? Hopefully not. The typical human response is to hold her gently, look into her eyes, and speak in a sweet manner. This cooing is called "motherese," and it helps a baby feel secure. This works with your partner as well. It doesn't require baby talk and high-pitched voices, just a calm tone. When people hear soothing speech, it activates sections of the inner ear and increases tone in cranial nerves that slow down reactivity. It sends a message to the brain that all is well. Professor Steven Porges has studied this phenomenon and says that couples who use reassuring, gentle expressions and intonation connect directly to each other's nervous systems. This provides a balm to frayed nerves and adds a healing dimension to the words.[103] There is an old saying that kindness is a language that the deaf can hear and the blind can see. If a partner is trying to help, they may fumble with their words, but their calm and sincere attitude will heal them both.

Main Points

- Anger is a powerful emotion and is damaging to relationships.
- Anger is a survival tool, meant to keep people safe.
- Anger can deceive us into retaliating out of a false sense of "protecting" ourselves.
- Even though anger may be an automatic response, we are not helpless against it. Our brains can exercise control over anger and allow us to choose a different response.
- Defusing anger usually requires learning how to soothe ourselves and our spouses.
- Anger is contagious, but so is calmness and comfort.
- Soothing of self and other happens through calm words and focusing on basic needs. Once we calm down, it is easier to see what is underneath the anger.

Discussion Questions

- What kinds of things tend to trigger your anger?
- What have been the results of anger in your relationship?
- When have you resisted anger? How have you calmed yourself down when becoming angry?
- Does your partner help to calm you down? How have you done this for your partner?
- What helps you feel safe in your relationship? Have you ever told this to your spouse?
- What does your spouse need to feel secure in your relationship?
- What steps can you take to create a calmer relationship?

Chapter 6
Defenses and Détente

Man hears what he wants to hear and disregards the rest.
Simon & Garfunkel, "The Boxer"

Michelle Knight was having a bad day, but it was about to become a nightmare. It was 2002 and she was a twenty-one-year-old single mother who had just lost custody of her son. She was anxious about a court hearing that would determine whether or not she could get him back. She left her cousin's house the morning of the hearing but never made it to the courthouse. She met a man who asked her if she was interested in a puppy she could give to her son. Michelle was curious, so she went with him in his car. He took her to his house, assaulted her, and tied her "like a fish," binding her hands, neck, and feet with an orange extension cord. He dragged her to his basement, where he wrapped a chain around her neck and bound it to a pole. It would be ten years before she saw her cousin, son, or any friends and family again.

Thus began a decade of hell, as Michelle's life now involved assault, humiliation, and degradation. For the first several weeks she was forced to wear a motorcycle helmet, which partially suffocated her and caused her to pass out. She was given a bucket for a toilet and rarely allowed to bathe. Eventually she was moved upstairs and chained to a bed in a room with boarded-up windows. In her first year of captivity she became pregnant, but her abuser punched her in the stomach with a barbell, causing her to miscarry. The next year, another victim, Amanda Berry, age seventeen, was kidnapped and brought to the house and another, Gina DeJesus, age fourteen, the year after that. They all experienced similar horrors, including filth, trauma, being locked in darkness, and sexual assault. In 2006, Amanda gave birth to a daughter, and Michelle was ordered to assist in the delivery. They used a small inflatable swimming pool as the birthing spot, and Michelle was threatened with death if the baby died. The baby stopped breathing during the delivery, but Michelle was able to resuscitate her.

In 2013 one of the doors was left partially unlocked. Amanda kicked a hole in the bottom of it, shouted for help, and was heard by a neighbor. The police came, found the women, and arrested their abductor, fifty-three-year-old Ariel Castro. He was eventually charged with kidnapping, rape, aggravated murder (for the miscarriage), attempted murder, and assault. At his hearing he was allowed to speak on his own behalf. The things he said disturbed and enraged those in the courtroom.

He began, "I just wanted to clear the record that I am not a monster. I did not prey on them . . . I just acted on my sexual instincts because of my sexual addiction. And God as my witness, I never beat these women like they're trying to say I did. I never tortured them." He excused his behavior based on his "addiction," but went further, mixing truth with lies, denying things that occurred, including the violence. He said, "I am not a violent person. I simply kept them there without being able to leave."

He also defended his actions based on his victims' recovery. "I see Gina through the media and she looks normal," he said. "She acts normal. A person that's been tortured does not act normal. They'd act withdrawn and everything. On the contrary, she's happy. Victims aren't happy." He continued, "Most of the sex that went on in that house, probably all of it, was consensual. These allegations about being forceful on them—that is totally wrong. Because there was times where they'd even ask me for sex—many times. And I learned that these girls were not virgins. From their testimony to me, they had multiple partners before me, all three of them."

Even compared to the worst liars, Castro's deception and denial is appalling. He lied, exaggerated, blamed the victims, and claimed to be a good guy. "I just hope they can find it in their hearts to forgive me," he continued, "because we had a lot of harmony going on in that home." He finished with an incongruous admission of guilt by asking for forgiveness, but then returned to his claim that they were all happy together.

Castro was locked up for life. But instead of remorse or responsibility, he played the victim. "I don't know if I can take this neglect anymore, and the way I'm being treated," Castro wrote in a journal while in prison. He complained about the food, his dirty cell, the toilet, and treatment from the guards. On September 3, 2013, he hung himself and died in his cell.[104]

Defending the Self

The extreme denial, rationalizing, and victim blaming Ariel Castro displayed was horrifying; unfortunately, it is also common. Perpetrators of atrocious acts excuse themselves, as do abusive and controlling partners.[105] In lesser ways, intimate partners do the same thing by claiming their bad behavior was acceptable or deserved. Like Castro, people get defensive after they harm others and then are in denial about what happened or the harm it caused.

Sigmund Freud brought the idea of defense mechanisms to cultural awareness, and since then, we have been using his terms. For example, when your friend downplays her fiancé's nine former marriages, you say she is "in denial." Freud observed, as many have since, that humans go to great lengths to keep "painful thoughts and emotions out of awareness."[106] People block out bad memories, ignore others who need help, and refuse to admit their flaws.

Although understandable, defenses have a cost. Author Daniel Goleman suggests that psychological defenses are analogous to protection from physical injury. Like going into shock, if someone experiences a psychic blow, they shut down and the pain abates, but they aren't feeling much else either.[107] The drug of defensiveness may help someone temporarily feel better, but it diminishes self-awareness and blocks connection. Numbness prevents both pain and joy and puts up a barrier.

In this chapter, we will talk about the ways partners build defenses and how these cause distorted perceptions and embellished accusations. We will review the best ways to come to peaceful resolutions and lower shields, which is called "détente" (day-taunt), which is a state of reconnection. By the end, we will see how small efforts to lower shields bring big benefits.

Defensiveness

Chronic defensiveness is a key predictor of divorce and relationship failure.[108] When your partner suggests a change, do you shift into a defensive posture? If you won't hear them out or you attack back, you are being defensive. This also occurs when you overstate victimization or see only your partner as the problem. Defensiveness can include whining, exaggerated indignation, blame, complaining, or distraction. Ariel Castro demonstrated extreme versions of these as he complained, downplayed his violence, claimed his victims were fine, and tried to change the topic to his addiction or his poor treatment in jail.

Nobody likes being accused or attacked, and we naturally protect ourselves. Of course we get irked when our partner points out our failings, but when defensiveness becomes habitual and unyielding, it's a problem. One woman I worked with responded to any concern of her husband by saying he was "being controlling." If he asked for help with the kids, brought up a concern, or requested snuggles, she bristled and told him to back off. She had an instant defense mode triggered by any approach. Defenses are strong because they are tripped by deep physical alarms, which cause strong protective reactions.[109]

Freaking

I was on a hike once in northern Michigan with my friend, Dale. It was isolated, but we camped in an area near a few others, including a woman and her dog. She told us there had been a bear nearby, so it was good to have the dog for protection. Properly cautious, we hung up our food, pitched a tent, and enjoyed the evening—both of us planning on outrunning the other if the bear showed up. Shortly before dawn, we were peacefully sleeping when suddenly, a few inches from our heads, there was loud growling, snorting, and snuffling as paws scraped at the tent. I shot up in a flurry of zippers and gear and ended up outside on the picnic table, still partially in my sleeping bag. Dale began shouting, and eventually through the chaos I heard what he was saying: "It's the dog—just the dog!"

You have probably heard the term "fight-flight-freeze," or just "fight or flight." These words describe defensive instincts that kick in when a threat appears. This happens when a beast growls near your head—your heart skips a beat and your body jumps and readies for action. This occurs instantly, before any reflection and thought occur. In the tent, I didn't take a few moments to ponder the snarling (*Gee, what could be going on this fine morning?*); I just reacted. I was outside before any thinking began, in a full throttle freak-out: heart racing, muscles tensing, and cortisol pumping. This didn't abate until Dale's shouting sank in. Defensive instincts are powerful and protective, but they can go awry. Some people activate with fight-flight-freeze modes when they feel criticized or emotionally unsafe. When this happens, a wife might internally react to her husband as though he is a slobbering grizzly. He raises his voice about the dirty dishes, and her body experiences things like panic, hypervigilance, restricted digestion, increased heart rate, and adrenaline. These are bad feelings that can lead to overreactions.

Remember Mad-Eye Moody from the *Harry Potter* books? His motto, shouted at the Hogwarts students, was "constant vigilance!" which is also the motto of your amygdala. The amygdala is an almond-shaped piece of your brain attuned to threat and emotional response. It is part of a system that watches, scans, and monitors surroundings. Like Mad-Eye Moody, the amygdala can be jumpy and quick to fire up at any threat. When the amygdala lights up, the prefrontal cortex—where we do our logical thinking and reflecting—is bypassed, and our emotional brain goes on high alert. A shout from the amygdala causes a lot of feelings but very little thinking. Does that ever happen to you? Most fights have lots of emotion and accusation and little reflection and problem solving.

Your amygdala also remembers bad events and is hypersensitive and prone to overreaction. Mad-Eye Moody lost a chunk of his nose to dark wizards and was twitchy and suspicious. Do you experience small things as big attacks of disrespect or disapproval? Do you heat up when someone is unhappy with you? Unless your partner is coming at you with claws and teeth, your freaking brain is taking you for a ride.[h]

---

h. Our responses to threat are compelling, because the information goes straight from the eyes and ears to a central switchboard in the brain, and the body instantly reacts. There is no comparable response for positive triggers. In other words, when we see something that might have a basic positive need-meeting function (like food or sex) we will respond physically, but it takes a few moments of evaluation and processing through the frontal cortex. If I had seen a bear and thought of it as food, I would have had to make decisions and then pursue them. But because it was a threat, the reaction was instantaneous.

Fighting

Jared was a tall, dashing stockbroker who would come to our sessions in suits and slicked-back hair. His wife, Joy, was a driven triathlete and consultant. They earned a lot of money and spent even more. They were also skilled debaters, with Jared claiming his seventy-hour workweeks were because she cracked the whip and Joy asserting that he was insensitive. Their back-and-forth jabs were quick and pointed.

> "If she could be happy with what we have," Jared would begin, "we wouldn't have this stress about money."
> Joy would respond, "If you hadn't lost so many of your accounts, we would be fine."
> "If the economy hadn't tanked, then I wouldn't have lost the accounts."
> "If you would try harder, then you would land new clients."
> "If you would get off my back, I might get more motivated."

Instead of hearing each other, they mobilized and counter attacked. This happened whether the concern was small or large. It may make sense to jump in a foxhole when real grenades are being lobbed, but Jared and Joy would hit the deck and return fire with no threats at all. Joy would make a comment about Jared's shirt, and he would tense up and snap back. He would sigh at her new purchase, and she would blame him for it: "You wouldn't approve of anything I get, so I just have to take care of it myself."

Defenses protect wounds, but they also keep them from healing properly. Like a badly set bone, some injuries remain sensitive, and people learn to keep others away through sharpness or aggression. Joy had watched her parents suffer years of volatile arguments about her father's infidelity and perpetual absence. He was a politician with money and power, and Joy had learned to despise him for his irresponsibility at home. She had built up emotional scar tissue, a rigid fortress to block out the repeated betrayals and embarrassments he caused. In her marriage this prevented calm discussion, even when Jared was waving a white flag. Jared would seek connection, but her amygdala would overreact and shut him out.

Freezing

Withdrawal is another natural reaction that is normal in the face of true threat but harmful in a relationship. When Jared felt like Joy was judging him, he would pull back and stop interacting. When researchers watch couples interact they can code withdrawal based on lack of eye contact, nonresponse to the other, or decreased emotion. Sometimes withdrawal is a kind of deadness, where people go through the motions of a relationship without having feelings for each other.

Gottman calls this stonewalling, and like defensiveness, it takes a toll. Men are more likely to stonewall than women and go into physical flooding in response to threat.[110] A typical response looks like this: Joy sees Jared surfing the web in the evening, becomes annoyed, and says, "Have you followed up with that guy that owes you four thousand dollars?" Jared stiffens and his heart rate goes up. He responds, "It is being taken care of." She isn't satisfied. "You said it was coming in last week. Have you even tried?" Jared's skin tingles and his face gets warm. "What I *said* was that it was under control. They were gone and I am not calling them on their vacation." He turns away from her and ignores her next response, which really bugs her.

Have you had someone stop listening or hang up on you? It's provocative and evokes a strong response. We are highly social creatures, and we want to see expressions of interest in others or sense their emotions to know where we stand. If you tell your spouse something important and he or she ignores you, it's upsetting. When experiments have been done with babies (and baby monkeys) where the mother puts a stiff non-expression on her face, the babies go ballistic. They cry and even attack the mother to get a response.[111] We hate non-responsiveness, because it sends the message, "You are irrelevant." To be ignored is devastating, and Joy hated it. When she saw Jared turn away, she stomped over and demanded he look at her. He glared at his computer screen then abruptly left to go for a drive. This is when stonewalling goes to the next level.

Fleeing

Flight is running away from a threat. Most don't like conflict and will avoid it, but for some it is particularly terrifying. Jared hated conflict and would sometimes drop clients at work when they became difficult or required hard conversations. Relationships and families can be loud and messy, and many people shift into the "get me out of here" mode during these times, and some deal with family problems by cutting off relationships completely.

When Jared would leave, this triggered Joy's aggression, and her escalating noises would further scare him off. This pattern is common and has been called "pursuer-distancer," or "demand-withdraw." The stereotypical version is for the female to pursue (80 percent of relationship discussions are brought up by females),[112] but it happens in any gender variation. The more demand-withdraw happens, the less satisfaction there is in the relationship and the more likely things are to progress to escalation, violence, and divorce.[113]

Lowering the Shield and Getting to Détente

Hopefully your relationship doesn't need thick steel defenses. If you need a shield to protect from verbal or physical abuse, then you should seek additional help, and the defenses are understandable. However, walls that spring up at minor threats or remain in place after the threat is gone damage relationships. Healthy partners lower their shields and resist impulses to fight, freeze, or flee. Partners need to get to détente, which means to call a truce, and back off after things have gotten tense. Even if an initial confrontation resulted in claws extending, these can be retracted and partners can calm back down and shake hands. When you feel defenses rising, it's time to check in with yourself. Are you resisting your partner's opinions? Are you having a hard time because you don't agree? Can you listen anyway? Would it help to ask for a peaceful negotiation?

Lowering defenses allows people to reconnect and grow. One of the many great things about love is that when you get close to someone, you get challenged. You bump up against other views, and you learn more about your own weaknesses. Hearing feedback takes vulnerability and trust, but is an opportunity to learn. Do you want to know how you come across, what you do that your spouse appreciates, and what you do that your spouse doesn't appreciate? Do you want to grow closer? Couples who thrive discuss concerns then try again. When one says, "It isn't okay for you to talk to me that way," it is a chance to smooth out rough edges and get better. Each has different views and strengths, and these combine to make a partnership that is greater than the sum of the parts. If both are the same, then one is unnecessary. Partners who open up and share with each other grow into something better.

Aaron learned this the hard way. He married Dayna when they were young, and he had a difficult time when she challenged his views. He had a sarcastic, hyper-manly approach to the relationship. When Dayna asked him to help with the baby or in the kitchen, he would scoff or ignore her. His attitude toward domestic duties could be summed up as "screw that." He was jealous of his still-partying friends who were living lifestyles incompatible with a committed marriage. And although he was a funny guy with a lot of energy, after a few years, Dayna calmly announced that she was taking their daughter and leaving.

Aaron was stunned and, to his credit, began a serious examination of his dismissive attitude. He agreed to marital therapy ("harder than a root canal"), and for the first time, looked at how his walls and selective attention to Dayna's concerns had shut her out. He realized he had been in a selfish mode, focusing on how hard he was working and what he had sacrificed to get married. This kept him from hearing or appreciating Dayna's experiences with the baby, and it started a bad cycle of her withholding affection to cope with his neglect. He realized that she felt alone and dismissed and that she protected herself by creating her own defenses. After the crisis, they began conversations about what they each needed. Dayna became more assertive in speaking up for herself, and Aaron tried to be accommodating and honest about his feelings.

Small Changes

What made the turnaround with Dayna and Aaron possible? How did they go from the verge of divorce to deep connection? It was the small, yet significant choices Aaron made to open himself to Dayna's input and take responsibility for his actions. This was like flipping a railroad switch that moved the track several inches, resulting in the train eventually going to Los Angeles instead of Las Cruces. Small choices can have big impacts, and it is always possible to move a few steps at a time. A complete overhaul of a relationship is unlikely, so try manageable changes, which can trigger positive chain reactions. Remember the old adage:

> *For want of a nail the shoe was lost.*
> *For want of a shoe the horse was lost.*
> *For want of a horse the rider was lost.*
> *For want of a rider the message was lost.*
> *For want of a message the battle was lost.*
> *For want of a battle the kingdom was lost.*
> *And all for the want of a horseshoe nail.*

Just like major fights can begin over who left the towels on the floor, happy cycles can start small. The butterfly effect says that when a butterfly flaps its wings in Phoenix, it can end up causing rain in Paris. Likewise, a sincere effort can change a relationship. This is partially because the *mindset* changes when someone tries to be helpful. This may be why one survey found that simple acts of kindness, such as putting the kids to bed, taking out the trash, or telling your loved one they look great were more important than flowers or chocolate (but those are also welcome).[114] These actions reflect an underlying attitude of care.

It is easy to talk of change but hard to create new habits. One minute we feel committed to our health, but then someone shows up with chocolate cake. We try to improve our marriage but then get provoked and are rude. Why is it so easy to do dumb things? This is partially because defenses and impulses originate in the oldest parts of the brain and are fast. However, our frontal cortex can help. It is the part of the brain that is most uniquely human and helps us choose and reflect. People with damage to the frontal cortex become impulsive, inappropriate, and carnal, like partying frat boys.[115] But if you are fortunate enough to have your brain intact, you can recognize your impulses and override them. The more you do this, the better you get at it. Even if you've had poor habits or past traumas, the brain is plastic and can change.[116] Like Aaron, your small and consistent efforts can become new habits.

But not all frontal cortexes are created equal. When my brother-in-law, Andrew, was a kid, he was part of an experiment at Indiana University. He was shown a plate of Nutter Butter cookies, then told the researcher would leave the room for a few minutes. If he waited until the researcher returned, he could have two cookies. But if he couldn't wait, he should ring a bell and the researcher would come back, but only give him one cookie. He recalled thinking it was silly—of course he would wait and get the bigger payoff. But it wasn't so easy for some of the kids, who ended up giving in. This experiment is part of some classic studies usually called the "marshmallow tests" that found that kids who delayed gratification were more likely as teens to get better SAT scores, get into higher ranked universities, and generally be more responsible. In many ways, the ability to put the brakes on impulses is more important than IQ and certainly helps a relationship.[117] Partners who can resist impulses to quit their job, lose their temper, or spend money indiscriminately will put less stress on their loved one.

It is good to keep trying, even when it is hard. Every time a partner attempts to make things better it benefits the relationship, and the willingness to try is more important than knowledge about healthy relationships. Studies have shown that just knowing the right thing to do doesn't improve behavior.[118] So forcing your spouse to read this darn book will not necessarily change him or her (worth a try though). You can lead your spouse to knowledge, but you can't make them drink in the information.

But most people *can* lower defenses and learn. If words and feelings get shared, then change can happen, and sometimes it happens fast. Like in the roadrunner cartoon where a door is painted on a wall and then opened, sometimes paths appear unexpectedly. Many times I have heard reluctant fiancés attend relationship classes and say afterward, "I didn't want to come, but I'm really glad I did. This was helpful, and I've learned things I will use." Partners who open themselves to each other grow closer and see each other more fully.

Main Points

- Becoming defensive is a common response to being challenged. Often people are defensive after acting badly.
- Defensiveness can happen in different ways, including whining, playing the victim, or expressing righteous indignation.
- When people block out emotion they might temporarily feel better, but they will have diminished awareness, which prevents other emotions as well.
- Bodies react to some triggers instantly, before reflection and thought occur. This is protective, but it can go awry when we misread threats.
- Defenses protect wounds, but they can keep them from healing properly. Some emotional injuries remain sensitive, and people learn to keep others away through sharpness or aggression.
- Stonewalling is shutting down emotionally and shutting out a partner.
- In healthy relationships, partners lower their shields and resist impulses to fight, flee, or freeze.

DISCUSSION QUESTIONS

- When your partner expresses a concern, asks a question, or suggests a change, what posture do you shift into? Is it one of defensiveness or openness?

- When conflict gets overwhelming, do you shut down emotionally? Do you shut your partner out when you are hurt?

- Do you run away from conflict or sweep it under the rug?

- What would it take for you to lower your defenses and resist any impulses to fight, freeze, or flee?

- What small changes would be helpful in moving your relationship in a good direction?

Chapter 7
Denial and Responsibility

It's not denial. I'm just selective about the reality I accept.
                              Calvin, from Calvin & Hobbes

A State of Denial

Some people would rather die than admit being wrong. In Pakistan, there are remote mountain villages that harbor the polio virus. These are among the last places on earth without immunizations, and the World Health Organization and UNICEF have worked with locals to send teams to vaccinate against this crippling and lethal disease. In 2012, the Taliban leaders in Pakistan started banning the vaccinations, saying it was an American plot. Not only did the Taliban refuse the vaccinations, they assassinated twenty-two of the professionals who were there to save their lives.[119] It is tragic, but people do similar things when they kill their relationships because they will not admit to being wrong. This is denial: when someone refuses to acknowledge reality.

Partners who are abusive can demonstrate dreadful levels of denial. One woman, Stephanie, would hit her husband, John, and blame him for it, saying, "I threw the keys at you because you were late." Sometimes she denied remembering the conflict: "He says I choked him, but I don't recall doing that. It was all a blur and we were both out of control." Denial also happens in subtle ways. When John would protest, Stephanie would discount him or change her story. She once started with, "I never called you a pansy," but John reminded her that their daughter heard it and had been talking about it. Then her denial shifted focus: "If I did, it was because you wouldn't stand up for me." That wasn't working either, so she just denied responsibility for it: "I only said that because I couldn't take it anymore." She finished by denying that her words were hurtful: "I could have called you something a whole lot worse!"

There is a joke about a depressed guy who goes to a therapist. He says, "Doc, I feel terrible. I have been living it up: boozing, sleeping around, and neglecting my family. Can you help?"

"So," she replies, "you want to change your self-destructive behavior."

"No." He says. "I don't want to feel bad about it."

Avoiding unpleasant feelings is a basic motivation. All creatures avoid pain. For humans this includes avoiding anxiety, shame, rejection, and inadequacy, and this aversion explains why denial is so common. Everyone has emotional pain, and we all want to avoid it. Some have had such miserable lives that denial is understandable. It is better to live in the land of denial than accept and absorb horrors of abuse, neglect, or trauma. This chapter will review how partners use denial to avoid feeling uncomfortable or unworthy or to avoid facing ambiguous or difficult situations. We will discuss how people can come back to reality and see clearer in their relationships.

Denial of Average

We all want to believe we are exceptional, worthy of love, and like the Lake Wobegone kids—above average. This "above average effect" is very common. Most high school seniors rate themselves in the top 25 percent (and 25 percent of those say they are in the top 1 percent). This isn't just a math deficiency. About 94 percent of college professors say they're above average in their teaching. It defies logic, but it doesn't surprise.[120] (What does seem odd are those bummed-out 6 percent who think they are below average. Maybe a therapy referral would help?) Other examples abound: doctors predict they will be better at diagnosing than they actually are, and corporate CEOs are confident they are worth every penny of their colossal salaries.[121] Incompetent people exaggerate their abilities the most. This is called the Dunning-Kruger effect and is found among undergraduate students taking exams, where the worst test takers are the biggest exaggerators of their abilities. It is also found among medical students doing interviews or clerks.[122] The worst of the group have the biggest need to embellish.

Lovers also have inflated egos, which can make it hard to come to a consensus. If you think your opinion is right (and of course you do), then why should you listen to your spouse's foolish idea? But your spouse is thinking the same thing, and this sets up a contest of wills.

Partners also overestimate. He says he will get home sooner than he does ("just fifteen more minutes, I swear"), and she thinks she will feel more amorous tomorrow. They both think they'll be ready to leave sooner than they are. Not surprisingly, partners overestimate how much time they spend doing dishes, and men particularly overestimate how much they help around the house. When partners are asked what percentage of housework they each do, the totals add up to about 120 percent.[123]

People are protective of their delicate egos. They happily believe flattery, which is often just as distorted as the criticism that they dismiss. Daniel Gilbert of Harvard had volunteers take fake personality tests that were "evaluated" by experts. The volunteers then got detailed, insulting feedback from a psychologist. The feedback was, of course, false. The participants—hopefully well compensated—were told they had few good qualities or that others liked them because they were not a threat (psychologists are really hilarious).

Of course, people were miffed. Who wants to be told their purpose in life is to help others feel better by comparison? But participants quickly found reasons to deny the credibility of the exam—or the psychologists. They told themselves, "They obviously don't know the real me" or "They are dumb to think that." They probably would have eagerly believed the fake feedback if it was that they were amazing. However, the researchers had another volunteer observe the psychologist giving the harsh results to the volunteer. The interesting thing was that the *witnesses* became more upset than the *recipients* of the rude evaluations. Why? The recipients were more likely to put up defenses and dismiss the feedback. The observers weren't being attacked, so they just heard the rude evaluations and didn't like seeing someone getting picked on.[124] But those receiving the beatdown simply "rejected the unbearable" (Freud's term) criticism from the psychologist.

Gilbert calls this the psychological immune system. Like our physical immune system, it mostly monitors the environment and springs to the ready when something happens, like a flesh wound or the flu. Similarly, when we are psychically attacked, our denial system activates and rushes the threats out the door. Minor irritants do not turn on the immune system, because it would be counterproductive to respond to every little thing. When the body's immune system is overreacting, as in the case of allergies or auto-immune inflammation, it's a bad deal. If the psychological immune system is hyperreactive then denial flares up at the slightest threat, and this results in a person who is constantly offended over any perceived slight.

When I talk with couples about denial, they can usually spot it. The problem is that they see it in each other, which is a kind of denial about denial. This is understandable, because admitting denial is hard. However, it is important to live in reality, and the reality of a relationship includes both perspectives. Using both eyes gives depth to your vision, and hearing both partners' perspectives brings more accuracy to your relationship.

Denial of Reality

In 1959, psychologist Milton Rokeach was interested in how denial could be challenged. He took three psychiatric patients who all thought they were Jesus and got them together. He figured if a guy thought he was Jesus, but then met two other Jesuses, then something would have to give. But he underestimated the power of denial. He had them live together, but arguments happened with each Jesus claiming he was the holiest, and according to Rokeach, one yelled, "You oughta worship me!" to which another responded, "I will not worship you! . . . Wake up to the facts!" One stated (logically) that the other two appeared to be patients in a mental institution, so their claims were sketchy. Their story was written up by Rokeach and later made into a play and two operas.[125]

Have you ever ignored something just because you didn't want to do it? Have you dismissed the news about the dangers of sugar or nicotine? A few years back, I was in a thrift store and found a used book from the 1950s arguing vigorously for the health benefits of cigarette smoking. When we don't want to change, we stick our heads in the sand. The satirical newsmagazine *The Onion* nailed it with their article, "New Study Finds Nothing That Will Actually Convince You to Change Your Lifestyle So Just Forget It." It said,

> Though it contains several significant discoveries with a direct bearing on human health, a comprehensive study published this week in *The Journal Of The American Medical Association* has found no data that will in fact convince you to change your lifestyle in any way, so what's the point of even telling you about it? 'Rigorous, controlled study of hundreds of volunteers has revealed a dramatic trend toward nothing that will make you take better care of yourself, or alter your behavior in a meaningful sense, thus leading us to conclude we're all wasting our time here,' said study author Dr. Janice Carlisle, who added that 85 percent of Americans probably tuned out the second they heard the word 'study' anyway . . .

The more we want something, the more we are tempted to ignore the truth if it gets in our way of having it. In twelve-step programs like Alcoholics Anonymous, the first step is to get past denial. This is because, as author Stephen King writes, "[Addicts] build defenses like the Dutch build dikes." King knows this firsthand, as he fought with alcohol and drug use. He told himself he "just liked to drink," or, as a sensitive artist, he needed the drugs to face the pain and challenge of writing. He thought he "could handle it."[126] It wasn't until his wife and family confronted him, and dumped out a garbage bag of evidence (beer cans, cocaine spoons, cigarette butts, Valium, Xanax, Robitussin, Nyquil, and mouthwash bottles), that his walls crumbled down.

Facing reality is painful, but it is better to address the warning signs instead of turning a blind eye. Sometimes spouses ignore signs of addiction (*she keeps coming home late plastered*), infidelity (*why does he abruptly shut the laptop when I come in the room?*), or general deception (*that story just changed again*). Excuses mount, and denial becomes enabling. It's easier to ignore warnings than have difficult conversations, but this leaves problems free to grow unchecked.

Much of the damage from child abuse is caused by those who looked the other way.[127] Many victims tried to tell a parent or teacher about mistreatment and were ignored, shamed, or pressured not to talk. When this happens, victims doubt their own sense of right and wrong. When someone is forced to accept a façade, reality gets lost.

This distortion occurs in domestic violence, where threats of being hurt cause confusion and self-doubt. One of my projects examined how the abuser's blame can persuade the victim to doubt her worth and think the abuse is her fault. One woman said, "[He convinced me that] if I would've just done this, he wouldn't have taken my debit card away, or . . . he wouldn't have yelled at me or said that I was stupid." These victims use denial to cope, because it is hard to admit the abuse or leave. Denial gives a victim a chance to come to terms with an awful situation, while trying not to feel worthless: "If you cannot focus on the negative, things are always better. If you live in your dreamworld with the rainbow, all that stuff, it's always much easier to cope. If he was bad about everything, then I had to be bad too."[128]

Denial of reality may be understandable, but problems don't usually change by themselves. If you are disregarding important concerns, it's time for a cold splash of truth. Ask yourself these questions: Am I avoiding a difficult issue? Do I sometimes rewrite reality in a way that becomes dishonest?

Denial of Ambiguity

One of my fellow graduate students was fond of Freudian psychoanalytic theories. At one point, he told me I was too quiet in class. He suggested this was because I must have come from a family that was uncomfortable talking about sex. I protested that he didn't know my family. "See!" he said. "Your reaction proves my point. You are using defense mechanisms because I am getting at underlying endopsychic conflicts." The more I pushed back, the more I proved to him that he was correct, and the more defensive I became. He saw what he was looking for.

Life is complex, but we like simplicity and certainty. We fill in gaps to confirm our biases and create a preferred reality. If we want to live in a dreamworld, we choose the rainbow. Since experience is often ambiguous, it's easy to find evidence that fits our views. Politics is an obvious example of this. The issues are loaded with ambiguity, complexity, and subjectivity. But that mess is often boiled down to a simple certainty: "Everything my side says is true, and you are an idiot if you don't agree with it." Have you been on Facebook during an election cycle? If so, you may have seen friendships disintegrate and confirmation bias run amok. Here is a post I saw during the last election: "How can any intelligent person vote for _____? I honestly am asking!" I don't think this was a completely "honest" question. I think he was saying, "What moron could support such a fraud?" Even this mention of politics may be firing up your emotions and biases.

As Voltaire said, "Doubt is uncomfortable, certainty is ridiculous," and he might have been talking politics, but he might also have been thinking about relationships. Partners can become very certain about their opinions, even when they are about subjective issues. Will and Kim were a quirky couple with lively eleven-year-old twin girls. Will was a health club manager, and Kim worked there as a masseuse. They were self-help enthusiasts and were both convinced they knew more than the other about how to raise the twins. They would find books and research that supported their views, and the kids were caught in the confusion as the parents implemented various (and sometimes extreme) interventions. Will would try time-outs and claim they were working, and Kim would suggest that his discipline was soul-crushing and caused depression. They would offer contradictory explanations for how the girls were turning out. For example, Kim would say, "The girls potty-trained early because we gave them freedom to develop at their own pace." Will would say, "The girls potty-trained early because I reinforced the idea and helped them learn."

Everyone likes to feel correct, and creating simple explanations for complex situations is one way to do this. Kim and Will liked reading advice books that gave prescriptions and claimed to know the one true way to make kids sleep through the night or learn to read. Given how different each child is, having one correct approach seemed presumptuous to me, but it was seductive to them.

The tendency to see what you want to see was shown in a classic experiment with the most irrational and violent of creatures: the sports fanatic. In the 1950s, psychologists from Dartmouth and Princeton asked students from both schools to watch film from an unusually rough football game and look for infractions of the rules. They were to rate the fouls from mild to flagrant. They all watched the same film but—I am sure you can guess—the students' ratings corresponded to their loyalties. The Princeton students saw more fouls from the Dartmouth players and rated their own players' fouls as much less serious, and vice versa. Each accused the other side of intentional rough play. Even back in an era when social scientists assumed people were rational, these researchers were forced to conclude there was no objectivity when perceiving events in which one has an invested interest.[129]

Motivated Reasoning

In the classic movie *Monty Python and the Holy Grail*, medieval villagers accuse a woman of being a witch, and they want her burned. In making their case, they cite sketchy evidence: "She turned me into a newt! . . . [awkward pause as people look at him] . . . I got better." The accused defends herself: "This is not my nose, it's a false one, and they dressed me this way!" The town expert questions their logic: "Did you dress her up like this?" They are indignant, shouting, "No!" which then changes to, "Yes," and then, "A bit." And then, "She has got a wart." Even when caught in crazy accusations, they refuse to change their view: "Well, we did do the nose, but she is a witch!" When people sort through evidence but have a preferred verdict, they are using motivated reasoning.

Reasoning becomes motivated when we want to prove a point. Remember the parenting battles of Will and Kim? One of their arguments was about religion. The twins were taken from church to church and used as pawns in the battle for righteousness. Will was a committed Evangelical Christian, and Kim was into New Age mysticism. They would gain support from their friends in each place and read things to convince themselves of their ideals. Will would give Kim literature about the benefits of youth programs, and she would skim it skeptically while pulling out articles about the dangers of organized religion. They didn't take the other's views seriously, because they were busy bulking up their own. One study found that people who read essays about values and political issues spend 36 percent more time on articles that align with their opinions.[130]

Young couples in love use motivated reasoning as they ignore red flags and run away together, and nearly all newlyweds think they will not be among the divorced.[131] When a person is invested in believing something, the limbic system gets involved. This is the part of the brain involved in moral decisions. When a person analyzes things objectively, the limbic system is cool and does not push for a certain action. When someone is making a decision about something they feel strongly about, the limbic system is very active.[132] The thinking process is less logical. One study had men review biographies of potential sexual partners. The men rated the most attractive people as having the least risk of STDs, even though no STD-related information was given. But in order to come to this illogical conclusion they used the evidence that was there to convince themselves. In other words, they felt like they were being rational if the bios gave them enough random details (she has a good sense of humor, likes pets) to consider. Even though the details weren't relevant to their conclusion, they helped the men feel like their decision was well-considered.[133]

We Don't Know What We Think

When motivation changes, we can easily switch opinions. Have you ever fallen for someone but then got rejected? Did you then come up with reasons why it wasn't going to work out in the first place? If you didn't get snubbed, you probably wouldn't have changed your mind. When motivated by blind love, people ignore common sense and reject advice from friends or professionals, creating explanations that support their desires, like, "If I am good enough I can change him. Love will conquer all."

Opinions change with circumstance and sometimes are created on the spot. One study showed that most people can completely switch their views without batting an eye. The researchers had 160 volunteers fill out two-page questionnaires asking them to what degree they agreed with morally-laden issues (such as individual rights or political conflict). The people filled out the form, then discussed and defended their answers. However, the researchers pulled a fast one. Each questionnaire was on a clipboard, and when the subject flipped over the page to fill out the second half, parts of the sheet stuck to the clipboard. When volunteers turned that page back over to discuss their first responses, the answer sheet had changed, containing different versions of two questions. But here's the thing—the volunteers' answers remained the same. So a person who originally had strongly agreed about the *benefits* of government surveillance now held a sheet that said they strongly agreed about the *problems* of government surveillance. The participants were interviewed about these views, including the ones that had changed. About two thirds of them defended the views they hadn't put down in the first place. They gave logical and coherent reasons but didn't realize they were supporting positions they hadn't originally given.[134]

The study shows that people can change their minds and retroactively create reasons and rationalizations for whatever they are feeling at the time. The authors suggest that the project shows "a dramatic potential for flexibility in our . . . attitudes" that back up behavior. This also indicates that many subjective decisions are made from emotion rather than logic. However, this study also shows we can be pretty darn flexible in our opinions if we are willing to have an open mind.

You think you wouldn't do what these volunteers did, but you might. A recurring theme in the deception literature is how most everyone agrees that deception occurs, but they usually don't catch themselves doing it. We are blind to our blindness. As author Dan Goleman said, "For self-deception, by its very nature, is the most elusive of mental facts. We do not see what we do not see."[135]

Denial of Responsibility

Why are *Homo sapiens* so prone to deny reality and logic? One reason is to avoid responsibility. It is hard to make changes or admit you screwed up. This happens with high profile cases, as powerful politicians, celebrities, or CEOs use denial when they misbehave. They get caught, but instead of apologizing they show indignation and give excuses. Eventually they might admit that "mistakes were made," then an underling is fired and the perpetrator goes to rehab.[136]

Couples do this, as demonstrated by Amoni and Dee Dee in our problem-solving project. Dee Dee was a waitress with heavily sprayed helmet-hair, and Amoni was a football coach who looked like he wanted to go to sleep. He always raised his hand with his finger pointing up when he wanted a turn to speak. He told Dee Dee that she yelled too much, which led to this exchange:

Dee Dee: "I can't control it."
Amoni: "I beg to differ."
Dee Dee: "I can't. You frustrate me sometimes."
Amoni: "But [points his finger at her] you don't have to yell at me."
Dee Dee: "It frustrates me that you don't take things seriously. Then I get upset about them and you don't understand why I am upset."
Amoni: "No, I do take things seriously. I just don't freak out about things."
Dee Dee: "I don't freak out about things."

Amoni: "Sometimes."
Dee Dee: "No."

Dee Dee first denied she can control her yelling by claiming it is Amoni's fault (he "frustrates" her). She then switched focus when he described her behavior as "freaking out." This was easy to deny, because it was ambiguous. She did admit to yelling, but since "freaking out" is undefined, she could deny that altogether.

Some people deny responsibility by always blaming others. This is a self-centered attitude that is often found when someone plays the victim. It shows up with those who are overly dramatic and make everything about them. If someone has a history of relationship failures but always says it was the other person's fault, he or she is probably denying responsibility.[137]

One husband refused to come back after one session with me because I had the audacity to ask what he might have contributed to their problems. In his mind, he was never at fault. His wife continued to come and eventually left him because he was controlling and mean. She wondered if he would ever change, and I told her that if change would happen he had to demonstrate responsibility for his behavior, especially when he was hurtful. He needed to be sincere and show this for a long time, not just give a quick apology and make empty promises. According to violence expert Virginia Goldner, denial is the main clinical issue to address with abusers, because until they take responsibility for hurting others, they will not change.[138]

Conscience and Reality

Even those who are hurtful usually feel bad about it, and nearly everyone values treating people with respect and dignity.[139] Unfortunately, sometimes when people get upset their humanity gets lost. This is why Terry Warner calls meanness "self-betrayal"—because when people are cruel, they aren't being true to their own selves, which is why people have to rationalize their bad choices.[140] One common therapeutic goal is to help people get back in touch with their goodness and values. This includes their kindness, commitment, and desire to do what is best for the relationship. If partners tune into their conscience and each other, they are engaging with reality. This is the opposite of denial.

Healing Your Raw Spots

According to Wynton Marsalis' great-great-grandmother, life has a board for every behind. Everyone has suffered and been hurt, and some of those experiences left marks. People experience shame, inadequacy, bullying, and sometimes abuse. Hard things happen in families and other places, and these experiences shape perceptions and create defenses. Sue Johnson calls these *raw spots*. These are areas of sensitivity where people overreact to signs of abandonment or threat.

If someone has been belittled, they may be oversensitive to criticism; if they have been sexually abused, they may feel pressured by intimacy; if they have been left at the altar, they will be hypervigilant about being abandoned. Many fight-flight-freeze reactions occur when a raw spot is touched.

It is good to be aware of your own sensitivities, because it makes it easier to talk about them and not blame others for your overreactions. It isn't fair to use raw spots as a blank check for bad behavior, so even though someone is sensitive to being bossed around, it doesn't excuse retaliatory screaming and name-calling. But it is important to know a partner's raw spots and not hit below the belt by going at them. It is a cruel person who grabs someone else's sprained wrist or rubs dirt in their wounds.

How do you recognize sensitive spots? Did you use one hundred pounds of dynamite to respond when ten would have been enough? Did your emotions shift abruptly? Did you become defensive or use denial? Johnson says this indicates that your basic attachment needs are taking over, pushing you to protect yourself and survive at all costs. Take care of past injuries and work to rehabilitate them. Work together to create a nurturing and protective relationship, and consult with professionals if necessary.

Have you attended to your own healing? Do you request healing from your partner? Most committed couples want to help each other but don't always know how. Think about what your sensitive spots are and what your spouse's are. Find a calm space and explore how they might have flared up in your relationship, then brainstorm the ways you use defenses and denial. Do you ignore problems or oversimplify situations to your advantage? Are there areas where you use motivated reasoning or ignore things you don't like? This kind of conversation doesn't often come up spontaneously, but it can be very important. The good thing is that most couples care about each other and can cut each other a break. Partners have their moments of denial, but they usually come back together and move forward in reality.

Main Points

- Denial is a refusal to acknowledge some painful aspect of reality or experience.
- Denial occurs because people don't like feeling discomfort or feeling average.
- When we are in denial about reality, we stick our heads in the sand, pretending that if we don't acknowledge it, reality doesn't exist.
- Life is ambiguous and uncertain, which is uncomfortable, so people prefer absolutes.
- Motivated reasoning is when someone sorts through the evidence and concludes something that benefits them.
- People are often changing in their opinions, depending on the circumstance.

- Denial of responsibility can lead to victim blaming or thinking that other people deserve bad behavior because of something they did.

- Everyone has "raw spots," or emotional injuries. These need to be acknowledged and addressed.

- Living in reality and being real with one another can change your relationship for the better.

DISCUSSION QUESTIONS

- In your relationship, do you assume that your way is the more correct one?

- Have you avoided a difficult issue that you should bring up?

- Do you sometimes rewrite reality in a way that becomes dishonest?

- In what ways do you see yourself tuning in (and out) and renewing your commitment to your partner?

- How is denial different than tuning in to yourself and your spouse?

- Consider your own raw spots. Have you attended to your own healing?

- What are the buttons that get pushed in your relationship?

Chapter 8
Emotion and Acceptance

When you're away, I'm restless, lonely
Wretched, bored, dejected, only
Here's the rub, my darling dear,
I feel the same when you are near.

Samuel Hoffenstein

As a junior high student, Nathan Zohner won first prize at the Greater Idaho Falls Science Fair. He presented some scary information about the chemical dihydrogen monoxide. He asked people to consider its dangers, including that 1) it is a major component in acid rain; 2) accidental inhalation can kill you; 3) it contributes to erosion; 4) it decreases effectiveness of automobile brakes; and 5) it can cause severe burns in its gaseous state.

Zohner asked fifty people if they would support a ban of the chemical. Forty-three said yes, six were undecided, and only one knew that "dihydrogen monoxide" was . . . water.[141]

This project showed how the truth gets lost when words mix with bad emotions. Fear and anger are persuasive and influential. This is particularly true in intimate relationships, where the close proximity of partners amplifies their emotions. Feelings pass quickly and change what is said and seen. The marriage changes the mood, and the mood changes the marriage.

Partners don't usually realize that emotion is causing them to see each other differently. It feels the other way around, like the person is causing the emotion. For example, maybe Vern is stressed about his looming credit card debts, and this leads him to unfairly see his wife Donna as the target for his stress: "If only you hadn't gotten that kidney stone and ended up in the ER, we wouldn't have spent all our savings on hospital bills!" Vern is implying that Donna was somehow selfish or responsible for their money strains, but the reality is that there were many factors, some caused by him. In today's busy world, there is a lot of stress and struggle, and this causes some emotional overreacting.

Is life draining your resources and leaving you low on energy for your intimate relationship? Are you worn out and stressed? This chapter discusses how depression, hectic jobs, processed food, and sleep deprivation can leave us depleted and cranky. We will learn the ways mood deceives us and how we can embrace emotion and learn from it. We will see how to slow down and care for ourselves and our relationships.

Emotion Changes What We See

When you feel good, you wear rose-colored glasses, and the relationship benefits. Every interaction seems better, and partners feel closer. Even small emotional boosts make a difference. In one study, researchers gave insignificant gifts to passersby in a mall. Shortly after, the people were approached with a "survey" about their cars and televisions. Those mall shoppers who were given the trinkets reported being happier with their stuff at home than those who weren't.[142] A random bonus of a set of fingernail clippers made people more pleased about their minivan. Other researchers have found that doctors diagnose more accurately when given a gift before seeing a patient, and another study showed that people have a better mood after finding a dime on the photocopier.[143] Small things make a difference, and a happy partner helps both partners. A rising tide lifts all boats, and a good mood improves all interactions.

However, the reverse is true as well. A bad mood can cause irritants to become big problems. Grouchy managers give worse performance appraisals, cantankerous teachers don't teach as well, and surly students don't learn as well.[144] A spouse in a foul mood sees the other spouse with a negative tint. If he leaves the seat up, it is a catastrophe. Her cute laugh becomes an annoying honk.

Feelings are filters that change how we perceive the world. This was found in one study where people were induced to feel an emotion, like frustration, and then shown pictures of faces. People usually thought that the other person was feeling what they themselves were feeling.[145] If the observer was angry, they thought the person in the picture was as well. Spouses do this when they are annoyed and then misinterpret the other's expression as annoyance, when it may have been nothing.

The Deception of Depression

Logan was a doctoral student studying ancient Italian poetry. His life was filled with shelves of old books and a teaching assignment where he was supposed to inspire lethargic freshmen. His advisor was difficult and inconsistent, and Logan was a people-pleaser who worried that others were always upset with him. He came to see me at the request of his wife, Yuko, who was starting to panic at his change in personality. "He used to be cheerful, fun-loving, and interested in his work," she said. "Now he is a zombie. He goes through the motions and doesn't talk to me or anyone. He comes home and goes to bed and then shuffles off in the morning. Even when he is in front of the computer or with a book he isn't engaged with it. He hasn't paid any attention to me in ages."

When we first met, Logan was hunched in his chair like he was trying to disappear. His voice was small and weak, and he listed so many things that were overwhelming him, I couldn't keep track. Life was squeezing him, and he was making whimpering noises.

Logan was seriously depressed. Changes in sleeping and eating? Check. Loss of interest in activities he used to like? Check. Feelings of guilt? Nonstop. And so on. He spoke in self-defeating terms: "I am dumb; why did I think I could do this? I am a disappointment to Yuko." And he described intense emotional pain and suicidal thoughts: "I will never finish and my family will be better off without me." Clearly his pain was killing both him and his marriage.

Depression can take the relationship down with the victim. Many studies show how this happens. For starters, depressed people often exude waves of negativity, which is hard for a partner to deal with.[146] They also make more bad choices when depressed, like driving drunk or saying mean things.[147] Non-depressed partners also worry or feel guilty for what is happening. One study found that when people looked at a depressed partner's face, it caused a depressed reaction in their own brains.[148] It is stressful to see another in pain, and this feeds a vicious cycle. When Yuko would become upset, it would trigger Logan's distorted perceptions. He saw her emotion as hostile, even when it wasn't. He assumed she hated him, when the reality was that she was worrying.

The cycle continues as the depressed partner is consumed by pain and can't feel affection or attend to the other person. When people are distressed, they lose touch with their intuition and can't understand others' expressions or body language.[149] The pain takes all the focus. There is a proverb that says a man with a toothache cannot be in love, and it is the same with emotional hurt. A throbbing ache in the soul leaves no room for anything else.

Logan demonstrated many altered, depressed perceptions. He "knew" his students thought he was a horrible teacher, when the reality was that most were tired and not into poetry. He thought Yuko and his advisor were scolding him when they weren't. His melancholy mood amplified his self-criticism, and his words became irrational and harsh. After his depression lifted, he saw things more clearly and was less inclined to extreme negativity, and his hope returned that he could continue his studies and his relationship.

Depletion

When people see a battery icon turn red, they look around for a recharge. Wouldn't it be helpful to have this same indicator on everyone's forehead? When partners are depleted, they are impaired, and this affects their relationship and everything else. Exhausted spouses are irritable, oversensitive, and reactive. Addiction recovery groups use the acronym "HALT" to remind participants that when they are hungry, angry, lonely, or tired they are vulnerable to relapse. We have talked about some of these issues in other chapters but will focus here on hunger and fatigue. We will see that frazzled spouses are not the best spouses.

Hangry

Imagine what your partner would look like as a doll. Now pretend you are given this doll, along with a pile of pushpins, and told to poke it depending on how angry you are. Researchers asked a group of participants to jab their spouse doll every night for three weeks, and they found that there was a strong correlation between the number of pins used and the level of the pokers' blood sugar. In other words, a hungry spouse was an angry spouse. The researchers tested their "hangry" hypothesis by inviting the couples to their lab at the end of the three weeks. Partners were put in separate rooms and told they were going to be competing in a game to see who could push a button faster when a target turned red (the partners were actually paired with a computer). They were told that whoever "won" the round could blast their spouse's headphones with a noise and make it as loud and long as they wanted. And—you guessed it—the lower a person's blood sugar was when they won, the louder and longer they blew their "spouse's" head off.[150]

Hunger is a typical deception, because most people don't realize it is changing their mood. When starving, people get annoyed at each other, but the problem isn't the person, it's the lack of a sandwich. Hunger clouds the judgment of even the most professional people. Demonstrating this, researchers followed a group of judges to see what time of day they were most likely to grant parole to offenders. Judges are supposed to be impartial and wise, but they were much more likely to grant pleading parolees a break when feeling full and comfortable. After a mid-morning snack, parole was granted about two-thirds of the time. Then the percentage dropped off continually until lunch, at which point it shot back up to the same happy two-thirds level.[151]

This worked for me when I was stressing about a thesis deadline. I was waiting to get feedback from a professor, and to encourage him, I brought him a plate of homemade cookies courtesy of my wife. He had the draft back within a day, with glowing reports about it—and the snickerdoodles. I have also heard many tales of food as marriage therapy. One couple reported that whenever they became crabby, they would stop and eat. It either solved the problem or left the pair too contentedly full to address it. In a men's group I was involved with, one guy said the secret to life was to buy his wife candy: "Dudes, sometimes you just gotta go to the Kmart for Junior Mints. It saved my marriage."

Food is energy, and relationships take a lot of energy (this is also why authors frequently stop writing to get snacks). One project found that when subjects were asked to interpret another's body language, they did better after having a drink of lemonade. This only worked with lemonade with real sugar, however, and not artificial sweeteners. The calories fueled the focusing ability.[152] Brad Bushman, one of the researchers on the voodoo doll study, has discussed how glucose is actual brain fuel, needed to control negative impulses. "Even though the brain is only two percent of our body weight," Bushman said, "it consumes about twenty percent of our calories. It is a very demanding organ when it comes to energy."[153] So ditch the diet when you are trying to improve your relationship, and work things out over steak and chocolate.

Tired and Worn Out

Francesca was tearfully reporting that she wanted to connect with her husband, Lee, in the evening, but felt rejected. "We used to talk and cuddle," she said, "but he is indifferent now. He just stares blankly at me then falls asleep."

"Her voice is so soothing," Lee said. Francesca was not buying this. "Evidently my words put him into a coma. I should come with a warning label: 'Do not listen to Francesca while operating heavy machinery.'" As we discussed the problem, I could see what she was talking about. He was getting slack-jawed and yawning. More questions revealed other clues. At night, he had been snoring at such extreme levels that she was worried about going deaf. "Once, I was having a nightmare about a motorcycle gang running me over," Francesca recalled, "but the roaring engines were his snores." She was now sleeping in another room, so I suggested a specialist. They discovered that during Lee's sleep he was congested and thrashing around, and he would often stop breathing until his face turned red and he gasped for air. Not too restful, and it was affecting the marriage.

Being wiped out isn't just being sleepy. All versions of fatigue, emotional and mental, leave people depleted.[154] Researchers have found that being worn out impairs judgment and weakens resolve. For example, tired people are more likely to be persuaded by commercials and to be selfish, judgmental, and mean.[155] This is why it is often a good idea to go to bed on an argument and come back to it fresh. Resolving a tense discussion takes emotional heavy lifting, and this is hard to do after a long day.

One project examined the connection between mental fatigue and impulse control. Researchers divided participants into two groups who had to remember numbers. One group was given short numbers ("12") and the other group was given long numbers ("8473029"). They were supposed to recite these to a staff member down the hall in order to get paid. While participants were keeping the figures in their heads, they passed by a cart with snacks—cake or fruit—and were asked what they wanted. Those who were sweating it with the seven digits chose the cake much more often than those recalling two digits. Ruminating on the long numbers used a lot of brain power, including their impulse control. They couldn't resist the cake because they were spending their mental energy elsewhere.[156] Another experiment found when people were asked to eat celery and ignore a plate of cookies, they did worse on a mental task afterwards.[157] Resisting instant gratification is also tiring.

It is draining to work on multiple things at once, and the brain isn't very good at this. I was working with a group of sex addicts many years ago. Armando was making good progress working the twelve steps but admitted to the group that he was going to lie to his wife that night. He said he was going to stop at KFC on the way home for a bucket of chicken. She had him on a diet, and he agreed that he needed it, but he didn't have the energy to abandon his relationship with extra crispy drumsticks at the same time he was giving up porn.

Mental fatigue is costly. Challenges coming from multiple directions leave people worn out and unable to keep their good intentions. As late-night host Seth Meyers sarcastically observed, "A new study has found listing calorie content on menus has almost no effect on encouraging customers to choose healthier foods. The study was conducted by looking around." When partners are depleted, they don't really care what the right thing is; they just do what feels good in the moment. Who wants to have a late-night budget meeting when it is easier to play video games or sleep? Partners need to have energy to see clearly and make good decisions.

Emotion as Connective Plasma

We live in a bath of emotion. Like fish unaware they are in water, we don't always realize that every relationship interaction has an emotional dimension. Freud said emotions "seep out of every pore."[158] Feelings pervade interactions and are felt from infancy, and babies (even blind ones) make the same emotional expressions of joy, disgust, anger, and fear that adults do.[159] These expressions and tones are how infants communicate. Babies can also read feelings and understand the emotional quality of words before they understand the meaning of the words.[160]

Tone Trumps Words

Unless a person understands the emotional subtext of a conversation, they might get confused or derailed. For example, take the question: "What is the matter?" This isn't just an objective inquiry. It can be a gentle expression of love or a sarcastic taunt. The *way* it is asked permeates the question and sinks deep into the hearer. The words mean something in the dictionary, but the speaker's attitude is what is most important. Tone trumps words. This is especially true when emotions are strong. A powerful emotion will trigger physical reactions, and that will influence a person's response. As discussed in other chapters, an aggressive tone triggers defenses and bias, and a soothing tone invites reconciliation. An old family therapy saying is that a person cannot *not* communicate: Even without words, messages are conveyed.

When Emotion Is Malfunctioning

People who claim they aren't influenced by emotions do not understand themselves. They may be tamping down feelings or ignoring them. This can lead to inappropriate or incongruent communication. This was the case with Davis, an oil-field engineer who fixed heavy mechanical equipment. He had a missing tooth and wore death-metal T-shirts, and when he was threatened he would do a strange thing—he would smile. He would grin, his eyes would get very wide, and he would sit up stiffly and talk. And then talk some more. The talking overwhelmed his wife, Jackie, and controlled the flow of the conversation. He did this in our sessions, steamrolling anyone else's attempts to contribute. "My wife knows her issues, and I don't have to go into that," he said. I began to ask for clarification, but he launched again.

"I will not take responsibility for her problems; she has to do that herself. She can't blame me," Davis said quickly. "I know I have my struggles, and I take full responsibility for those, but I won't be made the villain when she knows what she does."

"Help me understand what you are talking about," I said. "What specifically are the things you think she should change?"

"She knows, and I don't need to get into that," he said, eyes opening wider, with that strange smile. "I just work on my stuff. I work very hard, I put food on the table, and if she chooses to do her part, that is up to her."

He went on, but I stopped him, which made him grimace. "Do you know what he is referring to?" I asked Jackie.

"I have no idea," she said, glowering. "He makes blanket accusations, implying that I should magically know what he wants, but I don't."

"You see, that is what I am saying," he interrupted. "She knows what makes me angry but pretends she is innocent, when we both know that isn't true."

I was still lost and getting irritated at his condescending manner, so I pushed back. "Do you not want her to know? Do you like making accusations she can't do anything about?" I was trying to get clarity, but my frustration was coming through.

He shook his head and cleared his throat, "She cannot control herself with our son."

Jackie rolled her eyes. "He thinks that I yell at him or that I am 'illogical' with him. I don't yell, but I get frustrated when he leaves his football gear all over. When I try to talk with him, he acts disrespectfully toward me. And then Davis tells him he doesn't have to listen to me."

"I do," he said. "He does not have to listen to you when you rant and rave. It is a bad example for him, and I don't agree with it."

"But, do you see how that undermines any authority she has?" I asked. "Are you concerned that your disregard toward your wife will make it harder for both of you to parent your son?"

"I have no problems parenting my son," he smirked. "He respects me and does what I ask, because I have earned it. I don't make empty threats."

Jackie was now in tears and glaring at the wall. Davis had gotten under my skin, and I pushed harder about his motives or whether he valued his marriage. He pushed back and sat up straighter when I asked whether his work came before his family. "Obviously my work will help my family, and they understand that, so yes, work comes first."

It was one of those days, and although I normally was comfortable with negative moods in the therapy room, this one was getting to me. I tried to calm things down and generate a constructive conversation, but this session wasn't going to win any awards. I did want Davis to understand his thinking and examine his motivations. But I was also rationalizing my "interventions," since part of my motivation came from my annoyance.

That day, emotions were mixing with words in a potent combination. Davis's incongruent expressions—smiling and laughing while being aggressive—were provocative. It communicated more than rude words would alone. His emotions conveyed that he enjoyed being in control and hurting Jackie. The inappropriate facial expressions were also inflammatory. Additionally, my words were tinged with emotion, and Davis felt it. I was frustrated at him and protective of Jackie, who was being denigrated in front of me. I felt inadequate to stop the negativity, and this left me apprehensive and cross. Jackie felt run over and reacted with tears and flushed cheeks. She communicated through pained expressions, like, "Why do I even try?" Davis was feeling smug, because he was controlling the room, but he was also defensive from my challenges and Jackie's stories, which he responded to by becoming further entrenched in his entitled feelings. Negative emotions complicate all interactions.

Emotional Awareness and Self-Care

Emotions are a wonderful part of our lives. Singles pair up because of positive connections, and couples stay vigorous over the long haul because of all of the fun, connection, and joy that is part of their interactions. It is important to be aware how feelings live and breathe in your relationship. Are they expressed and understood? Downplayed? When emotions are denied, they usually surface in other ways, like Davis's cocky control. Emotions shouldn't be avoided but welcomed and managed. Sometimes emotions turn sour, because of a depleted physical container. A healthy body is more likely to produce healthy feelings.

Warren was in need of some emotional awareness and self-care. He was sixty and wore thick glasses and plaid button-down shirts with pocket protectors. He was often on edge and irritable, and his beleaguered wife, Bonnie, came with him to see me. "He cannot keep a job," she said. "He needs some serious psychological help."

"I have never been able to work with people." Warren told me. "I can't get along with idiots, and that's what I'm surrounded by." His last job was as a customer service representative helping people understand their annuities and insurance options. However, since he thought most customers and their questions were annoying, his "service" often included sighs, snappy comments, or unsubtle ways of telling them they were dense. This got back to his supervisor Ricardo, who sent him a stern email requesting a meeting.

"The email was in all caps," Warren said, "which is basically like yelling at me, and I am not okay with that. He's a punk." Warren stomped into Ricardo's office, which triggered the two-posturing-males-in-a-small-room scenario. Name calling began, and Ricardo made a comment about Warren's comb-over, and Warren punched him in the forehead.

"Fortunately, Ricardo didn't beat him down and kill him," Bonnie said. "He is thirty years younger." When I asked what they thought would help, Bonnie said that Warren was depressed and needed heavy medication. Warren wasn't sure, but he wasn't happy.

I asked some questions about depression, but the real story emerged when I asked about lifestyle. Warren was staying up most of the night surfing angry political sites, listening to angry podcasts, and playing Angry Birds. He was drinking a dozen cans of Mountain Dew a day, and his diet mostly consisted of two food groups: deep fried gas station lumps and Frito Lay flavor twists. His home office was a wreck, and Bonnie had forbidden him to come into certain rooms because he trashed them. Bonnie wasn't doing a lot better. She was a daily donut downer and would buy jumbo bags of peanut M&Ms and eat them in her closet. She also consumed ice cream while watching late night reality shows. I asked them if we could start with a different direction than medication.

Our Embodied Self—The Physical Container

Warren and Bonnie knew at some level their poor habits were affecting them, but they had a lot to learn. Emotions are housed in a flesh-and-blood body, and when it is being poisoned or neglected, the resulting emotional spew will be tainted. Many studies have found that poor self-care is connected to poor relationships.[161]

Eating Food

One of the first things we discussed were guidelines from food expert Michael Pollan. His first suggestion is to *eat food*.[162] The idea that we need to eat food puzzled Warren: "What else is there?" But he came to realize there is a big difference between meat, fruits, and vegetables, and the yellow dyes, corn syrup, and chemically processed combinations he was ingesting. I recall the moment when the light went on. His eyes widened. "So you are saying that a breakfast of eggs, a banana, and milk is better than a Mountain Dew and a Sam's Club muffin?"

That was exactly what I was saying.

Warren's first big change was to chuck the soda and start carrying around water. He became so faithful, he often had to slip out of our sessions to go to the boy's room. He and Bonnie worked on creating meals from fresh food. They focused, as Pollan suggests, on buying from the outer ring of their supermarket, not the inside aisles. They still had some treats or occasional nachos, but the majority of their nutrients now came from authentic sources.

Warren lost some weight and reduced his food comas and afternoon sugar crashes. He became enthusiastic about finding healthy options, and we had to restrain him from jumping on fad diets. One week, he came in with information on a coffee and tofu plan that promised fifteen pounds lost every week. Instead of this, we focused on basic changes that were sustainable and kept introducing new healthy foods over time.

Many people share Warren and Bonnie's challenge, and it seems as if everyone has a complicated relationship with food. It's hard to always feel good about what and how much you eat. This is why it's wise to be patient and kind as you work together to take care of yourselves. Focus on reasonable changes, and pay attention to what helps you feel the best. Warren and Bonnie had become disconnected from what their bodies were telling them in regard to being hungry or full. They practiced mindful eating, and one day Bonnie shared a breakthrough. She had become angry at Warren when he was asking her questions. Then she realized she felt lousy because she had come home ravenous and eaten four cupcakes, which led to vague nausea and cruddy feelings. Not only did these two learn to eat to avoid getting hangry, but they also learned to eat less of the edibles that punished them.

Getting Rest and Exercise

Without the caffeine flooding his system, Warren also did better going to sleep. He agreed to turn off screens at 10:00 p.m. and read books instead, and they both worked at recalibrating their sleeping schedules. Studies have found that those getting sufficient sleep improve work performance and have better health, less stress, and more willpower.[163] Another study shows that tired people are more likely to eat junk food.[164] These two decided that when either became cranky, they would try to grab a nap or go to bed early. Their evenings were shorter, but better. "His sense of fun has returned," Bonnie reported. "We watch shows together again, and instead of being critical, he makes his doofy jokes." They found, as the old Irish proverb states: "A good laugh and a long sleep are the two best cures for anything."

Another thing that helped their sleep and mood was a brief evening walk. Integrative medicine expert Andrew Weil considers it irresponsible for mental health professionals not to include physical exercise as part of a treatment program.[165] This is because exercise outperforms medication for many emotional problems, including depression, anxiety, attention deficit issues, and sleep disorders.[166] The walks became indispensable for Warren and Bonnie and when tense issues came up, they were better able to talk through them on the walk. If they finished the walk before the conversation, they saved the issue for the next outing. One study found that intentionally walking in a "happy" style, with arms swinging and head up caused the walker to feel more cheerful.[167] There is something about putting one foot in front of the other and being in the moment that helps to work out negative feelings. Eventually, Warren started going to the gym. Sometimes I saw him there, and it was kind of an amusing experience for him to eagerly come over in the locker room to report on his latest dead lifting accomplishments.[i]

Overall, exercise helps people better handle their emotions.[168] It slows down hair-trigger responses and strengthens self-control. It works well with meditation and stress-reduction techniques, because all of these help people be more in tune with their embodied self. As discussed previously, the most stable and long-lasting relationships have partners with lower physiological arousal; these folks don't get as reactive and out of control as the couples who are likely to split.[169] So take more walks, and dust off the elliptical machine. Use emergency interventions when you find yourself getting angry and burned out. Take a few minutes and breathe slowly, or go for a run.[170] Gym memberships, yoga classes, and meditation apps are all less expensive than divorces.

Setting Limits and Self-Care

Many partners are overwhelmed with ceaseless interruptions from work, bills, and errands. This can become a treadmill that won't turn off. Professor Bryan Robinson has estimated that about 25 percent of Americans are workaholics—actually addicted to the nonstop rush of tasks.[171] Vacations have shrunk and usually include checking emails and responding to "emergencies." Once I was at a cabin in the mountains. I agreed to join a conference call, because it was supposedly crucial and was for a large, funded project. I vividly recall watching a beautiful sunrise over a lake while my stomach tightened at the contention between callers and the tasks being added to my life. It spoiled much of that

---

i. This also brought up a unique ethical question to discuss with my students: what happens if a client comes to talk to you wearing only a towel?

morning, and, for me, was a wake-up conference call. It helped me set better boundaries in the future.

Saying no and protecting oneself is hard in today's world, but it's essential to staying balanced. Partners need to turn off phone alerts, leave the briefcase at work, and schedule time together.[172] The world will not come to an end, and the piles will be there for another day.

When people allow work to take over, they neglect things that feed their soul. This includes friends, family, hobbies, and spiritual lives. This had happened with Warren. I was surprised to learn he used to do woodwork, but his tools had been untouched in a dirty garage pile for many years. I asked him to bring me examples of his craft, and he did, showing me some small sculptures and pictures of tables he had made. His self-assigned homework was to break out the tools and spend some time each week with his projects. He re-subscribed to *Scroll Saw Magazine* and got back into the shop.

Taking care of yourself is not selfish and will benefit your partner. Are you neglecting your health, friendships, or a hobby you once loved? Take a walk in the woods, call a pal, or restart that saltwater aquarium, and your intimate relationship will also revive and grow.

Emotional Acceptance

Many people resist or ignore their bad feelings, and Warren was good at this. He was an emotional stuffer and would let irritations build up, then blow up. He had learned this through the typical male cauldron of being punished for showing weakness. He was harassed as a kid for being small, and then harassed again in the army. He learned to bite his tongue and not express himself, and this became a coping strategy. One of the things he didn't want to talk about in therapy was his adult son, who had become estranged. Through time and encouragement, he learned to accept and discuss this difficult situation. At first, Warren was dismissive ("It's his life; I don't care"), but eventually he was able to share the whole experience of self-blame, resentment, and sadness.

People hate negative emotions, but a healthy relationship can be a place to work them out. Accepting feelings, even bad ones, is part of engaging with life rather than running from it. As researcher Russ Hayes has said, "Higher levels of experiential avoidance, the technical term for trying to avoid or get rid of unpleasant feelings, are directly linked to an increased risk of depression, anxiety, stress, addiction, and a wide variety of other health issues."[173] Avoiding feelings often involves numbing pain and making poor choices. People drug themselves with prescriptions, alcohol, porn, work, phones, food, or shopping.

Warren and Bonnie had gotten into the habit of avoiding each other. Each evening they would lumber like robots toward food and screens, eluding eye contact and physical connection. To address this, they had to practice talking. They did this on their walks and during therapy. In the same way they learned to listen to their bodies, they also tried to understand what their emotions were telling them. For example, Warren learned his irritability was a warning sign to slow down. It indicated his need to examine his thoughts, which were prone to extremes. Bonnie also realized her resentments toward Warren had calcified and become bitter. She softened as she practiced bringing up concerns in a calm way and having Warren listen. They got better at receiving the ups and downs of the day. If they were stressed or had a frustrating interaction, they would talk about it if necessary, then move on.

Feelings need to be felt, not fought. Once I got a call from a client having a panic attack. She was a nurse who had been under intense stress about a job change. She couldn't stop worrying, and this had shifted into fast breathing and a sensation that she might pass out. I told her to not fight the unpleasant sensations, but to instead embrace them.[174] I suggested she take some slow breaths and observe her own reactions curiously, like she would if she was examining a patient. This was hard, but it works better than fighting back. She was panicking about the panicky feelings, trying to push them away, which is like tangling with a bully, making things worse. She found a quiet place, closed her eyes, and let the feelings and thoughts flow for a few minutes, noticing them. She grew calmer as she described some of the sensations and stepped back from the abyss.

Joe had a similar experience. He was a jazz pianist who was anxious and depressed about a serious relationship he was getting in. His previous marriage had ended badly, and he was terrified of a new one. He had kept journals during the rough divorce and couldn't look at them or think of his ex, because it caused fear and anger. He was having nightmares that his new girlfriend would hurt him. I asked him if he would be willing to look at his old journals and talk to me about it. At first he was dubious, but I told him sometimes the way to let go of old trauma is to reconsider it in a different time and a safer place. He returned surprised and relieved. "It wasn't that bad," he said. "Sort of unpleasant, but also cathartic. I was able to see how different that situation was, and that helped me to let go of hostility I had toward my ex." Emotional acceptance isn't always easy, but by allowing grief and pain to be felt, we let our emotional self do its work.

Accept What You Can't Change

A few years ago, I was attending a lecture by a Buddhist monk, who was leading us in meditation. She invited us to be present-focused, and keep a non-judgmental mind. We were asked to accept thoughts, feelings, and experiences without trying to change them. As I was settling in, a man began shuffling his papers and coughing. I was distracted but meditated on. He then started unwrapping a snack, which echoed in the quiet room. The monk continued with her exercise. I tried to give the loud eater surreptitious glances to convey my disapproval, but then a shift happened. I stopped wishing this man ill feelings and just started noticing. I observed his noise, my reactions, tension, and expectations. I became curious instead of frustrated. After a couple of minutes, the disrupter got up and exited, and I was left to reflect. My irritation became a learning experience once I accepted that things were outside of my control.

Partners can benefit from this lesson. Some resist the idea of acceptance, because it feels like giving up or giving in. But it doesn't mean you ignore problems or don't try to improve your situation. Acceptance just suggests that many things are outside of our control, and getting angry or bitter about it only makes it worse. Sometimes, difficult situations involve suffering. When there isn't a quick fix, it is an opportunity for patience and growth while continuing to work.

This is hard, because we all hate suffering. No one likes depression, bitterness, or pain. However, suffering can be a journey that couples take together. One time, a couple was talking to me about their adult son who was off the deep end abusing heroin. They had taken him in, but he had stolen from them and his siblings and was now homeless and self-destructing. I felt helpless to provide advice, but I tried to empathize and reassured them that if there was an easy answer to this situation, they would have already done it. They seemed dissatisfied and asked if there was anything else they should be doing. I commiserated and recommended some things to read, but reiterated that this was a very difficult situation. I tried to be encouraging and present, but I wondered if they got any benefit from coming.

I got an email from the wife a few days later. It said, "I cannot express now much better I feel after talking with you. I feel empowered to do what I know must be done. And I feel I can allow myself to be happy, if that makes sense. I have noticed a big difference in my attitude. I also know there will be tough times ahead. But I feel ready to face them."

I was surprised, to say the least. And I am not suggesting that simply being present and having a good cry will always make everything all better. I don't usually get those emails after tough sessions. But it is true that many things we deal with are just that—things to be dealt with. We aren't getting ripped off when we suffer. The trick is to engage with trials in a constructive and patient way and not add resentment to the problem by wishing it didn't exist. Growth happens as we embrace the fullness of life, with all of its uncertainty and challenges.

Expecting Reality and Showing Self-Compassion

One key to acceptance is having realistic expectations in a relationship. Partners who expect perfection will be disappointed. When partners think the other will always agree, they will be thwarted. If they expect to be waited upon, they are probably immature. At some level, all marriages are incompatible and all spouses are imperfect. This is reality, but it is okay. As one example, research shows that around 69 percent of the problems couples experience are unsolvable.[175] They don't go away easily, because they are connected to different styles or personalities. Successful couples live with these differences in a reasonable way and accommodate each other. Sometimes these challenges bring growth and help partners develop patience and unselfishness.

Some couples develop false expectations that things will always be amazing, because their early days of love are intoxicating. However, the heady rush of new love isn't sustainable, and most romance novels are fiction. There is a reason that *Romeo and Juliet* ended with death rather than a boring marriage with serious in-law problems. Highlights of a relationship are fun, but they are all the more enjoyable because of the challenges in between.

Perfectionism for your relationship suffocates love, and perfectionism toward yourself kills happiness. Kristin Neff studies self-compassion and has found that people who wouldn't dream of saying rude and demanding things to others often say these things to themselves. Have you ever called yourself an idiot or berated yourself for not following through with an exercise plan? Probably. Have you done that to a friend? Probably not. Neff has found those who are kinder toward their own imperfections are happier, more optimistic, connected to others, and emotionally resilient.[176] Self-compassion isn't just pumped up self-esteem or an inordinate focus on one's needs or issues. It is simply a willingness to extend empathy towards one's own suffering and inadequacies like you would a friend.[j]

Once I was talking with Neff at a conference about our respective sons who are on the autism spectrum. I was there presenting research with a student, Matt Brown, about the stresses couples experience when there is an autism diagnosis in the family. She began asking me some questions about our analysis and findings. Matt had left, and I was unprepared to adequately answer her, so I faked it as best I could. I felt dumb for days, but found it ironic that I was beating myself up for my weak responses to the self-compassion lady.

Having compassion for yourself is part of emotional self-care. Relationships work best when people are happy, so give yourself some tender, loving attention like you would for others. Don't be demanding, harsh, and contemptuous with yourself any more than you would with your best friend. Get professional help if needed, and allow your well-being to be a high priority.

---

j. To test your self-compassion see Kristin Neff's short assessment at selfcompassion.org.

Main Points

- Emotions change what people see in their relationship. Small things can make big impacts on emotions, which then change what people do.
- Often people don't realize that their emotions are coloring their interactions and perceptions.
- Depression is a particularly negative state that affects both partners.
- When partners are depleted, they are impaired, and this saps their relationship. Exhausted spouses are irritable, oversensitive, and reactive.
- Hunger and fatigue are subtle deceptions that drain emotional energy.
- When partners are depleted, they don't care what the right thing is; they just do what feels good in the moment.
- Tone trumps words. This is especially true when emotions are strong.
- When people get out of touch with their emotions, they often use them in inappropriate or incongruent ways.
- A responsible partner learns to understand and manage his or her emotions.
- Poor self-care is often connected to poor relationships.
- Emotional self-care involves eating a balanced diet, getting consistent rest, and exercising.
- Self-care also means setting limits and doing things that strengthen the couple and the soul.
- Accepting feelings is part of moving through life rather than running from it.
- It is healthy to realize that some things are outside of one's control, and that many parts of a relationship will not change.
- Having compassion for yourself is part of emotional self-care and will benefit the relationship.

Discussion Questions

- How have emotions influenced your interactions with your partner?
- When have negative emotions clouded your judgment or strained the relationship?
- When are you most likely to get in an argument with your spouse?
- What are your personal triggers related to being hungry, tired, or stressed?
- When does your body tell you that self-care is needed?
- What do you use to care for yourself emotionally, and what helps you stay your best self?
- How could you better care for your body, mind, and spirit? How might this benefit your relationship?
- What sort of expectations do you have for your relationship, and are these realistic?
- What ideas do you have for increasing your compassion for yourself and your relationship?

Part III
Authentic Connection

Chapter 9
Friends and Companions

We're all a little weird. And life is a little weird.
And when we find someone whose weirdness is compatible with ours,
we join up with them and fall into mutually satisfying weirdness—
and call it love—true love.

Robert Fulghum[177]

Jeanette and Alexander Toczko couldn't live without each other. They met when they were eight years old and fell in love. They got married in 1940 and moved around, settling in San Diego in 1970. They were married for seventy-five years, and at the age of ninety-five, Alexander was still playing golf every day. One afternoon, he took a fall, and soon his health began failing. He was put under hospice care, but the staff brought his bed to the Toczcos's home so that Alexander and Jeanette could sleep side by side, because their daughter Aimee said her parents couldn't bear being apart. Jeanette was holding Alexander when he passed away. She hugged him and said, "See this is what you wanted. You died in my arms, and I love you. I love you. Wait for me. I'll be there soon." Within a day, Jeanette died, and their son Richard said, "They both entered the pearly gates holding hands."[178]

Couples become one over time. An eight-year-old crush may be pretty strong, but for a relationship to last until age ninety-five, it needs to include much more. For a relationship to thrive over the years, it needs honesty, commitment, friendship, and confidence in each other. Committed spouses trust that the other has good intentions and won't be hurtful. Good friends believe each other, but also believe *in* each other.

This chapter will discuss what it means for intimate partners to be true friends and companions. The friend relationship is unique. It is different than short-term passion or temporary association. Intimate partners who are good friends respect each other and don't manipulate or treat each other as objects. They are kind, loyal, generous, and honest with each other, sharing their lives, laughing, and having fun.

Let's Be Friends

My grandfather used to travel a lot. In 1971, he went to Guatemala and visited Tikal, a site of ancient Mayan ruins. He wrote a book of his adventures and said, "The sites there were so astounding that I couldn't stop taking pictures." He carefully climbed to the top of one very old, steep pyramid. The steps were narrow and slick. He said, "There was a woman at the top who had climbed the pyramid with her husband some three hours ago and was too scared to descend." She said her husband had "left her up there in disgust. . . . She asked me to help her get down so I had her sit behind me and we descended with her hanging on to me. . . . It was quite an experience. If I had slipped, we would have both slid to our death."[179]

Props to Grandpa for helping out a damsel in distress, but I assume this lady's marriage took a hit from the husband's decision to leave her waiting in the wind. Three hours is a long time to be abandoned, and I imagine she had a lot to think about up there (maybe she pictured her husband sliding to his death). Imagine if you were with a good friend and you got into a comparable tight spot, like running out of gas in a scary neighborhood. What if, instead of going for help, your pal showed "disgust" and took off? Few friendships would survive that kind of disregard. However, many spouses are much more careless and cruel to one another than they are to their friends.

An It or a Thou

One way to capture the many attributes that go into a friendship is to talk about two ways of relating to others. French philosopher Martin Buber described these attitudes, suggesting people are either in an "I-Thou" mode or an "I-It" mode when they are with someone else. To be I-Thou is to view the other as an independent person with hopes, fears, desires, and opinions. An I-Thou partner sees another's needs as real and legitimate.[180] Feeling I-Thou can occur spontaneously, like when you have compassion for your partner's pain. At other times, it is a conscious choice, like when you try to listen and be empathetic. Grandpa responded to the stranded woman with an I-Thou approach. He saw her as someone who needed help, and he showed compassion. Friends do this also.

They see each other as valued and important, and they are usually respectful of differences.

To be in an I-It mode is to see the other as an object. The person becomes a thing, viewed only in terms of whether it helps or hinders, and the object is ignored or dealt with. The husband of the stranded woman in Tikal saw his wife's problem as his headache. She became an obstacle in his life rather than a person he wanted to help, and he moved forward without her.

We can't always be in an active I-Thou mode with everyone around us. Sometimes we are distracted by our own needs or problems. However, when we choose to see someone as a person, it affects what happens in that interaction. Another's needs become our needs, and this attitude is conveyed in many small ways. It colors the language and quality between people and generates good feelings. Duane Boyce described the effect of being in an I-Thou way of being: "People respond primarily to the way we feel toward them. More important than our knowledge, our skills, or our education, is simply our goodness—the quality of our hearts."[181]

How does it feel when you need something and your partner responds with warmth and empathy? When you want to talk and they listen? One contemporary philosopher of Buber's described this as responding to the "face of the other."[182] When your partner looks you in the eye and opens his or her heart, there is person-to-person connection. It feels good.

Contrast this with the experience of being seen as an object. Think of a time you were manipulated, dismissed, or used in a relationship. Perhaps your needs were treated as irrelevant, or you were pressured to feel or do something against your will. It is unpleasant. Instead of a companion, you become a thing, and a thing can't have a relationship. True friendships are between people who value each other, not between objects.

It is easy to ignore or even hurt an object. During World War II, Adolf Eichman was brought to Israel to stand trial for his crimes against humanity. He described how Nazi leaders used language to objectify Jews and other "undesirables." They were instructed to use euphemisms like, "final solution, evacuation, and special treatment," to describe genocide, murder, and torture. This I-It language made it easier for them to kill, because it turned human beings into problems to be solved.[183]

This happens in small ways in relationships when partners use cruel language to attack or disregard each other. Sometimes this is blatant, when hurtful names are called, but it can also be subtle. One client would dismiss his wife when he got frustrated by saying, "Women are just crazy." That phrase is condescending and puts her into a category. This had the effect of dismissing her, instead of engaging with her as a flesh and blood companion with valid feelings.

When couples are interacting in an I-Thou mode, they are open to each other's perspective, even if they are different. Friends who want to grab dinner can usually compromise and work out contrasting opinions. However, I-It partners are threatened by the other's ideas, only regard their own opinion as valid, and wonder why the other is so difficult. A dinner decision becomes personal: "Why is he being so insensitive? He knows that I would rather go to my favorite bar!"

Being Valued Instead of Used

Steve and Leticia changed their relationship by shifting from a dominant I-It mode to I-Thou interactions. They had been married for twenty years but had never fully connected as friends. Steve had been sexually abused by a baby-sitter and then struggled as a teenager with compulsive sexual behavior and pornography. He went to divinity school and became a substance abuse counselor and part time youth minister. He met Leticia in college while she was a senior in high school. They eloped after four months of dating. She had been raised in a domineering home, where messages about women were focused on subservience and guilt. Their attraction was real, but there were I-It dynamics on both sides. Leticia saw Steve as a ticket out, and he saw her as a girl who made him feel good, because she loved him and was willing to do what he wanted.

The marriage struggled from the beginning. Steve was often gone at work and sometimes objectified the women in his recovery groups by being flirty and inappropriate. Leticia, on the other hand, withheld sex and became sarcastic when she didn't get her way. When they had children, things settled into a routine, but their typical tone was resentful and resigned, and this went on for decades. Eventually, things came to a head when Leticia found out Steve had been secretly accessing pornography for years.

Leticia pulled up all of the files on Steve's computer and confronted him with it. He was embarrassed and defensive. She was angry, but also humiliated, and she kicked him out. Steve began attending a twelve-step group and came to me for therapy. He wanted to save his family, and he worked hard to be honest about his past struggles. For the first time, Steve carefully considered Leticia's life and opened up to her perspective. One of the days that stung hardest was when he was asked to consider these questions: "What if something strange happened and you were suddenly transformed into Leticia? Knowing how you treat her, how would you feel? What would it be like being married to you?" Steve thought about how awful it was for her to see all of his online activities, and he realized he had been condescending and dismissive of her. He apologized and kept working on his addiction but was frustrated with her resentment. She eventually let him back in but was still cool toward him. She was struggling with her own healing and began going to a therapist and studying women's empowerment and equality.

They were making some progress, and one day he called her to apologize for leaving abruptly that morning. He mentioned a speaking request he received for a vacation Bible school, and she became extremely angry. He became angry in return and asked what her "freaking problem was." He told me later what he thought, "I had been busting my butt for months trying to make this up to her, and she was hanging onto every little thing." He listened to her phone call, but gritted his teeth and walked outside where he could be away from coworkers. He was caught in thoughts of how hard he was working and how Leticia was being unfair.

She lit into him about how he was a crummy example for youth and had no business parading around telling others how to live. He got more defensive and saw her claims as exaggerated. "I was feeling sorry for myself—a poor, picked on husband who was doing the best that I could," he said. But then a shift happened. "Suddenly I recalled something I had been reading about how we are narcissistic and only see our own perspective. I thought of the question of what it had been like for Leticia to be married to me." It hit him like a cleft to the skull, and he sat down on a bench and realized that she was exactly right.

"I stopped trying to defend myself and wanted to hear about Leticia's experience," he said. "I became genuinely curious about why she was feeling what she was feeling." Steve then realized she was on target. "I *was* attached to praise from others. I was even using my recovery as a way to prove how noble I was—how I was some great model of an addict working a program. I used Leticia's lack of support to see myself as a henpecked husband who was enduring incredible odds."

As Steve listened, he became very emotional. Instead of feeling defensive, he felt a piercing sorrow for her pain and chagrin and that he was the source of much of it. He experienced her feelings of neglect and humiliation when he was schmoozing and laughing with other women, and he realized he rarely treated Leticia with this same fun and friendly attitude. He felt her shock at his betrayals. He attempted to convey this and asked for more details.

Leticia continued, recalling his stories of helping others, spending his evenings with them, listening and offering money. She pointed out how he would take depressed teens to dinner, then come home and snap at his own kids. She hated when others told her how much they loved her husband. As she unloaded, she felt Steve's sincerity and connection. She softened and apologized for her resentment and anger, and she expressed appreciation for his recovery efforts. They talked for a long time about their past and decided they wanted a new future.

The shift in their demeanor was palpable, and they saw each other with new eyes. "It was like a gift," Steve said. "That day outside of work, I didn't try to fix anything or prove something to her. I just saw her as she really was and tried to be as honest in my perceptions as possible. I allowed myself to feel her pain and emotion and it was like a dam broke and something started flowing between us again." Of course, this didn't solve all of their problems. They still had I-It moments where they became exasperated or irritable, but they were better about realizing it.

The Power of Modes

In this book, we have talked about how partners change from one mode to another. A mode is a way of operating that permeates the whole interaction. When a partner is deceptive, they think and act in dishonest ways. When angry, they see, feel, and act mad. When respectful, behaviors and words are conveyed respectfully. A complete exchange is colored by the participants' way of being. These are modes, and there are endless versions of them. Deceptive mode. Honest mode. Excusing mode. Angry mode. Defensive mode. Wiped out mode. Friend mode. Passionate mode. Each mode produces attitudes and actions that steer the relationship.

Steve and Leticia had a profound shift in mode the day of the phone conversation. However, this wasn't a permanent change. Each day they alternated between constructive and destructive ways of interacting. They got better at realizing what mode they were in, and they noticed the things that strained trust, caused tension, or brought connection and pleasure. John Steinbeck observed modes of relationships and commented on their power: "There are several kinds of love. One is a selfish, mean, grasping, egotistical thing which uses love for self-importance. This is the ugly and crippling kind. The other is an outpouring of everything good in you—of kindness and consideration and respect—not only the social respect of manners, but also the greater respect which is recognition of another person as unique and valuable. The first kind can make you sick and small and weak, but the second can release in you strength, and courage and goodness and even wisdom you didn't know you had."[184]

The Virtuous Friendship

The question for Steve about what it would be like to be Leticia was a key point in his progress. It was a variation on the "golden rule," which emphasizes treating others how you want to be treated. This principle is so fundamental to human relations that at least twenty-one of the world's major religions have some variation of it as a core teaching.[185] How do *you* want to be treated? That is your starting place for deciding how to treat your mate. This question is about virtues, not skills. Many marriage programs emphasize skills, like active listening or

I-messages. But these are insufficient without virtues like kindness and patience backing them up.

Some marriage scholars have discovered the critical role of practicing virtues in a relationship.[186] Attributes such as fairness, loyalty, and humility are not fixed traits that some have and others don't, but muscles that can be strengthened. Couples almost always exercise virtues while courting. They show understanding, forgive each other, and try to have fun. But too often after marriage, partners allow their virtue biceps to go soft. They get busy with other things or become complacent.

To stay strong, couples need to intentionally choose good attitudes and actions. Aristotle argued that it was through practicing virtues that couples feel closer. He said that virtues involved actions, but also feelings, and that they are cultivated through repeated choices to do right.[187] Aristotle said that to be good is not, as Kant was to later argue, to go against our nature, but it is our nature—our cultivated nature. We become good through persistently choosing kindness and unselfishness, but Aristotle did admit, "It is no easy task to be good."[188] Characters change over time as couples continue to try hard. Steve and Leticia changed their relationship by working on their character. Leticia chose to be kind and acknowledge Steve's recovery efforts, and he chose to be patient and unselfish and listen to her.

Fairness

The golden rule also addresses the virtue of fairness. We all want to be treated fairly, and this comes up frequently in relationships. It isn't cool if one does all the dishes while the other plays the Xbox, and no one wants to be the only one putting the kids to bed or apologizing after a fight. Abusive relationships are fundamentally unfair, where one person expects a servant or a target instead of an equal partner.[189]

We recognize injustice almost from birth. In one study, Paul Bloom showed babies a series of animated shapes and figures. Some shapes were "helping" others up a hill, and other shapes were being obstructive and getting in the way. When the shapes were presented to the babies as blocks, the babies nearly always reached for the helpful ones and rejected the hindering shapes.[190] This moral sense continues as babies become toddlers who complain that things aren't fair, and then become adults who don't like injustice much either. One study found that employees who felt they were being paid fairly compared to their colleagues were more motivated, happier, healthier, and more satisfied with their personal lives.[191]

Of course, exact fairness in a relationship isn't possible, and there are always differences in what partners think is fair. When couples keep score and argue about fairness, the relationship suffers. For example, early in their marriage, one couple would argue vehemently about whose turn it was to change their toddler's diaper. One would sometimes wait until the other was home if it was the other's "turn," which ended up punishing the soggy kid for the adult's pettiness. This is a selfish focus on "what's in it for me?" rather than, "what's the right thing for us?" Marriage scholar William Doherty calls this a consumer marriage, where the partners approach the relationship with an attitude of getting the best deal. They become dissatisfied if they think they could do better, and instead of committing to the process, they consider trading up for a new model.[192] This is not fairness but an immature debate.

In contrast, healthy partners both contribute to the relationship. They are each willing to give extra and rebalance when needed, and they put energy toward the greater good, even when it takes sacrifice. Steve and Leticia learned this as they were changing into a generous mode. For example, Steve didn't always feel like listening to Leticia when she wanted to talk about her anger. But when he did, she appreciated it, and it was good for the relationship. Leticia didn't always want intimacy when Steve did, but when she was willing to get together, they usually had a good experience and felt close.

This doesn't mean that either *had* to do what the other wanted. They had freedom to refuse and negotiate each other's requests. They also worked on not pouting and punishing the other person when they didn't get what they wanted. These small efforts had big benefits for them individually and as friends. As Buddha said, "Drop by drop is the water pot filled. Likewise, the wise one, gathering it little by little, fills oneself with good."

Loyalty

Being loyal is a virtue that keeps partners feeling safe. During her marriage crisis, Leticia had been confiding in a male friend at work. She didn't tell Steve, and she excused her deception because she was still furious about his betrayals. After Steve and Leticia began working on their relationship, she told him what she had done. He was stung but appreciated her honesty, and this helped him admit more of his own mental and emotional disloyalty. This new level of honesty increased their accountability to their values and each other. They became vigilant how they talked about their marriage with their friends and family. Leticia also helped their son become more loyal in his new marriage. He had been making jokes about his wife's cooking and teasing her in front of the family. Leticia told him his first priority now was his spouse, and he needed to show this in his actions.

Gratitude

Partners have an amazing capacity for taking each other for granted. In most relationships there are all kinds of things to be happy about—why else would people partner up? But how often do couples stop and think about all the great things they have together? The comedian Louis CK was discussing how quickly people become entitled and ungrateful. He described being on an airplane where they offered high speed internet for the first time. People tried it and it was great. He said, "And then it breaks down. They apologize and the guy next to me says, 'Pfffff! This is $#@*!' Like, how quickly the world owes him something he knew existed only ten seconds ago!"[193]

Unlike the ungrateful flyer, couples who express gratitude to each other feel valued and content. Family scientist Ted Futris found that appreciative words increase relationship commitment and stability, and expressing gratitude is the most consistent, significant predictor of happy marriages.[194] Algoe Fredrickson and colleagues found that grateful words to a spouse inject enjoyable feelings that persist until the next day and decrease the odds of breaking up.[195] Choosing to be grateful makes people happier.[196] Positive psychology guru Martin Seligman suggests a proven method to increase gratitude: "Every night for the next week, set aside ten minutes before you go to sleep. Write down three things that went well today and why they went well . . . have a physical record of what you wrote. The three things need not be earthshaking in importance. Next to each positive event, answer the question, 'Why did this happen?' Writing about positive events in your life may seem awkward at first, but please stick with it for one week. It will get easier. The odds are that you will be less depressed, happier and addicted to this exercise six months from now."[197]

It feels good to be grateful, and it is nice to be appreciated. It is a sign of being valued. I tell my wife when I have cleaned the garage, because I want her to tell me I did a good job. We all do things that go unnoticed, so it is nice when someone does notice. Try an experiment where you thank your partner for what he or she does. Notice when your partner makes your life better, and express your appreciation. This will be welcomed by your spouse and benefit you as well.

Exercising virtues does not take specialized training. As Aristotle realized thousands of years ago, it is a matter of commitment. When people come for couples therapy, it isn't usually because they need to learn a technical skill; it is because they have gotten disconnected from their best self—from their heart. Steve and Leticia worked on finding and sharing their best selves, and this created a surprising effect. "Not only are we better than we were before the problems came to light last year," Steve said, "we are better than we have ever been. We are more unified, more open. It feels like a real partnership instead of two people who are just dealing with each other."

Humor

A relationship without humor goes stale. Humor adds fizz and fun and can help a couple survive the storms. Being connected over time creates inside jokes, and hilarity is a natural emotion booster. As comedian and musician Victor

Borge said, "Laughter is the shortest distance between two people." Research supports this, showing that couples who laugh together feel closer than those who are more serious.[198] Laughter is a social glue, and it is contagious. People laugh thirty times more often with others than they do alone, and only 20 percent of laughs between people come from humor or jokes. Most laughter emerges from good feelings and inviting words, like: "Hey baby!" or "Wait until I tell you what our kid said today!"[199]

Humor signals enjoyment, playfulness, creativity, and intelligence. It doesn't work if laughter is fake (listeners can discern a real laugh from a phony two thirds of the time).[200] This is why a nervous laugh is awkward: people feel social pressure to laugh along, even if they are not amused. Humor should be fun, not cruel. One husband in therapy would crack sarcastic jokes when we addressed sensitive issues. He had learned to be a clown to deal with stress, but it was preventing honest discussion and was sometimes annoying. However, when appropriate, humor can defuse a difficult situation and reconnect partners.

Fun and Romance

Think of your closest friends. What do you like to do together? Sit around and Netflix binge? Argue over who should vacuum the car? Probably not. Most friends have fun together. One thing that can get lost in marriage is the kick of early dating. Alice Zhou did a statistical word analysis of all of her text messages between herself and her boyfriend as they progressed from dating to marriage. The most frequent words in their texts while they dated were "love, fun, soon." After two years of wedded bliss? "Ok, home, yeah."[201]

Novelty and surprise help people feel connected. Arthur Aron found when couples do a simple challenging task together, they feel more in love than do couples who do a boring task. He also asked couples to spend ninety minutes a week doing unfamiliar activities like rock climbing or taking Italian lessons. After ten weeks of the interesting dates, couples felt closer than couples in another group who had stuck to the traditional dinner and a movie.[202]

Marriage scholar Teri Orbuch found that about 42 percent of spouses feel "in a rut," and these couples have higher distress levels nine years later than non-rut marriages. She suggests that partners need to "knock each other off balance" in fun ways by introducing new things, like small gifts, taking a role they don't normally have at home, or spicing up their intimate life.[203] My wife surprised me once by calling me at work and telling me to meet her at a nice restaurant. There she presented me with tickets to a hilarious theatre production and an overnight bed and breakfast. This was memorable for many reasons, including when I accidently turned the heater off in the middle of the night, so we froze and had to use the towels as extra blankets. The next morning we went to a beautiful canyon and watched hawks circle below us in the crisp fall air. Unique memories stick out in the consciousness more than routine ones, and novel events fill a relationship with texture and life.

Even a movie can be therapeutic if used to share and connect. One study divided 174 couples into three groups. One group went to relationship education classes, one did nothing different, and the third set went to see movies. The twist was that the movies were those depicting realistic challenges and joys of intimate relationships (*Twilight* was not included). After watching, the couples discussed assigned questions to spur conversations about the characters and their good and bad relationship choices. Couples were asked to think about how the movie relationship was "similar to or different from [their] own relationship" in certain areas. The movie watchers were prescribed one movie a week for a month, along with some questions. This combination of film and conversation was just as helpful in reducing the chance of divorce as the relationship education classes.[204]

The next time you feel flat in your relationship, skip the Walmart and dinner date. Instead, go together to a trampoline park, take a pottery class, or discuss a weepy relationship movie. Act like friends and have a fun time building an authentic long-term relationship. Maybe you will make it to seventy-five years together and die in each other's arms with a smile on your face.

Main Points

- Successful relationships include friendship. This involves honesty and respect.
- Partners are either in an I-It or I-Thou mode with others. An I-It mode is viewing another person as an object to be ignored or used, whereas in I-Thou mode, others are seen as legitimate and important.
- Even though partners get distracted with their own needs, when they choose to see the other as a person, it changes the way they interact.
- The mode someone is in permeates their attitudes and behaviors.
- Virtues such as fairness, loyalty, and gratitude need to be consciously exercised in a relationship.
- A relationship without humor is dull. Humor can ease tension and bring partners closer together.
- Friends laugh together, have fun, and genuinely enjoy being around each other. Those who choose to do novel and interesting things together often feel closer.
- Be intentional about exercising virtues and having fun building a lifelong relationship.

Discussion Questions

- What does a quality friendship consist of? How is friendship part of an intimate relationship?
- When have you felt like you were treated like an object? When have you been treated like a person? What was the difference?

- When are partners likely to shift into I-It or I-Thou attitudes with each other?
- What kinds of modes do you or your partner get caught in? Which are helpful and which are not?
- What virtues do you see in your relationship? Which would you like to strengthen?
- How does humor play a role in your relationship?
- What can you do to strengthen the friendship you have with your spouse?
- How have you tried to "knock each other off balance" in the past to keep things interesting in your relationship?
- What are some of the most fun and memorable experiences you have created together? What would be good to try next?

Chapter 10
Heart and Mind

Educating the mind without educating the heart is no education at all.

Aristotle[205]

When Your Boyfriend Gets Married without Telling You

Imagine you are in a lovely long-distance relationship. You Skype and text every day, meet up every few months, and plan your life together. One day, you are surfing Facebook and find fresh wedding photos of a happy couple with their family and friends. The strange part is that your boyfriend is the groom, and his ex-girlfriend is the blushing bride. Surprise! Now what do you do? Call him and scream until you burst a blood vessel? Hire a hitman to take him out?

This was the predicament of a woman we will call Tammy. In the summer of 2015, she was surfing Facebook and saw wedding pictures featuring her current boyfriend as the groom. After the shock subsided, she called him up. But he reassured her it was just a misunderstanding. Tammy's head was now spinning, and she sought help. She posted her situation on the website *Ask Metafilter* to get feedback on whether she was just being "silly" to think something was wrong. Here is what she wrote: "He told me that it was from a video that his university is making for new students to show how glamorous graduate school life can be (he's a professor and an alum). Am I being irrational in doubting him?"[206] She wanted to believe him and explained, "He said he thought it wasn't important enough to mention to me. . . . If I think about all the time we spend IMing and calling and Skyping, he couldn't possibly also be married, right?" She was asking for a second opinion because she didn't want to pester him and "fall off a cliff of crazy and alienate him." She even complimented his handling of her questions: "He was understandably reluctant to talk about the photos, but he took the time to be patient and to explain . . . [saying that] if he were married, she would be with him at home, and he wouldn't have been able to Skype."

So that solves that, right? Well, uh, no. The responses on *Ask Metafilter* were swift and searing. Although many tried to be respectful to poor Tammy, they were overwhelmingly skeptical of her boyfriend's claim. Some of the more polite questions included the following:

"Does it make sense to you that your boyfriend wouldn't mention being involved in a PR photo shoot? With his ex-girlfriend?"

"No school I've ever gone to or heard of uses footage of a fancy wedding to entice students or faculty. They especially don't create extra family photos to include as props."

And, "Either you are in a romantic comedy Adam Sandler couldn't pull off or you're dealing with sociopathic-level behavior."

One wrote, "Please listen to your gut on this one." The problem was that her emotional entanglement, or what could be called her gut, was part of her self-deception. She was so smitten, she couldn't see reality. Her infatuation was talking her out of her common sense. In this battle between emotion and logic, emotion was winning. The battle began when she first saw the Facebook posts. Her rational mind cried that something was very wrong with this posted picture. But this warning was drowned out by her heart—*No! He loves me. This cannot be real!*

She likely spent some painful hours with these two voices arguing back and forth. Fortunately, her logical brain had enough persistence to reach out for help. After she got a boost from crowdsourced common sense, she again called her boyfriend. After more dodging, he finally admitted that he "was engaged." This was a weird response since Tammy had already seen his wedding, but clearly the truth wasn't a key feature of this relationship. Tammy was crushed as reality started to sink in, but her internal war continued. She wrote a follow-up post: "I'm angry and heartbroken, and I don't know what to do when part of me is so betrayed and the other part still loves him. Crazily enough, that part of me that cares about him is even a little glad that he found someone he really loves. But I don't know what my tomorrow morning will be like without a good morning text from him, without hearing his voice. Everything is so surreal. He asked me for another Skype tomorrow, and I think it really, really needs to be the last time we talk for a long time."

Tammy's experience of going back and forth between her emotional heart and her logical mind is a good example of how people react in relationships. This two-part process and the impact it has on love lives is the topic of this chapter. We will discuss how the brain processes in two ways, and how these can be likened to a *heart*, which is intuitive and quick, and a *mind*, which is reflective and rational. We will compare the heart and mind to a horse and a rider. Each has as role in helping partners connect in honest and meaningful ways. We will learn how to listen to the wisdom of both and what they each do in relationships.

Our Bifurcated Brains

Daniel Kahneman is a Nobel-winning scientist who has devoted his career to understanding the two ways that the brain processes information. According to Kahneman, we have one type of processing that is rapid and automatic. He calls this System 1. It is quick and intuitive, controlling simple tasks like driving someplace familiar or solving easy math problems. We will call System 1 "the heart." The heart encompasses many automatic and emotional reactions. The heart is useful and strong and drives much of our behavior, but can be prone to overreaction.

System 2 is reflective and rational. This system involves effort, and it engages when we are carefully driving in a blizzard, solving hard calculus problems, or struggling to understand another person. We will call System 2 "the mind." The mind is associated with the front sections of the brain and has the ability to reflect, reason, and evaluate. The mind can override and retrain the heart. The heart and mind work together, sometimes in harmony, and other times in conflict.

These two systems are active during relationship interactions. For example, consider a tense exchange between Taylor and Ree. Taylor is stressed out because of a bad performance review at work and a long day. After traffic, fatigue, and hunger, Taylor gets home and is grumpy. Ree's immediate reaction is defensive, and she thinks Taylor is being obnoxious. Ree's "heart" is responding to the tension with annoyance and an angry face. However, after Ree's initial reaction, she engages her "mind" and calms down and reevaluates the situation from a different perspective (*Taylor is way tired. Time to administer some caffeine*).

Kahneman says, "Conflict between an automatic reaction and an intention to control it is common in our lives. We are all familiar with the experience of trying not to stare at the oddly dressed couple at the neighboring table in the restaurant . . . and every human being has the experience of not telling someone to go to hell. One of the tasks of System 2 [the mind] is to overcome the impulses of System 1 [the heart]. In other words, System 2 is in charge of self-control."[207] The impulses of the heart are strong, but the mind can override them.

The Heart as the Horse

Imagine the heart as a horse, with the mind as a rider sitting in the saddle. The horse is handy. It is strong and moves forward with efficiency and speed. But the rider is important too. It trains the horse in basic tasks that eventually become natural and automatic. However, the horse can become unruly. At times it overreacts to noises, gets distracted by squirrels, and might even bolt. The horse is a vital helper, but it isn't as logical or as smart as the rider.[k]

---

k. Plato suggested that the mind was like a chariot driven by two horses, intellect and emotion. Jonathan Haidt and others have used similar metaphors, like the example of an elephant and rider, to describe the parts of the brain. This suggests that the deeper sections of the brain are the more reactive and instinctive, with the frontal cortex more reflective. This chapter uses this metaphor of the two beings, which loosely fits with Kahneman's typology of the systems.

In relationships, the heart is the center of emotion and moving forward. Love is a fun ride, and the heart can get people together, but it can also take over and get misdirected. Take Tammy, whose heart was ignoring the fact that her long-distance boyfriend became someone else's husband. Tammy's horse was galloping in a happy frenzy right toward a cliff. Then came the photos, which kicked off a vigorous debate between her horse and rider:

> Horse: "I love him so much. I think about him all the time. Wait, there he is on Facebook!"
> Rider: "What the heck! In a tux with his ex? Nooooo! Wait, slow down, horsey!"
> Horse: "No way, I am still bolting forward. I don't believe this!"
> Rider: "Something is wrong, woah!"
> Horse: "I'm running and you can't stop me!"
> Rider: "Anyone! *Ask Metafilter*, help me!"
> [Skid! . . .Crash!]
> Rider and Horse: "Ouch."

When the Horse Is in Charge

When people are in love, they are on an exhilarating ride. But hasty hormonal decisions are not always well thought out. Often the rider is just hanging on to the horse. When someone falls in love the feelings drive the behavior, and the thinking comes later. A lover might explain their feelings by saying, "She was so beautiful" or "I loved his confidence." But these statements don't adequately account for the emotion, because there are a lot of beautiful and confident people that aren't eliciting this love. The heart is deciding who to love, and the mind is giving reasons to explain why it is happening.

Our assumption that we are logical and in control is what neuroscientist Josef Parvizi refers to as a "corticocentric bias."[208] Because your rider is smart and can steer the horse, it feels like it is always doing this. But the rider is often just going along for the journey and commenting on it. The deep brain initiates many actions before the conscious brain is aware of them. The heart sends you toward your spouse to connect, and this initiates back-and-forth reactions like touching and happy expressions. These occur without thought.[209]

The upshot is that the horse is helpful and has good instincts. It perceives and organizes reality and acts automatically so the rider doesn't have to overthink every action. But the instant nature of this process can cause problems in early love. Pre-marital counseling can slow this down and invite the riders to weigh in on important issues like finances, family planning, and values. These discussions may not occur if the horse is given free rein to run. Both horse and rider should be involved when making commitments.

The Horse Overreacts

A bolting horse ignores the rider, and a strongly reacting heart ignores the mind. Couples rush to passion when feeling lust and rush to catastrophe when feeling anger. The heart often jumps to conclusions and overreacts.

A few years ago an alarm went off at East Carolina University. A man wearing a white hat with a rifle strapped to his back was spotted near campus. Emergency personnel mobilized, danger notifications flew out, and a shudder went around the country as many of us watched the news with concern. After several hours, it was determined the guy was just carrying an umbrella.[210] Similarly, angry couples sometimes go on alert and gear up for a fight when there is no real threat.

Overreactions can happen because of past wounds. My colleague Doug Smith and I looked at how traumatic experiences leave an imprint on the brain. We wondered whether we could see differences in brain activity in women who had been in violent relationships, as compared to those who had not. In order to see the brain in action, these women went into a claustrophobic fMRI machine. The fMRI uses strong magnets—no jewelry or braces allowed—to produce a series of images of the brain reacting as it is presented with a stimulus. (I also suggested stuffing angry couples into the machine on top of each other to see what their brains did, but that was voted down).

As each volunteer lay still, we showed her a series of pictures. There were various photos of happy couples, tense couples, and angry and threatening couples. For example, a picture might show an enraged man with his fist raised. What we found was the women who had *not* been in violent relationships had an active prefrontal cortex as they looked at the threatening pictures. This is important, because the prefrontal cortex is the part of the brain associated with thoughtful decisions and self-control. It is the rider. The women with no history of violence kept their rider in the saddle while looking at the angry pictures. This suggests these women are better able to process during tense interactions and make better judgments on how to handle them. The women who had been in abusive relationships were not using their prefrontal cortex when they saw the scary couples. It was dormant, which implies they had less control of their thoughts and actions while viewing tense situations.[211]

Everyone overreacts at times, and we each have our hot buttons. Have you jumped to conclusions or gotten upset for the wrong reason? Assumed your partner was mad at you only to find out later he or she just had indigestion? Have you gotten upset at a laugh when it had nothing to do with you? When might you be responding to a false alarm? How do you decide whether something is a concern or a non-issue? It is important to distinguish real firearms from harmless umbrellas.

The Horse Is an Eeyore

The horse is especially sensitive about bad stuff. Psychologists call this the negativity bias—we are likely to see and remember bad things more than the good. Like Eeyore, the glum donkey in *Winnie the Pooh*, the horse can be touchy and pessimistic. This can bring a relationship down. Have you been complimented by your partner but then critiqued? "Great singing—you were only flat that one time!" The criticism probably had more impact than the compliment. The inner Eeyore hears accusations in a partner's words that aren't there and worries about things that will never occur. He hangs on to past slights and forgets the happy moments. Relationships need a lot of fun and bonding to compensate for the negativity of fights and hurt feelings, and the healthiest relationships have a ratio of at least five good things happening for every bad one.[212]

The negativity of the horse is protective. The brain monitors the environment constantly in a process known as neuroception.[213] This is because a body needs to react instantly if there is a problem. This can lead to overreactions. Once, in the middle of the night, my wife blurted out, "Oh my gosh!"

My eyes flew open in the dark, and she got louder. "Do you see that!?"

I was alarmed. "Honey?" What is it?"

She escalated further. "Oh my gosh! Oh no! Do you see that?"

I sat up and grabbed her shoulder. "What? What is it?!"

Then she rolled over asleep, having just been shouting at a dream.

It took me a while to recover from this nonthreat. My heart beat fast for several minutes until I had walked around the house in my jammies to check everything.

When a threat is present, it dominates the heart and mind. The brain can't engage socially and partners literally can't relate to each other in this protective mode. This is because the brain operates like a set of doors. Some are open when things are safe but slam shut during a threat. This happens even if the danger is imaginary, like a nightmare. Professor Steven Porges describes this in his Polyvagal Theory, where these modes operate through vagal (neural) pathways of the autonomic nervous system.[214] When a threat happens, an alarm goes off. Heart rates go up, emotions become flooded, and the relationship becomes irrelevant. The alarm is a feature of the brain, and it is loud. Like any alarm, this vagal noise is disruptive and sometimes goes off just to be safe. But this means that your brain can be like an annoying smoke detector that beeps every time you make toast (we had one). Alarms give false positives to keep people safe, but the noise prevents conversations. A horse will naturally be anxious with an alarm going off.

It is important to get Eeyore some professional help if the negativity becomes pervasive (*Oh, bother!*). When partners see only the bad about each other, it is called "negative sentiment override." This means that people who once gave each other a break (*He is running late. I wonder what is going on?*) now see malicious intent (*He promised he would be here. What an insensitive liar!*). In this negative state, partners claim the relationship was doomed from the beginning (*I should have listened to my friends when they told me she was a selfish diva*), and are hyper-vigilant for put-downs. In one study, unhappy couples watched an interaction but only saw half of the positive events that objective observers saw.[215] Dark glasses of negativity make everything more sinister.

Getting a traumatized horse retrained includes unlearning old habits, practicing looking for the good, giving others a break, and giving credit where it is due. This takes deliberation, since negativity is a natural tendency. However, when couples shift into a more positive way of being, they see each other differently and are much more likely to succeed. Wally Goddard and James Marshall summarize this body of research: "Happily married couples aren't smarter, richer, or more psychologically astute than other couples. They are simply willing to keep their negative thoughts and feelings about one another from overwhelming their positive thoughts and feelings."[216]

That's One Lazy Horse

When a happy couple buys their first home, they should be thoughtful about where they hang pictures and put silverware, because they might stay there for decades. Moving day decisions end up becoming permanent, because we are biased for efficiency. People keep the same seat in class or pew in church because it is easy. The brain saves energy where possible, and as Kahneman says "Laziness is built deep into our nature."[217] Our brains have a lot to do, and many things happen automatically and beneath awareness.[1]

When people meet for the first time, they make snap judgments about the other's likability, trustworthiness, and aggressiveness in a tenth of a second.[218] Try to count a tenth of a second. It is quicker than conscious thought. These first impressions are persistent, and people are hesitant to revise them even in the face of new information. One study found that first impressions closely predicted how people would feel about each other months later. Have you ever liked someone and then later found out they were awful? Or disliked someone and then became friends? That revision process takes time because of the power of first impressions. The laziness bias is one of the reasons that height and attractiveness are influential, because those attributes are easily seen. One feature of a person

---

1. As one writer put it, "The brain has 100 billion neurons amid another trillion support cells. A typical neuron connects with 5,000 other neurons, adding up to about 500 trillion synapses. The number of possible combinations of those 100 billion neurons is more than 10 to the millionth power—that's a one followed by a million zeroes. As a comparison, the number of particles in the universe is estimated to be a one followed by a paltry 80 zeroes."

gets generalized—*because he is tall he must be skilled.* This may be why you don't often see a gorgeous person doing menial or degrading work—they have moved up the corporate ladder because they benefit from this halo.[219]

This perceptual bias is called *anchoring*, where a person builds a whole theory from one bit of data.[220] This works against couples when they hold onto one thing and ignore others. For example, long-distance lover Tammy clung to her boyfriend's assurances and ignored the blatant evidence that he had, in fact, become someone else's husband. When partners anchor onto each other's glitches, these negative things seem like character flaws. Dishes left in the sink become a sign of hostility or narcissism. Clothes on the floor show arrogance, and frustration with the clothes on the floor shows rigidity and obsessiveness. It is easy to anchor, but it's often wrong.

There are many ways the heart is seduced by ease. People are more likely to believe statements when they are in a clearer font or easy-to-understand accent.[221] This is known as the "fluency heuristic," which means that if something is easier, people will think it is preferable.[222] People fall for those similar to them, and they are more likely to marry someone with a name that sounds like theirs.[223] Brett Pelham of SUNY Buffalo showed that people named Dennis are more likely to become dentists than those with other names, and people named George disproportionately move to Georgia.[224] This effect is small, but real. If you ask Dr. Wizwell why he became a urologist, he will have many reasons, but the subtle association of his name may be one of them. Marketing researchers exploit the laziness bias by making it as easy as possible to buy things. Merchants put goods at eye level at the store and create one-click buttons because this makes it easy for customers to fill carts.[m]

Snap judgments are easy. It takes effort to really get to know someone, and this is why we stereotype. Grouping is an efficiency function of the brain, and we have specific neurons in our prefrontal cortex associated with categorizing.[225] This helps us make sense of life when we are young (*that fuzzy thing is a cat*) and save energy when we get older (*white coat means a medical doctor*).

Partners can help each other to steer things in a good direction, especially when snap judgments are going awry. In Tammy's case, she needed a reality check from her *Ask Metafilter* community. After their feedback she said, "I still want too much to believe him when he tells me he loves me. But really, really thank you. Without everyone, I would have just ignored the photos." Reach out for help when you need it, and loan your brain to your partner when they need

---

m. An example of making things too easy to buy are the in-app purchases that are the default on devices. My friend Sean didn't change this setting before he let his kid use his iPad. It didn't take long for his daughter to rack up more than $120 on a Farsi language version of a Dora the Explorer app.

it. We all have horses that can go bonkers, and we need to rein things in before we gallop into a mess.

The Mind as the Rider

It is easy to steer a calm, well-trained horse. A nudge keeps him going in the right direction, and a strong tug will correct him when he is going off track. In healthy relationships, partners regularly rein in their impulses, and work hard to correct mistakes. Kahnenman has found when people engage the rider, it shows up in the dilation of their eyes.[226] Training a reactive animal takes determination but it can change the direction of a relationship. One woman came from a family where everyone yelled, so that is what she did in her marriage. Her husband was calm, even in the face of conflict, and this took her by surprise. She decided this was how she wanted to be. It took months of practice and some relapses, but she became a non-yeller. She retrained her heart.

To bridle a horse does not take away its passion; it directs it toward something good. It is fine to have strong feelings, opinions, and interests, but partners should govern these. For instance, if one hates the taco restaurant the other suggests, or desperately wants the yellow couch, he or she should be reasonable and assertive, but not obnoxious. Benjamin Franklin said, "If passion drives, let reason hold the reins."[227]

When partners aren't willing to reflect, it causes problems. One day a man was going on in session, basically saying, "I don't care what the issue is—she is the problem." This demonstrated that he was missing a brain—a reflective brain—because he was not willing to admit that he played a role in any of their difficulties. This, of course, *was* a key problem in their relationship. His heart was usually biased and angry, and he thought that it was correct. He wasn't willing to do the work to control and calm the unruly horse.

In situations where the rider is literally incapacitated, the horse can run without restraint. This happens when someone's personality changes from brain damage from dementia or frontal cortex injury. This can result in impulsive, demanding, sexually aggressive, and otherwise animalistic behavior.[228] In cases where a brain is organically whole, partners don't have an excuse for letting impulses go undirected.

Wisdom of the Heart

Although a horse needs to be trained and guided, it brings wisdom and direction of its own to the relationship. This is why we get better at relationships as we move out of awkward teenage interactions into more mature ones. An experienced heart grows in self-control and judgment. A horse may be better than the rider at finding its way back home if it is given the reins, and the heart is well equipped to respond to others, and is usually intuitively appropriate in social situations.[229]

It is often good to listen to the heart in matters of love. For instance, no logical formula can perfectly match up a person with their soul mate. People are led to good matches by following their feelings. Helen Fischer is an anthropologist who has studied mating and attraction, and she suggests that our mental intuition—our horse—often provides the best algorithms for leading us toward love.[230]

Both heart and mind are needed to be wise. The mind may rely too much on matchmaking formulas or logic, and the heart may be too easily swayed by emotion. This is what happened with Tammy, who wasn't getting enough complete information to make a good decision with her long-distance boyfriend. Her virtual reality relationship became distorted by the biases of a lonely heart. I have seen many clients who rushed into relationships before spending enough face-to-face time together. A common remark of these speedy lovers is that they didn't know each other well enough. They were influenced by heart biases without getting heart wisdom.

The heart may detect warning signs that the mind misses. Creepy or dangerous vibes are often discernable, and if you are getting a bad feeling, you should take heed. Sometimes nice people get talked out of their feelings or rationalize away their good sense (*I didn't feel comfortable going home with him, but he seemed so nice!*).[231] Manipulative dates can talk someone out of their intuition, or override "no" answers by being persistent and confusing. When things are ambiguous and troubling, it is often good to listen to the heart.

Healing the Heart and Training the Mind

Dan Siegel is a psychiatrist who studies how the brain changes when partners override their initial impulses and choose to be calm. The rider can overrule the horse and change bad habits.[n] For example, couples get better at letting things go and not getting impatient with each other. They do this through biting their tongue and being patient, which eventually becomes part of their nature. Mark and Katelin learned how to do this. They met in a ballroom dance class in college, got married, had kids, and after seven years had become tired and distant. One night, they came home to a messy house and Mark said he was going to bed and Katelin tensed up. Each of them now had options for their horse and rider. Katelin chose to be snippy: "Just because we are tired doesn't mean that we should let the place become a dump." Mark now had a choice. He could go with his first urge of criticism and self-pity: "You haven't helped, and I have had a horrible day." Or he could redirect his brain into something constructive. He had

---

n. For those that like brain jargon, his more technical description is that "a cortical override process can occur in which subcortical activations are overridden by the inhibitory input from the cortex, especially the prefrontal region." This area "integrates social, somatic, brain-stem, limbic, and cortical systems all into one functional whole."

several options: 1) Take a deep breath and respond calmly: "Yes, it is pretty bad. I am tired, but will help tomorrow" or 2) say something caring: "I know you are wiped out." He ended up using option 3), humor: "Let's go watch *Hoarders*, which will help us feel better by comparison."

This made Katelin laugh and give him a playful shove and is an example of how a distressed partner "can use the subjective inner aspect of reality [Mark's perception] to alter the objective physical structure of the brain."[232] Katelin was cranky, but Mark didn't have to be. When he responded in a good way, it changed his brain, which then altered her brain as well. Couples who work at this develop stronger minds.[233]

Kevin Ochsner is a psychologist at Columbia University who watches the brain change as people engage their rider. He put volunteers into an fMRI machine and showed pictures of emotion-laden scenes, such as a woman crying in front of a church. When volunteers saw this, their amygdala activated instantly, and they felt sad. However, at this stage they were asked to reappraise the situation, or think about it in a positive way by imagining that the woman is crying tears of joy at a wedding. When the new thought occurred, the brain changed accordingly.[234] The amygdala quieted down and new emotions were generated. Ochsner says that this shows that our first emotional reactions can be improved with effort. "Reappraisal alters our emotional response," he says. "When we do it intentionally, we gain conscious control of our emotions."[235] Katelin and Mark worked on this process of reevaluation when they became upset, and they got better at it. This was the beginning of new efforts that felt awkward to try: "It was like trying a new toothbrush that feels funny in your mouth at first," Katelin said. "But you adapt quickly, and then it feels natural."

Many couples who feel hopeless are able to turn things around, and things that begin with conscious effort become automatic.[236] It is possible for spouses to teach their old horses new tricks. One of the ways Mark and Katelin focused on their relationship was getting back to the dance floor. At first they had to think about each step, but they soon were performing complex moves gracefully and automatically. Their hearts were again beating in sync, and they were dancing and relating to each other better than ever.

Main Points

- We have two processing systems. System 1, or "the Heart," is automatic and quick. System 2, or "the Mind," is more reflective and conscious. It can override System 1.
- The heart and mind can be compared to a horse and rider, where the horse is strong and instinctive, and the rider is logical and governing.
- The heart controls more perception and behavior than most people realize. It drives people forward and automatically makes many decisions. However, the heart also can be biased and overconfident.

- The heart is prone to overreaction and may see threats that don't exist. It also overreacts when it has been hurt by specific things in the past.

- The heart is especially sensitive to negativity, and will notice and retain bad things more easily than the good. It also is biased for efficiency and laziness.

- The mind can train and restrain the heart, especially during moments that are provocative. The mind doesn't take away feelings and opinions but bridles and expresses them in a reasonable way.

- The mind and heart work together to evaluate situations and make decisions. As couples spend time together, they increase their ability to understand each other's emotions and opinions.

- The two-part process of perceiving can improve as people intentionally act. The mind can rewire the brain through conscious choices to reflect and slow down. Emotions can also change as they are reconsidered by the mind.

Discussion Questions

- When has your heart run wild—like a horse without a rider?

- In what circumstances have you overreacted or gotten too focused on negative events?

- When have you jumped to conclusions or gotten upset for the wrong reason?

- What can you do to help your mind and heart work together?

- How have you been able to change habits or override impulses that might have gotten you into trouble in your relationship?

- Think of a time when you have spent time with your spouse and truly listened to him or her. How did that change the way you viewed your spouse and the conflict you might have been having?

- Have you had times where your emotions changed as you reconsidered a situation? Have you been able to choose to do that?

Chapter 11
Responding and Conversing

Good communication is as stimulating as black coffee and just as hard to sleep after.

Anne Morrow Lindbergh[237]

Every couple that comes to therapy is different, but this one was *more* different than usual. The wife, Jill, told me they were seeking help for "communication problems." She was a chain-smoking, no-nonsense manager at the 7-Eleven. Short and stocky, Jill had a gruff demeanor and bright stripes on her pants. Her husband, Santiago, was a genial roofer who doted on their toddler, frequently taking him to the McDonald's PlayPlace. When I first met them, I was surprised to see they brought a friend, Mateo. I asked if he would be joining us, and Jill said he was their interpreter. I assumed she meant he was an impartial friend who could help, but Jill clarified. With a load of gravel in her voice, she said, "I don't speak Spanish, and Santiago don't speak English. Mateo is here to interpret for us and for you."

We did our best, but it was an unusual session with Mateo translating rapid-fire for all, and he probably understood their relationship better than any of us. But he didn't have to translate Jill's exasperated sighs or the laughter of Santiago that often followed Jill's accusations. This aggravated her, which would make Santiago shrug and laugh again.

I have worked with many couples that misunderstood each other, but Jill and Santiago were the only pair I helped who literally didn't understand a word the other said (other than a few choice phrases). They were having a hard time but reported being in love. They both claimed they didn't need to talk, because they "just got each other" and "had a sturdy connection." Such is the power of love—it transcends verbal communication.

Relationships *should* be deeper than words. Love should include feelings, looks, touches, and energy. However, words are important. They are connectors that bind souls together. In this chapter we will discuss conversations that happen between partners. We will evaluate how people react to each other and discuss ways to be present and respond. We will also see how memory can be unstable and deceive partners and cause misunderstandings. Things will conclude with a discussion of practical steps to help errant conversations get back on track.

Be Responsive

When your partner says something to you, what is your typical response? Do you grunt and growl like Jill? Laugh it off like Santiago? Ignore it? Engage? Spouses have a stream of opportunities to react to each other, and the way they do reveals the health of the relationship. Shelly Gable is a psychologist who studies interactions. She looked at how partners react to something good in the other's life. She had seventy-nine young couples do a five-minute task. Her team watched how partners responded when one shared something positive. They classified the responses into four types: active-constructive (energized support), passive-constructive (minimal support), active-destructive (negative), and passive-destructive (ignoring what was said or changing the subject).

For example, suppose that Dartel comes home and tells Josie he got a raise. Josie can respond in many different ways. An active-constructive response might be, "Awesome! It's great that you're being recognized for your work." Or she could give a passive-constructive response: "That's cool" [briefly glancing up from Instagram]. She could be active-destructive: "What if they expect you to do more? Can you even handle your job now?" Or passive-destructive: "I am so mad at your mom right now."[238]

Gable followed up with the couples two months later and found that the difference between those doing well and those who had broken up was the amount of active-constructive responses. Partners showing genuine interest in each other's lives had the healthiest relationships. This is because active-constructive responses are not just words; they convey information about the relationship. If Josie gives Dartel a verbal high five ("Awesome"), it shows that he is valued, safe, and supported. The positive impact isn't from the literal meaning of her words, it is from how she feels about Dartel, and this comes across to him.

John Gottman calls relationship interactions that expect a response "bids." When a partner says something, it is a bid, and the reaction is revealing. Say that Josie and Dartel are driving in companionable silence. Josie looks out the window and says, "I used to have a purple Ford Taurus like that in college, only it was rusted through." Her comment isn't about the clunker, it is about connecting with Dartel. If his response is positive ("That is one sweet ride!"), it is an example of a partner "turning toward" the other, in Gottman's terms. If the response to the bid is negative ("You have told me that a million times,") then it is a "turning away" moment. It is also a turn away if the bid is ignored or greeted with an eye roll. The response shows whether the feelings are caring or dismissive. The accumulating turns toward each other are adhesives for the relationship.

A while ago my wife texted me, "The iPad is missing. Any ideas?" I was busy, but texted back, "No, sorry." I got back to work. A few minutes later, I saw she was calling. I sighed. I was busy writing a book about connecting with your spouse, so I didn't want to answer. I did answer, but my first impulse was to be snarky and say something like, "Did you just want to *tell* me verbally that it was gone?" But fortunately I thought better. She was irritated and having a stressful day, and we talked for three minutes. I listened and asked a couple of questions ("Maybe the kids put it somewhere?"), and it was fine. This was a small example of a bid, and it could have gone several ways. If I was condescending it would have caused distance and resentment. I tried to be present, so it went okay. Maybe I could have been more sympathetic and it might have generated more of a connection. She wasn't necessarily asking me to solve the problem (although that would have been welcome), but wanted a few moments from me to listen to something that was taking her energy.

Bids come frequently, and couples who manage them in a reasonable or encouraging way do much better than those who don't. Gottman followed couples for six years after they got married and found that those who had divorced responded positively after a bid only 33 percent of the time. The couples that were still together had responded positively about 86 percent of the time. This is a big difference, and it has been found in many kinds of couples—rich, poor, gay, and straight—and is key in predicting which relationships will survive.[239]

How often do you respond positively to your partner's bids? The healthiest couples are encouraging or constructive nine times out of ten. The struggling couples are turning toward each only about a third of the time. What is your typical response? How does your partner invite you in? Do they ask for attention, act playful, or want help? All of these are opportunities to show interest, support, and make connections.

Be Positive

Connecting takes a good attitude. One day with Jill and Santiago I was trying to generate hope and focus on strengths, but Jill wasn't feeling it. "I love him, but we don't have anything in common," she said. "Maybe we shouldn't have got together." After the translation, Santiago protested vigorously, saying that they had a lot in common. "Name one thing," Jill snapped. Santiago thought for a moment, then brightened and spoke.

[Translation] "We both like . . . pizza!"

Jill stared at him like he was dumb as a brick. "Everyone likes pizza! That don't count!"

Santiago laughed.

I had a hard time keeping a straight face, and then Mateo lost it. Soon we all were laughing.

I am not sure if this interaction was helpful to them, but I appreciated Santiago's efforts to accentuate the positive in a tense situation. Couples who focus on the good cope better with challenges and feel better individually.[240] In Shelly Gable's observations, it was the positive responses that made them feel closer. The passive responses were not much better than the negative ones. She also found that when partners discussed happy events together they felt closer throughout the rest of the day.[241]

People like positive energy, and the brain will shift into a better gear when prompted with good things. Consider, for example, these questions: "What attracted you to each other in the beginning?" "Why do you love your partner so much?" These inquiries prompt you to recall fun experiences, excitement, and traits you value in your mate. What if you were asked, "What are your partner's least attractive qualities?" "What would make you consider divorce?" These questions lead your brain in a different direction and cause you to think about your partner's unfortunate tendency to throw his underwear on your sink, or how she avoids feelings, or that one awful fight comparing whose mom was worse. This tendency to follow an emotional prompt is called the positive test strategy, which is a type of confirmation bias. When a conversation starts down one path it tends to continue that way, which is why it is important to steer your comments.[242] The more you focus on good things, the better you feel and the more likely good will continue.[243]

With Jill and Santiago, we found some strengths. I asked them what it was like when things had been going well. "This sounds silly," Jill said, "but we used to hold hands and pray together. I miss doing that." Santiago thought of another thing. They shared an electric toothbrush, but they each had their own head for it. After one would use the toothbrush, they would change the brush for the other and leave it that way. They weren't doing this anymore (they did, however, confirm that they were still brushing their teeth). These sound like small things, and they were. But the negative changes indicated that something was dying. Like leaves turning brown on a rosebush, the negative developments in their relationship symbolized deterioration at the roots. I asked them to act like things were going well and do things they used to enjoy with each other. They took this seriously and returned to the easy, nonverbal relationship they started with.

Be Present

People can be on the same couch and be miles apart. For connection to happen they need to give attention to each other. The brain is a nonlinear organ—it produces thoughts spontaneously and bounces around like an ADHD puppy in a field of squirrels.[244] The ability of the brain to make random connections is part of being flexible and creative, but it makes focusing difficult. This is particularly true in the modern world, which is humming with distractions. Conversations compete with emotions, physical needs, dogs barking, and text alerts chirping.

One woman described her husband's evening ritual, which began with a grunt, as he sat on his recliner and embraced his smartphone, tablet, and TV remote control. She would try to talk with him—ask about his day or tell him of hers—but his responses to her bids were monosyllables and shrugs. When she got peeved and asked him to put down the devices, he claimed they helped him focus on her. His argument was silly, of course. The brain can't pay attention to multiple things simultaneously. It can jump quickly from thing to thing, but it can't focus on two processes at the same time.[245]

Pretending to be present doesn't work very well. Think of times when you were on the phone and could tell the other party was preoccupied. There were vague noises ("Um hmmm") and wimpy responses while they rewound your statements to try and keep up ("Wait, oh, yeah, right"). When people are distracted, it weakens the connection. This happens in meetings as workers furtively check their phones and daydream about vacations. It happens in relationships when partners' heads wander.

An old proverb says a man who chases two rabbits won't catch either one. Likewise, a couple trying to solve a problem won't have success unless they give it dedicated attention. It is especially hard to focus on a problem when there is a threatening or loud distraction. For instance, it is nearly impossible for partners to follow the meaning of a conversation if they are being shouted at. It is like trying to do a crossword puzzle while prodded with a Taser. A threat takes all the energy in the brain, and it needs to be removed before attention can be on something else.

But a distraction doesn't have to be threatening to interfere. Electronics are designed to grab attention, and they do, quite successfully. One study looked at how partners snub each other with their smart phones. This phenomenon, known as "phubbing," may be familiar to you. Have you ever stopped a conversation to check an alert? Glanced at your phone while talking? Pulled it out during a lull? Kept it visible while you are in the bedroom? The researchers found that the more often these phubs happen in a relationship, the worse the relationship does, which often leads to dissatisfaction and depression. About a quarter of survey responders said that phubbing had caused a fight.[246] Other researchers have labeled this phenomenon "technoference," because technology interference has become ubiquitous as devices encroach upon conversations, dates, and intimate lives.[247]

Being present takes some coordination and effort, and one estimate is that partners are distracted about seventy percent of the time. This means that they are aware of each other about thirty percent of the time, leaving the chance that they both are available at the *same* time about nine percent.[248] If you want to connect, it will take more than just putting down devices and blankly staring. Be active. Take a curious approach to what is passing between you. Put yourself in your partner's shoes, and ask yourself what your partner is feeling in that moment. Pay attention to facial expressions and body language. Take an interest, ask questions, and be positive, like you would on a first date.[249] Be aware when your mind is wandering, and avoid comparing your partner's experience to yours ("Wow, you think your ex is bad, listen to this . . ."). Instead of pointing out your efforts or opinions, try to understand the other person's first. In a world of inner and outer distractions, it is a gift to give the present to your partner.

Have a Voice

Endless are the explanations for relationship failure. Authorities cite specific issues like money, housework, or sex, as the "number one" reason for divorce. However, these phenomena by themselves don't *cause* anything. They are just places to have different opinions. If each partner takes one hundred dollars to Walmart, they will buy different things. If both set out to clean the house, they will start in different places. No lovers agree on how often and how exactly to get intimate. That is the reality of relationships. How couples deal with these differences is the trick. Both want, and should have, an opinion in what happens together, and successful conversations include a give-and-take of views, listening, and compromising.

In one of our studies, we examined the ways couples balanced the back-and-forth requests in their conversations while discussing a concern. We analyzed these, rating each time the conversation changed from one to the other. If the partner was asserting something or directing the conversation, we gave it a one. If acquiescing, or going along with the other's direction, it was rated as a negative one. For example, here is a section of a conversation where Alexis was expressing a concern to Nicole because she had lied about talking with a former girlfriend.

Alexis: "That is one of our biggest issues: trust. But you know why I can't trust you."

Nicole: "I know. I know why you can't trust me. That's my fault. And the sad thing is I know you [can't] . . ."

Alexis: "I feel like I am checking up on you all the time. . . . It frustrates the hell out of me sometimes, because I have to take time out of whatever I am doing at work just to call you and see what you are doing."

Nicole: [laughs] "I know."

In this instance, Alexis's segments of the conversation were assertive, and Nicole's were acquiescing, or accepting. Over the course of a conversation, these turns create a pattern that can be plotted visually, and this shows whether the conversation is balanced in give-and-take. What we found was that in healthy couples there was equity between suggestions and agreements. In couples where there was abuse or control, the conversations often looked different. The pattern was more hierarchical, with one side giving most of the dominating statements.[250]

It is not healthy if one always controls the discussions and the other squelches his or her feelings. A relationship takes two voices, and both have important things to share. One study found that when people hide their feelings their relationship suffers. This was particularly true for extroverts.[251] Partners who are phony or sweep things under the rug build up resentment. Both should be truthful and address issues in a kind and constructive way. Some have a fear of standing up for themselves, and women sometimes get mixed messages in this regard and are pressured to not rock the boat or hurt others' feelings.[252]

To interact and converse takes time, and this is often in short supply. Yet people spend a lot of time on unimportant things: TV, traffic, fantasy sports, or phone surfing. It seems reasonable to think that partners who play Candy Crush or check what their high school friends are eating on Facebook could take a few minutes with each other.

Most couples wait a long time before addressing problems, so one researcher examined what would happen if they were forced to face their issues. James Cordova gave 216 married couples questionnaires to assess their strengths and weaknesses. He assigned half the couples to visit a therapist twice to review their relationship and to create a plan to address the trouble areas. The remaining couples were left on a waiting list. The researchers checked in with the couples after one year, then two, and found that those who had done both check-ins had higher relationship satisfaction, better intimacy, more feelings of acceptance, and less depression symptoms than did the waitlist couples.[253] That is a lot of benefit from two focused, honest conversations.

State Intentions

It is good to address relationship weeds before they spread and take root. Working on concerns is stressful, so it is good to set the stage. A conversation will go better if a partner says, "I don't want us to fight, and I don't want to have bad feelings, but I do want to talk about something." This primes both for an accurate conversation and helps defenses stay lowered. In one of my studies on escalation, we watched couples problem-solve, and when one "stated intentions," it generally had a good effect on the process. Examples included questions like, "So, how should I confront you about your house?" "What do we need to do then to get . . . to where there doesn't have to be someone around to keep us from fighting?" They also made requests like, "Talk with me about it. Ask me why I am mad." And, "I wish you would just speak your mind a little bit more and . . . I'll try to see it your way. I just want you to be a little more open."254

It is crucial to start a conversation well, because then it will end well. About 96 percent of the time, a conversation will end the way it begins in its first three minutes.[255] If you start with a controlled question it will have a different outcome than if you accuse with guns blazing and emotions erupting. Staying in control is crucial. And as we have discussed in other chapters, it is important to be honest, kind, and responsible for words. One way to take ownership is to use "I-messages." This means you speak about your own concerns and feelings rather than accusing the other.[256] For instance, it is better to say "I am annoyed when you won't get off your Instagram when we are talking" than "You phubbing jerk!"

Partners should also avoid extreme statements. Ultimatums like, "If you are late one more time, we are through!" make negotiation impossible. When divorce is used as a threat the brain becomes negative and preoccupied with splitting up. This makes it more likely that partners will dwell on how great other potential mates seem to be and how annoying their current one is.

Conversing partners also need to stick with the issue of concern and not throw in every complaint they have had since the day they met. The brain can juggle multiple things, but when too many are put on the table, awareness shuts down.[257] This is especially true when the issues are tense. A fire hydrant of words will not persuade, only flood the room and the listener.

When Not to Say Anything

Conversations are important, but it is good to know when to leave things unsaid. Many irritants in a relationship are simply part of two imperfect people living together, and if each minor bump is brought up, it gets exhausting. When your partner leaves crumbs on the desk or talks to the waiter in a way you aren't thrilled with, it might not matter. Many frustrations will pass, and some are caused by your own emotions or biases. Mature couples let things roll and are judicious when choosing which issues to hash out. The next time you find the socks folded the wrong way, you can decide whether it is worth pointing out or whether you take three seconds and fix it.

Lola Walters learned this lesson as a newlywed when she read in a magazine that in order to strengthen a marriage, a couple should tell each other all the things that bothered them. She said,

> We were to name five things we found annoying, and I started off. . . . I told him that I didn't like the way he ate grapefruit. He peeled it and ate it like an orange! Nobody else I knew ate grapefruit like that. Could a girl be expected to spend a lifetime, and even eternity, watching her husband eat grapefruit like an orange? . . . After I finished [with my five], it was his turn to tell the things he disliked about me. . . . [He] said, "Well, to tell the truth, I can't think of anything I don't like about you, Honey."
>
> *Gasp.*

I quickly turned my back, because I didn't know how to explain the tears that had filled my eyes and were running down my face.[258]

Like Lola, sometimes we are unnecessarily critical. When you address a concern, are you doing it for the wrong reasons? To prove something? To put the other in his or her place? Or, are you genuinely trying to work through something important?

Beware Your Memory

One deception that throws off couples as they interact is memory. Partners assume their recollections are accurate, but memory is not as reliable as it seems. Shelby and Stan were illustrating this one day as they argued over an incident at her parent's house. "We went there for a family barbecue after we first started dating," Shelby reported. "Stan was just getting to know my family, and he ended up losing his temper and embarrassing me in front of everyone. It was a catastrophe!"

"Her little brother is a twerp, and he came up and pulled my shorts down around my ankles," said Stan. "He thought this was hysterical, but I was mad."

"So you hurt him," Shelby said. "You Hulked out and tackled him and he ended up with bruises and is now freaked out by you. My parents were wondering what kind of guy I brought over."

"Your parents should have been wondering about what kind of teenager they were raising." Stan snapped. "Your brother was a spoiled punk, and I didn't tackle him. I just chased him and put him in a headlock. He needed to learn his lesson, and he wasn't hurt; he just had a couple of scuffs."

"He was bleeding and crying! You almost killed him!"

"I barely touched him, and he only had scrapes and was laughing!"

"Everyone was shocked at what you did!"

"No one cared! They thought he deserved it!"

Have you done this? Recounted the same event but had different versions of it? Have you become frustrated at your partner's inaccuracies in memory? How could your partner be so wrong about basic facts? Is your spouse lying or just confused? He or she is probably just doing the same thing you're doing, which is remembering something incompletely. Memory is not a video that replays the same way each time. It is like an improvisational play, where themes and events are reworked slightly with each performance.

Professor Ulrick Neisser did an impromptu experiment after the space shuttle Challenger exploded in 1986. The day after the disaster, he asked his class of 106 students to write down where they were when they heard about it. Three years later, he asked these students the same thing. Over 90 percent of the accounts changed, and about half of them were inaccurate in at least two-thirds of the details. The revised memories had supplanted the earlier, more accurate ones, but the new ones *felt* true. One was shown her first description, written three years earlier, and said, "I know that's my handwriting, but I couldn't possibly have written that."[259]

The late Oliver Sacks, a neurologist, was curious about the malleability of recall. He studied false memories, self-plagiarism, and the way events are "transformed, disassembled, reassembled, and recategorized with every act of recollection."[260] He also experienced this firsthand. Sacks wrote a memoir of his childhood in London where he recalled intense and scary bombings during the end of World War II. After it was published, his older brother talked with him about his stories.

"My brother immediately confirmed the first bombing incident, saying, 'I remember it exactly as you described it.' But regarding the second bombing, he said, 'You never saw it. You weren't there.' I was staggered by Michael's words. How could he dispute a memory I would not hesitate to swear on in a court of law, and had never doubted as real? 'What do you mean?' I objected. 'I can see the bomb in my mind's eye now, Pa with his pump, and Marcus and David with their buckets of water. How could I see it so clearly if I wasn't there?'

"'You never saw it,' Michael repeated. 'We were both away at Braefield at the time. But David [our older brother] wrote us a letter about it. A very vivid, dramatic letter. You were enthralled by it.' Clearly, I had not only been enthralled, but must have constructed the scene in my mind, from David's words, and then appropriated it, and taken it for a memory of my own."[261]

Both of Sack's memories had the same quality. Both felt real.° The emotions attached to the memories were strong, and this influenced the recollections.[262]

Memories are shaped by feelings that existed at the time, but also by the way the memory is retrieved. For example, how someone asks a question will influence details of an event. Elizabeth Loftus showed participants a short movie of an auto accident and afterward asked them questions, but she discovered that the words she used influenced what observers remembered. For instance, she asked people how fast the car was going when it hit the other car. But when she changed the word "hit" to "smashed," the estimates of speed were higher. More people remembered seeing broken glass when she asked the "smashed" version as well.[263]

---

o. He suggests that although our memories are fallible and creative, this is part of what helps us connect with others. He suggests that the tendency of our memories to pull from various sources "allows us to assimilate what we read, what we are told, what others say and think and write and paint, as intensely and richly as if they were primary experiences. It allows us to see and hear with other eyes and ears, to enter into other minds . . . [it] arises not only from direct experience but from the intercourse of many minds."

If Memory Serves . . .

If a partner recalls a story while angry, the details will be more negative. Brains fill in gaps to support the angry version, and memory serves its owner. Details that don't fit are dropped, and others are added to make the memory coherent and pleasing.[264] It only takes a few days after an event for the details to change.[265] Stan and Shelby may have had similar initial memories of when Stan mooned the barbecue, but their current marriage problems were darkening these recollections. Now Stan remembers Shelby being biased and critical, and she remembers him as extreme and violent.

This negative filter was a bad sign. Couples who are not doing well say things like, "We got married too young; I didn't see what a slob he was then." Or, "She tricked me into thinking she would actually be excited about sex." In one study, researchers interviewed fifty-six couples, none of whom were planning divorce. However, the team accurately predicted the seven couples that would divorce based on the negative way they talked about their history.[266] After relationships fail, exes are inclined toward "retroactive pessimism," where they recall the problems in a way that sounds like they were inevitable: "It was doomed from the start."[267]

The reverse is true as well. When couples feel loving, they recall things more generously. Satisfied partners describe their history in positive terms and will laugh about previous bumps and misunderstandings. When President Kennedy was assassinated, there was an outpouring of grief in the United States. In a poll following the assassination, two-thirds of respondents recalled voting for him in the previous election, when only half really had. People's memories changed to be consistent with the positive emotions they felt about their martyred president.[268]

Not only do memories feel true, but they aren't easily corrected. When someone is attached to a story, challenging it with contrary information can entrench it further. This tendency is called "belief perseverance," which is when a person refuses to change even in the face of contradictory data.[269] Stubborn partners are often wrong, but they are rarely in doubt.

Belief perseverance is self-protective. When couples attack each other's recall, even with evidence, it feels like an attack of the person. Stan and Shelby were implying the other was incompetent, not just inaccurate. Even if each brought witnesses from the barbecue to testify for their version, it would not convince the other. When a partner tries to browbeat the other into agreement, it doesn't work and causes resentment. Imagine an argument where one comes away grateful for having been forcibly corrected. "Gee thanks, Shelby, for helping me see how wrong I was! Now I can go forward in truth and light!"

Nietzsche captured this egocentric version of recall. He said: "'I have done that' says my memory. 'I cannot have done that,' says my pride, and remains inexorable. Eventually—memory yields." In this sense, false memories are similar to other deceptions we have reviewed, like motivated reasoning, exaggerating, or lying. All types affect one's self-image.[270]

Workability and Repairs

It helps when partners are willing to recognize their fallible memories and be humble. History is subjective, and truth is in motion in a relationship. Instead of arguing over facts, it is better to spend energy on solutions. One therapy approach calls this "workability." This is a focus on what helps, instead of worrying about who did what.[271] It may be true that he acted like a toddler, slamming the door and stomping his feet, but it might be more workable to focus on what would improve the current mood. It may be accurate to say she has put on thirty-two pounds since the wedding, but is that helpful to say? Is it moving the relationship forward? In throwing out opinions about who is right and wrong, it is good to consider the old advice: Is it true? Is it kind? Is it necessary? And is it workable? Workability does not ask "Who is right?" but "What is the right thing to do?"

One of the most workable actions in a relationship is a repair. Time will heal many wounds, but injuries heal faster with treatment. This can happen in a kind conversation or other conciliatory efforts. One study looked directly at the power of healing gestures. People filled out questionnaires and gave interviews describing incidents when they had recently been emotionally hurt. The researchers followed participants for several weeks to find out what the offender did to make things right. Some did nothing, but others apologized,[p] made recompense, and had a peacemaking attitude. The more steps the offender took, the more the hurt party forgave.[272] Positive attempts changed the way that the hurt person viewed the relationship and the aggressor. Trying to make things right always makes a difference.

Sue Johnson offers guidelines for addressing injuries that are not healing on their own. First, speak about the hurt honestly and simply. This should focus on the feelings, not the fault of the one who caused it. The listening partner acknowledges the pain without getting defensive or making excuses. Second, the injurer needs to take ownership of what he or she did. This needs to be done without downplaying what happened. A real apology is needed, not a "Sorrrrreeee! Sheesh!" Even if the pair doesn't agree on every particular—and they probably won't—it is important to not get stuck rehashing details. Instead, partners should converse about what needs to be done next. This will provide a sense of moving forward and will be reassuring. If couples can talk through the events without getting upset, it helps to rework the memory into a less bitter version.[273]

---

p. Brian Gaar has tweeted, "Relationships are mostly you apologizing for saying something hilarious."

It is important to nurture and treat wounds, but that doesn't fix things immediately. Someone can apologize profusely for breaking another's arm, but the pain will still last for a while. The offender has to allow this and not get frustrated ("I said I was sorry. Just go use your arm already!"). They also must feel regret for the pain, not just the issue it has created. Sincere apologies help couples recalibrate and commit to do better. They help partners become more aware and honest for future conversations.

Stan and Shelby had to work at this, but they finally realized that no amount of arguing would convince each other whose story was most correct at that fateful poolside day. As they improved at having positive conversations, they were better able to laugh and admit their stories had become warped. They heard each other out and agreed to drop the issue. They also agreed to avoid pool parties at her parent's house until her brother left home.

Main Points

- Partners interact frequently, and the way they respond to each other shapes the relationship.
- Successful couples turn toward each other, or offer positive responses, almost 90 percent of the time.
- Those who attempt to be positive with each other will feel closer.
- Partners improve their connection by giving full attention to each other when interacting.
- Electronics are designed to grab attention, and "technoference" often disrupts relationships.
- Successful conversations include both partners having a voice and sharing opinions, as well as listening and compromising.
- Stating intentions includes being honest about what you hope to accomplish, avoiding extreme statements, and knowing when to leave things unsaid.
- Memories are faulty and often change in a way that is favorable to the one recalling them.
- It helps when partners are willing to recognize their biased recollections and be humble.
- Instead of arguing over facts, it is better to spend energy on solutions.
- Repair attempts include apologies, reconciliation, and a constructive attitude.
- Sincere efforts to make things better help couples recalibrate and become more aware and honest.

Discussion Questions

- How do you usually respond to your partner's bids? How often are these responses positive and supportive?
- What helps you stay positive and focus on the good things in your relationship?
- What tends to pull at your attention the most? Electronics? The kids?

- What can you do to minimize mental distractions while spending time with your partner?
- What can you do to increase the balance between suggestions and agreements in your conversations?
- When have you realized that your memory was faulty?
- When is it important to focus on the future rather than argue over the details of the past?
- How as attempting repairs or apologizing benefited your relationship?

Chapter 12
Passion and Compassion

*And he took her in his arms and kissed her under the sunlit sky,
and he cared not that they stood high upon the walls in the sight of
many.*

J. R. R. Tolkien

John Ronald Reuel Tolkien is known worldwide for his fantastic characters and creations. His hobbits, dwarves, elves, and warriors have changed the face of literature and culture. As a boy, he had unusual interests. He loved reading mythology, playing chess, and drawing fierce dragons, and by age nine, young Ronald (as he was usually called) had invented several languages. Well-known is Tolkien's prodigious geek cred, but less known is that he was a hopeless romantic.

He grew up in England in the early 1900s in difficult circumstances, having lost both his father and mother by his mid-teens. Taken under the guardianship of Father Francis, a Catholic priest, young Ronald became lonely and contemplative. At sixteen, he and his brother moved into a small apartment, where downstairs was a girl that would change Ronald's life. Edith Bratt was a pretty nineteen-year-old, with light gray eyes and a flair for music. Ronald was lovestruck. Edith's interest was piqued, and she began to befriend the Tolkien brothers. Ronald would lower a basket from his window, and Edith would load it with snacks. The food depletions must have puzzled Edith's guardian, Mrs. Faulkner, as Edith was slender and less than five feet tall.

Over time, Edith was won over by the younger Ronald, and they began spending their spare time together. They made each other laugh. One amusing pastime was to meet at a rooftop tea room in Birmingham and throw lumps of sugar into the hats of those walking below. When one bowl was empty, they moved to the next table. Their companionship was so consuming, it caused the alarm of Father Francis and Mrs. Faulkner (assigned the code name, "The Old Lady" by the pair). The guardians thought the relationship improper and were upset that Ronald was not attending to his studies. To skirt this disapproval, Edith and Ronald invented a whistle call that would summon the other to the window, where they could talk into the night.[274]

One weekend, the two conspired for a meeting in the countryside. They rode and returned separately but were spotted by a caretaker, who mentioned it to the cook back at the church. Around this same time, Ronald failed his Oxford entrance exams, and Father Francis put his foot down and insisted there be no more courting of Edith. The pair could not be kept apart, however, and they again planned a rendezvous. They plotted well, met secretly, and boarded a train for a getaway. The retreat was to another town where they shopped at a jewelry store, buying gifts for each other's eighteenth and twenty-first birthdays. Unfortunately, their luck was again cursed, as an observer recognized them and word got back to Father Francis. This time, the priest was firm and unambiguous—Ronald was to have no contact with Edith until his twenty-first birthday.

Tolkien was depressed but dutiful, and obeyed his guardian's wishes. Over the next three years, he passed his college exams and began life at Oxford, playing rugby and studying Gothic, Anglo-Saxon, and Welsh. He did not, however, forget about his Edith.

On the eve of his twenty-first birthday, he sat in bed watching his clock. The moment it struck midnight, he began a letter to Edith, pouring out his love and proposing marriage. After a few anxious days, he received a letter back with the devastating news that she was engaged to a more suitable prospect, George Field. She was getting old (almost twenty-four!) and felt the urgency of time. She also had assumed their long separation had cooled Ronald's fancies and that he had moved on.

Ronald jumped on the first train to Cheltenham, where Edith met him at the station. They walked out into the chilly countryside along the railway viaduct. He made an impassioned case that melted Edith's heart. She agreed to ditch George and throw her lot in with the college boy with the strange interests in Beowulf and linguistics.[275]

Their marriage was filled with joy, laughter, and four children. One day, the lovers had an experience that lodged so deep in Ronald's soul that it became a key story in his books. He and Edith were walking in the woods and came upon a clearing filled with flowering white hemlock. She began to dance in the sunshine and it took Ronald's breath away. Recounting this story to his son many years later, Tolkien wrote, "In those days her hair was raven, her skin clear, her eyes brighter than you have seen them, and she could sing—and *dance*."[276] This event inspired the romance between Beren and Luthien, a mortal man and an elf-maiden. In his book *The Silmarillion*, he wrote of the pair, "But wandering in the summer in the woods of Neldoreth, Beren came upon Luthien, daughter of Thingol and Melian, at a time of evening under moonrise, as she danced upon the unfading grass in the glades beside Esgalduin. Then all memory of his pain departed from him, and he fell into an enchantment; for Luthien was the most beautiful of all the children of Iluvatar."

When Tolkien submitted his *Lord of the Rings* manuscripts to his publisher, they questioned his inclusion of any romantic elements. Specifically, he was told that the story of Aragorn and Arwen, which parallels Beren and Luthien, was "unnecessary and perfunctory." The publisher didn't think that a chest-pounding story of men and magic needed any mushy stuff. Tolkien pushed back, citing the stirring nature of love. In his letter to publisher Rayner Unwin, he pled the case for including the doomed lovers: "I still find it poignant: an allegory of naked hope. I hope you do."[277] His passionate heart again prevailed, and Tolkien kept the romance in the story.[q]

Edith died in 1971 at age eighty-two in Bournemouth, Hampshire, England, and Tolkien had the name "Luthien" engraved on her headstone. When he died twenty-one months later, he was buried with her, with the name "Beren" added to his name.

The passion between J. R. R. Tolkien and his beloved Edith is moving, because we all have passion within. Their fierce connection demonstrates the depth of love humans can attain. Passions bind people together and includes physical drives that thrill but also intellectual, spiritual, and emotional intimacy.

This chapter is about the ways partners connect through emotions, body language, and chemistry. It discusses how two people who are open and honest can literally become one—two parts of a whole. We will also review the importance of compassion, which is the ability to feel another's emotions.

Connecting and Transforming

Connection isn't just a metaphor. When people share emotions and space, they start to bond and alter each other. They literally become different. This was demonstrated in the unusual arena of fire-walking. Every June in Spain, thousands gather in the village of San Pedro Manrique to watch brave individuals walk barefoot over smoldering oak embers in front of cheering crowds. One year, researchers strapped heart monitors on some of the fire walkers and spectators. As volunteers stepped onto the glowing coals their heart rates synchronized with the heart rates of their family and friends watching. Strangers, however, did not synchronize with the fire walkers.[278]

Invisible chemical processes were connecting those who cared about each other. In other settings, lovers whose hearts beat together feel closer and more stable,[279] and clients whose hearts synch with their therapists' hearts report better sessions.[280] Scholars have also found that tense emotions are jarring to the heart rate. One wrote, "During the experience of negative emotions such as anger, frustration, or anxiety, heart rhythms become more erratic and disordered, indicating less synchronization . . . between the parasympathetic and sympathetic branches of the autonomic nervous system (ANS)."[281] In other words, out-of-sync emotions produce out-of-sync heart rates. The heart isn't just a metaphor

---

q. The quote at the beginning of the chapter is from another brief love story that Tolkien snuck into *The Return of the King*: the eventual romance of Faramir and Eowyn.

for love, it is part of it. Another study found that high-conflict couples tend to have thicker carotid arteries,[282] which suggests being hard-hearted is bad for marriage *and* health.

However, positive emotions from one partner can act as a healing force. When one simply projects a caring or concerned feeling toward another, it results in measurable changes to the recipient's heart.[283] Good feelings are palpable, and they spread from people who are connected. Another study at a wedding found that the oxytocin levels of the bride, groom, close relatives, and friends all surged together.[284]

Love connects and changes partners. Have you ever laughed about how old married couples look alike? Science backs this up. Robert Zajonc showed volunteers pictures of couples, some in their first year of marriage, and some in their twenty-fifth year.[285] The researchers removed extra information in the photos to leave only faces. Volunteers were able to pick the long-term spouses more often than unconnected people or short-term spouses. People's faces did grow more similar over time, and the researchers speculated that one of the reasons was that lovers look at each other and empathize together for years, mimicking and reflecting what they see. Long-term couples also have unusually similar kidney functions, cholesterol levels, and grip strength.[286]

Deep and Painful Interdependencies

People are made to love—it is built into their cells. This is why it is distressing when connection is blocked or goes bad. Many mental disorders are diagnosed because of connection problems. For example, when someone has no empathy, they are diagnosed as sociopathic, and when one is overly suspicious of others, they are paranoid. The extremely indifferent are schizoid, those in highly unstable relationships are borderline, those who can't read emotions are autistic, and so forth. It can be a diagnosable concern when healthy connections aren't happening.

Take the issue of loneliness. People are living alone at higher rates than ever, and some research has found that loneliness is associated with health risks that rival those correlated with obesity or smoking.[287] According to the University of Chicago's John Cacioppo and William Patrick, around 20 percent of individuals feel isolated enough for it to be a major source of unhappiness in their lives. For older Americans, that number is around 35 percent. People need people. The sentimental statement "You complete me" is real. Two people paired is a more natural state than one isolated. However, this pairing up creates a new entity, and if it shatters, it hurts. Partners who bond and then break are not just experiencing a transition, but a rupture.

Matthew Lieberman has found the sting of a breakup is experienced in the brain like physical pain.[288] One study surveyed 5,700 people about "post relationship grief (PRG)" and found that breakups can be brutal, and men often experience them more deeply than women.[289] Despair can persist for years and lead to mental and physical health problems. Brain scholar Lucy Brown suggests that romantic rebuffing is more primal than other refusals. "Other kinds of social rejection are much more cognitive," she says. "[Romantic rejection] is a life changing thing, and involves systems that are at the same level as feeling hungry or thirsty." In other words, love is connected to our deepest self. This is why new love is so thrilling and can cause delirium and poetry writing. But the loss of love is like a withdrawal of a drug.[290] Like an addict climbing the walls, a jilted lover may act crazy with heartache and loss.

The Pathways of Connection

Growing together is a process, and there are a lot of mechanisms involved. Two people connect through visual, tactile, chemical, verbal, and biological means. These pathways are like rubber cement—designed to stick two separate things together. Often, connection begins with a look.

Your Face Is Showing

I was sitting in church one day as a newly-married man and noticed a nice-looking woman on the piano bench up front. She was staring my direction and caught my eye. She had an intense look that startled me. She gave a coy smile. I was surprised and alert—but I didn't recognize her and was getting uncomfortable. I glanced at my wife beside me, who didn't notice what was going down. I looked back at the woman who laughed, then winked. I felt extremely awkward and started to sweat. I glanced around to see if anyone was watching this steamy exchange, and then realized her husband was right behind me gazing sappily and waving back at her.

The face is a beacon and transmitter. There are about forty-six facial muscles whose sole purpose seems to be communication of feelings.[291] These muscles make an infinite variety of expressions and are players in the mating game. Sexual attraction and interest is broadcast by facial expressions, including flashing eyes and smiles.[292] Those with attractive faces have a significant advantage in this arena, and a good-looking person will always have others willing to jump into a relationship with them.[293] A John or Jane might be cruel or have a room temperature IQ, but if they are beautiful, then breathless pursuers will follow them around like dogs.

Humans are astonishingly good at recognizing and remembering faces—even those we haven't seen for years. We can differentiate faces based on tiny variations in symmetry or arrangement of features, and we generally agree on which configurations are desirable, even though the differences between lovely and homely are miniscule. We easily distinguish between a cold stare, a blank stare, a come-hither stare, an in-love stare, and an about-to-attack stare. When our eyes fasten upon one of these expressions, our body reacts instantaneously. Strong emotion in others triggers tiny responses in our facial muscles. If you watch someone pulling out a splinter, you cringe too, and if you see someone beam with joy, your expression unconsciously follows, as you mirror the other's face.[294]

There is a specific part of the brain that recognizes and interprets emotional expressions. Fearful and angry looks get the most response, but any face gets this section of the brain going.[295] One study found that people looking at faces scan from the eyes to the nose to the mouth. However, women make about twice the number of these scans, which may be why women are better at recalling details of faces.[296]

We are drawn to the eyes because of their power, which is why one client presented a particular challenge for me. She was a paranoid woman who always wore wrap-around Terminator sunglasses. This wasn't because of vision problems. She changed her explanations for why she couldn't remove the shades, and despite a few gentle requests, I never did see her eyeballs. This was disconcerting, because it is important in therapy to closely track emotion, and the movements around the eyes and eyebrows convey a lot. It is hard to connect without eye contact, because gazing eye-to-eye is a bonding experience. Opening these windows to the soul invites others in.

Expectations and Attitude

Signals pass between people through faces, gestures, words, and tone of voice. In one classic experiment, teachers were told that some of their students were gifted and others normal. Although the students were actually labeled at random, over time, the expectation of the teacher changed the students. Of the children designated as brilliant, 80 percent gained at least ten points in their IQ, and 20 percent gained an amazing thirty or more points.[297] Simply treating pupils like they were smart made them so. Even more surprising was a study where research assistants were assigned to watch rats make their way through a maze. Again, the assistants were told that some were high-achieving rodents and others were not, even though there was no difference. And again, something about how the assistants treated the "smarter" rats made them that way, and they performed better in the maze.[298]

This has profound implications for intimate relationships. Partners who see each other as amazing will convey encouraging expectations. These lovers see each other with enthusiasm, and the support is like a protein shake filled with nutrients for the soul. Mark Robert Waldman and Andrew Newberg have found that the brain is hardwired to respond favorably to loving speech. They suggest that even a single positive word like "love" or "peace" alters the brain and strengthens self-control, motivation, and resiliency.[299]

Unfortunately, expectations work the other way as well. When a partner is contemptuous and scornful, the other will be dragged down. Spouses do this in subtle ways through sarcasm, sighs, raised eyebrows, or derisive laughter. Sometimes negativity is extreme and causes real damage. In repeated studies, women who suffer domestic violence report that psychological abuse is the worst part.[300] Even though some had horrendous beatings or physical injuries, the verbal beat down left long-term emotional scars. One of the volunteers from my research sadly described the damage she felt from verbal abuse. She said, "One day I went to the mall, and I had no idea what I liked anymore, nothing. And that's when I realized you just totally lose your whole person."[301]

Navigating Signals

Most people are innately skilled at reading and responding to others, and this makes romantic success possible. Take the example of James and Dinah. James was a friendly and funny anthropology major with unruly blond hair and freckles. He was an impulsive, live-for-the-moment guy who played bass in a Ska Punk band. He was taking a break at a party when he saw Dinah across the room. She had dark eyes, curly hair, and a wide smile, and it was one of those times, as James recalled, "I saw her looking at me across the room, and suddenly I couldn't see anything else. I know it's cheesy, but the noise stopped, everything went blurry, and I was drawn toward her against my will. This was one of those moments I knew nothing was ever going to be the same" [cue the Aerosmith power ballad].

A sequence of actions followed that linked these two, and the majority of these connectors were outside of their awareness. As James floated his way through the crowd, he unconsciously read the body language of the mob, feinting and dodging. Others responded to his body signals, parting to make way for his goal-directed movement. He watched Dinah for indicators as he approached, and she met his eye and smiled, then turned away. As they got close, he cleared his throat, which signaled that he was about to speak. She looked up and gave an expression of welcome. Had she frowned or rolled her eyes, James would have immediately changed strategies. But so far, their wiring was active and attaching.

"He was pretty awkward," Dinah laughed, "but very polite." His courtesy and interest was communicated through words and expressions. He was playful and he repeated her name, drawing it out: "Diii-nah. Cool." She laughed, "Yeah, my grandparents are from Israel." They navigated small talk, which was mostly meaningless but had the effect of gauging interest: "Some party . . . ," "Your band is really good," "What are you studying?" Each tracked signs regarding how the interaction was going and used unspoken protocols of turn-taking. For instance, when finishing a comment and passing the verbal baton, they slowed their words a bit, talked softer, stopped making gestures, and looked expectantly at the other.[302]

They followed each other's behavior with enthusiasm, sharing nods, laughs, and verbal prompts to keep going. If these hadn't happened, the direction would have shifted. For example, if Dinah got warning signals or odd vibes, then she would have indicated disinterest or completion, again using signs that most understand, like, "Well, good luck with the rest of your songs." But she was enjoying the conviviality and went with it, taking it further. She implied future possibilities by saying, "Maybe I can see you guys play another time." She also made unconscious physical flirting movements, including tilting her head to show her neck, crossing her legs, and leaning toward James. He also preened by sitting up straighter, sticking out his chest, and running his hands through his hair.[303] She gently teased him, "You must have a lot of girls interested in you since you are a rock star!" This sent a tiny tingle through him, and he shifted into a cool flirt, which was almost a fatal blunder.

This style includes a calm tone, but can be harder to read.[304] "I thought he got turned off," Dinah recalled. "Right when I was getting interested, he got all chill and started asking me hard questions about my music knowledge."

"She said she liked Ska Punk," James laughed, "So I was trying to bond with her." She wasn't really interested in Ska Punk, but she was in James, so they forged ahead over the bumps and talked late into the night. Their interest was ignited by a look, and tinder was added until their relationship burned bright.

It is impossible to pick apart all the things that happened between James and Dinah as they formed a bond, but it is important for partners to practice this dance. It is a natural but complex process, and this is why people need to work at it. Knowledge about love is important, but trying to master relationships without spending time with others is like trying to become a brilliant dancer by reading about it. Only in the presence of people do humans experience all dimensions of relationships. So it is good to put down the devices and strengthen relationship muscles through interaction.

Misreading Cues

The path from casual to friendly to intimate is beset with obstacles. If it wasn't for the force of passion, people might not pair up at all. Some are skilled at navigating these roads, and they have an advantage in games of love. Just like athletic or intellectual talents, some have aptitude and others don't. Even kindergartners show different levels of social skills, and those with more natural ability are more popular among their little peers.[305] Life is harder for those who struggle to read others.

Take the example of autism. Although this condition has a thousand variations, there are a few key features. One is the presence of social deficits. Those on the autism spectrum often have a hard time reading emotions or facial cues. Prominent autistic professor and advocate Temple Grandin said that during her childhood, she wondered if other children were telepathic, since they easily grasped other's thoughts and feelings that were eluding her.[306] Kamran Nazeer, describing his experience with autism, said that conversations with strangers were his version of "extreme sports" because they were so far out of his comfort zone.[307]

One name for the inability to read social cues is dyssemia.[308] The term comes from the Greek roots *dys* (difficulty) and *semia* (signal). This deficit can strain a marriage. One couple was seeing me because of communication problems, but much of it stemmed from the husband, who had traits of autism and constantly misread his wife's signals. He would go on and on about his work problems and not realize that her expression was pained or disapproving, sending the message, "I don't care. I am bored to tears with what you are saying." She also got frustrated when he missed her messages. She would have a hard day and complain, but what she was saying was, "Pay attention to me." This was too indirect for him.

They identified with a story I told them of a couple driving together. In the account, the wife asks, "Are you thirsty?" The husband ponders for a moment, and says, "Nah," and keeps driving. Later he notices that she is upset, and is puzzled. She wasn't, of course, just asking him a question about his thirst, but was making a request. She was telling him she wanted to stop for a drink, but doing it in a way that required him to interpret her underlying needs. Some partners are not good at making these connections, and this requires more direct communication.

One classic study suggested that in conversations about 55 percent of the emotional meaning of a message is communicated through facial expressions and body gestures, and about 38 percent is transmitted through the tone of voice. This leaves only 7 percent of the emotional meaning conveyed by the words.[309] A person relying only on words might be missing 93 percent of the message, and that isn't going to go well in a relationship.

Some partners struggle to understand feelings, because they have had their emotional radar damaged. Peter Fonagy has found that some who misread emotions grew up in families where they were overwhelmed.[310] When a child experiences a scary world they sometimes respond by shutting down. The feelings are so intense that a psychic tourniquet is created to stanch the pain.

Emotional misreads also happen in the presence of danger, because high arousal makes a person blind to another's emotional state. Author Malcom

Gladwell calls this being "temporarily autistic," because social cues cannot be read during strong arousal.[311] When couples fight they lose the ability to connect or understand each other.

Deep Compassion

Passion works best when paired with compassion. Physical passion is a magnet to bring people together, but it is a temporary pull. Ongoing intimacy takes investment in the well-being of the spouse and a willingness to be open to their joys, as well as their pain. The term "compassion" is derived from Latin words that mean "to suffer together." In this sense, compassion is more than sympathy for a stranger. It is taking on a partner's burdens, feeling what they feel.[312] When partners are one, this comes naturally.

Compassion and Co-Suffering

James Coan has watched compassion appear in the brain. He put participants in an fMRI machine and presented a series of *X*'s and *O*'s. If an *X* appeared, there was a 17 percent chance the person would get a mild shock on their ankle, but if an *O* showed up they were safe. When a shock was possible, the threat centers of the brain would activate. However, Coan tried a variation on this setup. He had participants hold the hand of a friend, and in these instances, the friend would receive the shock. Interestingly, the brain of the person in the fMRI machine activated as well. They felt the same fear for their friend as for themselves. When a stranger held their hand, they didn't activate. Coan said, "The correlation between self and friend was remarkably similar. The finding shows the brain's remarkable capacity to model self to others; that people close to us become a part of ourselves, and that is not just metaphor or poetry. It's very real. Literally we are under threat when a friend is under threat."[313]

This is another reason a partner feels remorse for being cruel. If one is hurtful, both are damaged. It doesn't feel right to hurt a loved one, and it initiates movement in two brussels-sprout-sized parts of the brain called the lateral frontal poles. These activate when people reevaluate and feel sorry for their actions.[314] Humans are the only organisms with this brain component, and this may help explain the moral feelings common to all people.[315] Solid relationships have partners attuned to their sense of conscience. Spouses know that being hurtful is wrong and that being fair and kind is right.

Compassion and Healing

Compassion has power to heal. Harvard's Ted Kaptchuk examined the curative force of a warm, interested person. Patients with irritable bowel syndrome signed up for an "acupuncture treatment." One group was welcomed by a caring, friendly researcher who asked each participant about his or her life, pain and symptoms. After this, they received the treatment. However, the acupuncture needles were a sham and didn't pierce the skin. Then came the comparison group. Patients got the same trick needles, but were treated abruptly by the assistant—no kind inquiry, no sympathy—just a quick in and out. Neither got any actual medical help for their flaming bowels. However, the symptoms of those who received kindness and compassion got significantly better than those who were blown off.[316]

It wasn't the treatment that helped, but the presence of a caring person. This is one reason spouses in a healthy marriage live longer than those alone or in unhealthy relationships.[317] This isn't just because wives insist their husbands go to the doctor to "get that thing on your neck checked out." It is also because love is healing. It is an allover tonic that lowers stress, soothes pain, and is not sold in any store.

This was found in another fMRI study where participants were strapped down in a confining tube and shocked with a searing pain (what is it with these fMRI scientists?). Arthur Aron watched the brains of those in new and still-passionate relationships as they looked at pictures of either 1) their partner, 2) an attractive person of the same age and gender as the partner, or 3) a neutral word association designed to distract from pain. The viewers watched these pictures while being zinged on their hand, but as they were looking at their lover, their brains had a unique response. Not only was there less pain (the word distraction also had that effect), but there was a "pharmacologic activation of reward systems." In other words, the partner acted as medicine, with their face triggering the reward centers of the brain that light up from other kinds of thrills like cocaine or winning money.[318]

A similar study found that love stimulates the brain's cannabinoid neurotransmitters. That groovy buzz you get from touching and connecting with your lover really is like medical marijuana.[319] This calming effect counteracts the stress hormones that damage the cardiovascular system and wear out the body, so a good relationship is good medicine.[320] If you are feeling stressed, take two doses of love and call your therapist in the morning.

Creating Passion and Compassion

What can be done if the feelings aren't flowing? One bummed-out partner posted this question online:

> So . . . my boyfriend and I have lost the "spark" for each other. I know we really love each other so I was wondering if this is normal. We're really close . . . even though only a year has passed. I guess we moved pretty fast. . . . If this isn't normal, then I feel like I should find another boyfriend since I would be denying myself a love life filled with passion. . . . I just wonder if it's normal to lose a spark or if it's possible to keep a spark going forever?[321]

Fear not, *Yahoo!* chat room person! It is normal for relationships to experience ebbs and surges in their "sparks." Flames that burn hot will eventually cool down to coals. However, chilly feelings can be warmed back up. Couples can touch, laugh, or do fun things together, or they can try to reignite loving feelings through conscious effort.

Psychologist Barbara Fredrickson has found that love can be rekindled. She studies the vagus nerve, a connector between the brain and heart that triggers tiny facial muscles that create eye contact and emotional expressions. Like most parts of the body, the vagus nerve can be strengthened through exercise. Fredrickson asked volunteers to practice feelings of love and kindness in a meditation. They reflected upon thoughtful phrases and wished people peace, well-being, and happiness. This reinforced vagal tone, which improved capacity to track moods and feel love.[322] Stronger vagal tone helped partners self-soothe, control their moods, have empathy, and feel love.[323] These results were so impressive that the Dali Lama took an interest in the project.

The Power of Sharing

Couples who share meaningful conversations feel more love. One study had random volunteers pair up and ask each other specific questions about meaningful thoughts and feelings that became more personal as they progressed. After a deep forty-five minute talk, the couples looked into each other's eyes for four minutes. These pairs that began as complete strangers became bonded, and one couple eventually got married.[324]

If strangers can turn up the heat through meaningful words, it should be easy for a committed couple to rekindle the flames. Ask your significant other good questions. Try to understand their hopes, concerns, and goals and show concern, which will sync up your heart rate and breathing with theirs.[325] Practice looking at your spouse's face and sending warm feelings. Their experiences are important to them, and they like sharing them. About 30 to 40 percent of spoken words are about one's own experiences, and on social media this is about 80 percent.[326] One study found that the pleasure centers of the brain warm up during self-disclosure, and that participants are often willing to forego money in order to continue to talk about themselves.[327]

Another benefit of processing is that it helps people let go of old hurts. James Pennebaker found that those who wrote about a traumatic experience like a death or assault had better physical health than those that didn't. The most in-depth written efforts were associated with the fewest visits to doctors and highest levels of antibodies.[328] Another study found that when couples considering divorce talk through their difficulties with someone else (like a friend, minster, or therapist), around 80 to 90 percent of them find it helpful.[329] People are built to reflect and explain, and this is a healthy way to cope with life's challenges.

I have my students read a short story by Anton Chekov called *The Lament*. It begins on a snowy evening in Russia in 1908. Iona Potopov is a cab driver who is silently hunched next to his horse. He is roused from his thoughts by a man requesting a ride. He slowly shakes off the snow and they set off. Iona mentions that his son Barin died during the week. The rider gives minimal response and mostly disregards Iona's comment. Later, he picks up some other young men, and again mentions the death of his son. The riders are loud and cruel, and they mock him. The evening continues as strangers absorbed in their own lives pass by, unconcerned about the cabdriver's overwhelming grief. At the end of the day, he stands with his pony and is overcome. "The little horse munches, listens and breathes over its master's hand. . . . Iona's feelings are too much for him and he tells the little horse the whole story." Sometimes people need to talk, and it is nice to have a partner that will quietly listen.

Passion beyond Words

Some people find intense conversations to be as comfortable as a bed of nails. As important as deep discussions are, they do not have to dominate a relationship. Passion can be generated in nonverbal ways, such as touch, generosity, and fun. Gary Chapman's concept of love languages has found many enthusiasts, because it speaks to the idea that there are many ways of giving and receiving love.[330] Some partners want to talk and listen, while others prefer gifts or cuddling. J. R. R. and Edith Tolkien loved fussing over each other's health and would take great care in wrapping and choosing birthday presents. In their later years, they talked together endlessly about their children and grandchildren.[331] Some couples love going to concerts and surprising each other with tickets for shows or travel. Others stay home reading in front of the fire. Getting this balance right and honoring each other's style is an important part of staying close.

Robert Epstein is an expert on the psychology of love, and he recommends a few interesting nonverbal tactics to awaken passion. First, he suggests that couples have sustained gentle eye contact. Not creepy staring, but kind, face-to-face connection. He also advises a warm embrace, where both try to synchronize their breathing. Another option is the monkey task, where spouses stand face-to-face and imitate each other's movements, slowly getting closer every few seconds.[332] These activities are designed to jumpstart the chemical and emotional signals that draw people together.

Love and Vulnerability

Passion is exciting, but scary, because love requires vulnerability. Partners literally put themselves into each other's hands and trust they will be handled with care. Having intimate conversations, sharing secrets, and being in close proximity are all exciting, but risky. Opening up to another leaves one exposed.

One graduate student, Kay, wrestled with this. "I came here to school to get away from a really unhealthy relationship," she said. "I needed time to clear my head and heal, but now I have a problem." I asked her what it was. "I have met a really wonderful guy who is interested in me. He is kind, funny, gentle, and well-grounded in his goals. He comes from a great family and isn't putting any pressure on me when I asked for time to think." So, what's the problem?

Kay was afraid of being hurt again, which was understandable. However, she also had found something wonderful and didn't want to pass it by. Joseph Campbell said, "The cave you fear to enter holds the treasure that you seek." Kay didn't want to barge into this cave just because she was fleeing a storm, but she knew that a leap of faith can move things forward. She was brave and transparent with her new beau, even though it was hard to tell him her fears. "What if he thinks I'm an idiot," she wondered, "because I stayed with my last boyfriend for so long? What if he leaves?" As she honestly revealed her feelings and uncertainties, she was reassured by her new friend's reaction. She was vulnerable as she moved forward, but she ended up with the treasure.

As relationships mature and become safer, the risks go down. People become more secure with each other, which actually frees them up to experience more fun and passion. Sue Johnson uses the analogy of a zip line. People attach themselves to a high rope and race down at insane speeds, screaming with delight. However, if the zip line became unstable or started to break, the screaming would take on a very different tone. It is only *because* of the secure connection that the rider can let go and enjoy the thrill. In a relationship, you trust the other person to not let go.[333]

True Love

As passion buds and flowers, it changes people. On the TV show *Psych*, Shawn Spencer is a consultant to the Santa Barbara police department, where Juliet O'Hara is a junior detective. Over the years, they swing between romantic interest and frustration with each other. Eventually their feelings of attraction become too powerful to ignore. Shawn does his best to grapple with this, and he tries to explain his feelings to her:

> Shawn: "I have a motorcycle."
> Juliet: "Yes . . . you do."
> Shawn: "Yes, I do. And you know what: it is the purest form of freedom that I have ever experienced. You zip through traffic; you park anywhere. You never have to take anyone to the airport. You certainly don't have to help anyone move. Easily the best purchase I have ever made in my life, and I have never regretted it. Not for one second."
> Juliet: "Great, you love your motorcycle. Is there a point to this?"
> Shawn: "Yeah. There's a point. My point is . . . since I met you, I've been thinking about getting a car."

True love involves giving up a part of yourself to become something bigger. This sacrifice can be hard, which is why honest love must include commitment and willingness to work through challenges. J. R. R. Tolkien said, "Nearly all marriages, even happy ones, are mistakes in the sense that almost certainly . . . both partners might [have] found more suitable mates. But the real soul mate is the one you are actually married to." Despite Tolkien's passionate nature, he understood that relationships take work. "No man, however truly he loved his betrothed and bride as a young man, has lived faithful to her as a wife in mind and body without deliberate conscious exercise of the will, without self-denial."[334] Authentic love isn't just attained by a flash of ecstatic desire. It takes effort and trust in the relationship and each other.

Let's return to Dinah and James, who bonded over his gnarly music. After a tumultuous period of dating that included excitement as well as agony, they were sinking fast. "She gets depressed and clams up," he said. "And I hate that, so I push her to talk, and it makes it worse." Dinah's quiet style would set him off, which would cause her to lash out and run away. Dinah loved James fiercely but was exhausted. "In my past relationships I would think I could do better, or want my freedom, but it has been different with James," she said. "I don't even think of other guys. He is everything to me, but when we fight it turns vicious."

Their passion and friction sometimes produced fire, where they would be having fun but then someone would get offended, then names would be hurled and feelings torched. After the ashes cooled, they would apologize but eventually fall back into the same routine. After one particularly nasty fight, they broke up, and this broke their hearts. James couldn't sleep and would lie on his floor for hours staring at the ceiling, rehashing his mistakes and agonizing over his possessive tendencies. Dinah was miserable as well, and she missed their crazy fun and James's ebullience and energy.

The intense quality of their connection was their blessing and their challenge. Their passion *for* each other became passion *against* each other. James and Dinah hated being apart but weren't sure how to be together. They were desperate, though, so they committed to one last try. Through raw self-examination, they learned a lot and became more honest with themselves and each other. They matured, acted nicer, and learned to slow down and listen. Their initial efforts took hold, and the love returned, only with a new sense of safety. They eventually got married.

It wasn't all happily ever after, though. They started sturdy but occasionally slipped back into petty spats. However, they would quickly try to correct things, talking into the night, persisting until they made up with passionate love and a resolve to try again.

One night, they were wiped out from another misunderstanding. Out of the silence, James asked, "Do you trust me?" Dinah was taken aback, but responded, "Of course."

"No," he said. "I am not talking about cheating on you or lying. I am asking whether you can be completely honest with me about your pain. Can you share your darkest times or your deepest fears, even if I am causing them?"

She considered, and asked, "Can I trust you to hold me, including being gentle with my feelings? Can you honor them, and not cast them aside?" James looked at her intently, as if seeing her for the first time, and she continued, "Can we be real with each other? If I share those ugly moments, those flaws that I already beat myself up over, can you still love me? Can I come out of my cocoon and know that you won't scare me back into it?"

James pledged his best. "I want to be with you. I want us to be emotionally naked and real and safe."

Dinah was touched and began to weep. "I know we can. I love you."

James became emotional as well and couldn't talk for several minutes. He held her close and thought about all they had been through. "I am so lucky to be married to you. Really. I don't ever want to be apart." They didn't know what the future held, but they wanted to go there together. They were feeling true love.

Main Points

- When people connect emotionally, they are transformed by each other—two partners become one.
- Connections mean that breakups are literal. When people are alone or separated it is a less natural state than being in a relationship.
- There are many pathways of connection—we can bond visually, tactilely, chemically, and biologically.
- Faces are like beacons, transmitting signals to others and to our partners.
- Voices convey expectations that can either build up or tear down a partner.
- Partners are intuitively good at navigating signals that create relationships. Those who are not good at this skill will have a harder time understanding others.
- Passion works best when paired with compassion, which involves sharing feelings.
- Compassion has a healing effect and can be generated through effort.
- When love isn't flowing, couples can talk about meaningful things, touch, laugh, or do fun things together.
- True love requires being open and vulnerable, but this requires safety and trust. As couples grow closer these risks go down, and couples are free to let go and experience more excitement.
- True love involves giving up a part of yourself in order to become something bigger. It requires honest sharing and commitment.

Discussion Questions

- In what ways have you experienced the transforming power of connection?
- When do you feel most "at one" with a partner?
- What nonverbal signals do you give and receive in your relationship?
- Can you describe a time when you experienced compassion—either giving or receiving? What effect did that have on your relationship?
- When was the last time you shared a meaningful conversation with your spouse?
- How do you connect with each other in nonverbal ways?
- When do you feel most open with each other? When do you feel honest and safe?
- What are the greatest strengths of your relationship?

Afterword *and* Acknowledgments

Relationships are tricky, and the principles in this book will apply in different ways for each couple. Science can help us learn about love, but it is sometimes a blunt or biased tool. Couples who attempt to apply these lessons will have the most success when they are patient and kind with themselves and with each other. The most rigorous science cannot create a loving heart, and relationship knowledge always works best through relationship virtues.

I am responsible for these ideas and stories, but I got by with a little help from my friends. For starters, there would be no book without my best friend and wife, April. She has an amazing capacity for love and wisdom and demonstrates this in all her relationships. She was also the sharpest editor I have ever worked with and lovingly refused to accept murky or mediocre prose. She is my inspiration, lover, and provider of material by being who she is.

Others who provided invaluable feedback (including for painful early drafts) include siblings Kim Wells, Jeremy Whiting, and Katelin Morton who have always told me what they thought without reservation, as well as friends and colleagues Sean Davis, Steve Fife, Kay Bradford, Megan Oka, Jaclyn Cravens-Pickens, Jeremy Boden, and Lisa Merchant. I owe these readers much for their insightful words and suggestions.

My colleagues and administrators at Texas Tech University also provided key support, including a sabbatical, without which I would still be on chapter two. I have been fortunate to work with many diligent graduate students over the years who have helped gather resources and pick research gems out of heaps of material. Rachael Dansby in particular provided heroic service with her reference formatting skills and has forever changed my use of the word "that."

The Cedar Fort team provided important professional guidance and help along the way, and particular thanks goes to Lynnae Allred, who had faith in the book and opened the door to make it possible.

Many others deserve thanks for indirect or direct support, including my children, friends, colleagues, students, mentors, and community, all of whom demonstrate kindness and life lessons. I watch and learn from all of these associates. I also appreciate the brave individuals and couples who have opened their hearts and worlds to me and engaged in the life-changing work of creating loving relationships.

Sources

Introduction

1. Pamela Owen, "My Big Wedding Day Was Ruined by a Bomb Scare — Phoned In by My Bumbling FIANCÉ," *Mirror*, December 1, 2013.

Chapter 1

2. Bella M. DePaulo and Deborah A. Kashy, "Everyday Lies in Close and Casual Relationships," *Journal of Personality and Social Psychology* 74, no. 1 (1998): 63.

3. Robert S. Feldman, James A. Forrest, and Benjamin R. Happ, "Self-Presentation and Verbal Deception: Do Self-Presenters Lie More?" *Basic and Applied Social Psychology* 24, no. 2 (2002): 163–70. Feldman reviews this and many other related phenomena in his book *The Liar in Your Life*.

4. Kim B. Serota, Timothy R. Levine, and Franklin J. Boster, "The Prevalence of Lying in America: Three Studies of Self-Reported Lies," *Human Communication Research* 36, no. 1 (2010): 2–25.

5. Bella M. DePaulo and Deborah A. Kashy, "Everyday Lies in Close and Casual Relationships," *Journal of Personality and Social Psychology* 74, no. 1 (1998): 63–79.

6. Tim Cole, "Lying to the One You Love: The Use of Deception in Romantic Relationships," *Journal of Social and Personal Relationships* 18, no. 1 (2001): 107–29.

7. Bella M. DePaulo, Deborah A. Kashy, Susan E. Kirkendol, Melissa M. Wyer, and Jennifer A. Epstein, "Lying in Everyday Life," *Journal of Personality and Social Psychology* 70, no. 5 (1996): 979.

8. Robert S. Feldman, James A. Forrest, and Benjamin R. Happ, "Self-Presentation and Verbal Deception: Do Self-Presenters Lie More?" *Basic and Applied Social Psychology* 24, no. 2 (2002): 163–70.

9. Ty Tashiro, *The Science of Happily Ever After: What Really Matters in the Quest for Enduring Love* (Ontario, Canada: Harlequin, 2014).

10. This was a British poll taken in 2013. See Andrew Hough, "Why Women Constantly Lie About Life on Facebook," *The Telegraph*, March 12, 2013. A follow up article argued with some nonscientific data that men are just as guilty. See Emma Barnett, "It's Not Just Women: Everyone Lies on Facebook," *The Telegraph*, March 13, 2013.

11. Stephanie Rosenbloom, "Love, Lies and What They Learned," *The New York Times*, November 12, 2011. See also Katherine M. Hertlein and Markie L. C. Blumer, *The Couple and Family Technology Framework: Intimate Relationships in a Digital Age* (New York: Routledge, 2013).

12. Most of these findings are reported in Günter J. Hitsch, Ali Hortaçsu, and Dan Ariely, "What Makes You Click? An Empirical Analysis of Online Dating," *Society for Economic Dynamics 2005 Meeting Papers*, vol. 207, 2005. Another illuminating study about online deception in dating sites was from Christian Rudder, "The Big Lies People Tell In Online Dating," *OkTrends*, July 7, 2010, https://blog.okcupid.com/index.php/the-biggest-lies-in-online-dating/.

13. Robert Feldman, *The Liar in Your Life: The Way to Truthful Relationships* (New York: Twelve, 2009).

14. Shaul Shalvi, Ori Eldar, and Yoella Bereby-Meyer, "Honesty Requires Time (And Lack of Justifications)," *Psychological Science* 23, no. 10 (2012): 1264–70.

15. Amy Choate-Nielsen, "True or False? 96 Percent of Americans Admit to Lying," *Deseret News National*, March 28, 2014, http://national.deseretnews.com/article/17952/true-or-false-96-percent-of-americans-admit-to-lying.html.

16. Katlyn Elise Roggensack and Alan Sillars, "Agreement and Understanding about Honesty and Deception Rules in Romantic Relationships," *Journal of Social and Personal Relationships* 31, no. 2 (2014): 178–99.

17. Susan D. Boon and Beverly A. McLeod, "Deception in Romantic Relationships: Subjective Estimates of Success at Deceiving and Attitudes Toward Deception," *Journal of Social and Personal Relationships* 18, no. 4 (2001): 463–76.

18. John Gottman has distilled his research on couples into some handouts and lay books. One of his points on his "Marriage 101 Tips" is to edit yourself in how you speak to each other, especially when frustrated. He also discusses this in his book, *The Marriage Clinic: A Scientifically Based Marital Therapy* (New York: W. W. Norton & Company, 1999). The idea of editing yourself and exercising restraint is also discussed by Blaine J. Fowers in his book, *Beyond the Myth of Marital Happiness: How Embracing the Virtues of Loyalty, Generosity, Justice, and Courage Can Strengthen Your Relationship* (New York: Jossey-Bass, 2000), 111.

19. Mary Elizabeth Kaplar, "Lying Happily Ever After: Altruistic White Lies, Positive Illusions, and Relationship Satisfaction," *Psychology Ph.D Dissertations*, Paper 2, http://scholarworks.bgsu.edu/psychology_diss/2.

20. Bella M. DePaulo, Deborah A. Kashy, Susan E. Kirkendol, Melissa M. Wyer, and Jennifer A. Epstein, "Lying in Everyday Life," *Journal of Personality and Social Psychology* 70, no. 5 (1996): 979–95.

21. Bella M. DePaulo and Deborah A. Kashy, "Everyday Lies in Close and Casual Relationships," *Journal of Personality and Social Psychology* 74, no. 1 (1998): 63.

22. Douglas C. Derrick, Thomas O. Meservy, Jeffrey L. Jenkins, Judee K. Burgoon, and Jay F. Nunamaker, Jr., "Detecting Deceptive Chat-Based Communication Using Typing Behavior and Message Cues," *ACM Transactions on Management Information Systems (TMIS)* 4, no. 2 (2013): article 9.

23. Bella M. DePaulo et. al., "Lying in Everyday Life," *Journal of Personality and Social Psychology* 70, no. 5 (1996): 979–95;

24. Douglas C. Derrick, Thomas O. Meservy, Jeffrey L. Jenkins, Judee K. Burgoon, and Jay F. Nunamaker Jr., "Detecting Deceptive Chat-Based Communication Using Typing Behavior and Message Cues," *ACM Transactions on Management Information Systems (TMIS)* 4, no. 2 (2013): article 9.

25. Sandra Petronio, *Boundaries of Privacy* (Albany, NY: State University of New York Press, 2002).

26. Dan Ariely, *The (Honest) Truth About Dishonesty: How We Lie to Everyone—Especially Ourselves* (New York: Harper, 2012).

27. Francesca Gino, Michael I. Norton, and Dan Ariely, "The Counterfeit Self: The Deceptive Costs of Faking It," *Psychological Science* 21, no. 5 (2010): 712–20.

28. Sam Harris, *Lying* (Opelousas, Louisiana: Four Elephants Press, 2013).

Chapter 2

29. Karen Wilson, Brent A. Mattingly, Eddie M. Clark, Daniel J. Weidler, and Amanda W. Bequette, "The Gray Area: Exploring Attitudes toward Infidelity and the Development of the Perceptions of Dating Infidelity Scale," *The Journal of Social Psychology* 151, no. 1 (2011): 63–86.

30. Katherine M. Hertlein and Fred P. Piercy, "Internet Infidelity: A Critical Review of the Literature," *The Family Journal* 14, no. 4 (2006): 366–71; and Jennifer P. Schneider, "A Qualitative Study of Cybersex Participants: Gender Differences, Recovery Issues, and Implications for Therapists," *Sexual Addiction & Compulsivity: The Journal of Treatment and Prevention* 7, no. 4 (2000): 249–78.

31. "Is Facebook Killing Your Marriage?" *Facebook Cheating*, www.facebookcheating.com.

32. Jaclyn D. Cravens, Kaitlin R. Leckie, and Jason B. Whiting, "Facebook Infidelity: When Poking Becomes Problematic," *Contemporary Family Therapy* 35, no. 1 (2013): 74–90.

33. Susan D. Boon and Beverly A. McLeod, "Deception in Romantic Relationships: Subjective Estimates of Success at Deceiving and Attitudes toward Deception," *Journal of Social and Personal Relationships* 18, no. 4 (2001): 463–76.

34. Jaclyn D. Cravens and Jason B. Whiting, "Establishing Boundaries on Social Media for Couples: A Story Completion Method," (forthcoming).

35. Carlos Perez, "How Christian Couples Maintain a Relationship After an Affair: A Grounded Theory of Forgiveness and Trust" (doctoral dissertation, Texas Tech University, 2013).

36. Stephen T. Fife, Jason B. Whiting, Kay Bradford, and Sean Davis, "The Therapeutic Pyramid: A Common Factors Synthesis of Techniques, Alliance, and Way of Being," *Journal of Marital and Family Therapy* 40, no. 1 (2014): 20–33.

37. Zoë Chance, Michael I. Norton, Francesca Gino, and Dan Ariely, "Temporal View of the Costs and Benefits of Self-Deception," *Proceedings of the National Academy of Sciences* 108, supplement 3 (2011): 15655–59.

38. Bennett L. Schwartz, "Illusory Tip-of-the-Tongue States," *Memory* 6, no. 6 (1998): 623–42.

39. John M. Gottman, *The Science of Trust: Emotional Attunement for Couples* (New York: W. W. Norton & Company, 2011), 14.

40. Catherine A. Cottrell, Steven L. Neuberg, and Norman P. Li, "What Do People Desire in Others? A Sociofunctional Perspective on the Importance of Different Valued Characteristics," *Journal of Personality and Social Psychology* 92, no. 2 (2007): 208.

41. Amanda Szarzynski, Rob Porter, Jason B. Whiting, and Steven M. Harris, "Low-Income Mothers in Marriage and Relationship Education: Program Experiences and Beliefs About Marriage and Relationships," *Journal of Couple & Relationship Therapy* 11, no. 4 (2012): 322–42.

42. Sue Johnson, *Hold Me Tight: Seven Conversations for a Lifetime of Love* (New York: Little, Brown and Company, 2008).

43. John M. Gottman, *The Science of Trust: Emotional Attunement for Couples* (New York: W. W. Norton & Company, 2011), 6.

44. Hugh LaFollette and George Graham, "Honesty and Intimacy," *Journal of Social and Personal Relationships* 3, no. 1 (1986): 3–18.

45. Gila Ruth Shusterman, "Honesty in Marital Communication" (doctoral dissertation abstract, Brandeis University, 1995).

46. Dan Ariely, *The Honest Truth About Dishonesty: How We Lie to Everyone: Especially Ourselves* (New York: Harper Perrenial, 2013).

47. Jason B. Whiting, "The Role of Appraisal Distortion, Contempt, and Morality In Couple Conflict: A Grounded Theory," *Journal of Marital and Family Therapy* 34, no. 1 (2008): 44–57.

48. Brené Brown, *The Gifts of Imperfection: Let Go of Who You Think You're Supposed To Be and Embrace Who You Are* (Center City, MN: Hazelden, 2013) 9.

49. Timothy D. Wilson said, "One of the most enduring lessons of social psychology is that behavior change often precedes changes in attitude and feelings." From his book, *Strangers to Ourselves: Discovering the Adaptive Unconscious* (Cambridge, MA: Belknap Press, 2004) 212

Chapter 3

50. Jason B. Whiting, "The Role of Appraisal Distortion, Contempt, and Morality In Couple Conflict: A Grounded Theory," *Journal of Marital and Family Therapy* 34, no. 1 (2008): 44–57.

51. Carol Tavris and Elliot Aronson, *Mistakes Were Made (But Not By Me): Why We Justify Foolish Beliefs, Bad Decisions, and Hurtful Acts* (New York: Mariner Books, 2007).

52. Roy F. Baumeister, Arlene Stillwell, and Sara R. Wotman, "Victim and Perpetrator Accounts of Interpersonal Conflict: Autobiographical Narratives About Anger," *Journal of Personality and Social Psychology* 59, no. 5 (1990): 994.

53. Jason B. Whiting, Megan Oka, and Stephen T. Fife, "Appraisal distortions and Intimate Partner Violence: Gender, Power, and Interaction," *Journal of Marital and Family Therapy* 38, supplement 1 (2012): 133–49.

54. James W. Pennebaker, *The Secret Life of Pronouns: What our Words Say About Us* (New York: Bloomsbury Press, 2011).

55. Daniel T. Gilbert, Elizabeth C. Pinel, Timothy D. Wilson, Stephen J. Blumberg, and Thalia P. Wheatley, "Immune Neglect: A Source of Durability Bias in Affective Forecasting," *Journal of Personality and Social Psychology* 75, no. 3 (1998): 617.

56. See Susan M. Johnson, *Emotionally Focused Couple Therapy with Trauma Survivors: Strengthening Attachment Bonds* (New York: The Guilford Press, 2002).

57. Beatriz Lia Avila Mileham, "Online Infidelity in Internet Chat Rooms: An Ethnographic Exploration," *Computers in Human Behavior* 23, no. 1 (2007): 11–31.

58. Zoë Chance, Michael I. Norton, Francesca Gino, and Dan Ariely. "Temporal View of the Costs and Benefits of Self-Deception," *Proceedings of the National Academy of Sciences* 108, supplement 3 (2011): 15655–59.

59. Dan Ariely, *The Honest Truth About Dishonesty: How We Lie to Everyone—Especially Ourselves*, (New York: Harper Collins, 2012); Zoë Chance, Michael I. Norton, Francesca Gino, and Dan Ariely. "Temporal View of the Costs and Benefits of Self-Deception," *Proceedings of the National Academy of Sciences* 108, supplement 3 (2011): 15655–59.

60. Katia Vergetti Bloch, Carlos Henrique Klein, Nelson Albuquerque de Souza e Silve, Armando da Rocha Nogueira, and Lucia Helena Alvares Salis, "Socioeconomic Aspects of Spousal Concordance for Hypertension, Obesity, and Smoking in a Community of Rio de Janeiro, Brazil," *Arquivos Brasileiros de Cardiologia* 80, no. 2 (2003): 179–86; Peter T. Katzmarzyk, Louis Perusse, D. C. Rao, and Claude Bouchard, "Spousal Resemblance and Risk of 7-Year Increases in Obesity and Central Adiposity in the Canadian Population," *Obesity Research* 7, no. 6 (1999): 545–51.

61. Faby M. Gagné and John E. Lydon, "Bias and Accuracy in Close Relationships: An Integrative Review," *Personality and Social Psychology Review* 8, no. 4 (2004): 322–38.

62. Sandra L. Murray, John G. Holmes, and Dale W. Griffin, "The Benefits of Positive Illusions: Idealization and the Construction of Satisfaction in Close Relationships," *Journal of Personality and Social Psychology* 70, no. 1 (1996): 79, doi: 10.1037/0022-3514.70.1.79.

Chapter 4

63. Steven Pinker, *The Better Angels of Our Nature: Why Violence Has Declined* (New York: Viking, 2011) 490.

64. Susan D. Boon and Beverly A. McLeod, "Deception in Romantic Relationships: Subjective Estimates of Success at Deceiving and Attitudes toward Deception," *Journal of Social and Personal Relationships* 18, no. 4 (2001): 472.

65. Jason B. Whiting and Jaclyn D. Cravens, "Escalating, Accusing, and Rationalizing: A Model of Distortion and Interaction in Couple Conflict," *Journal of Couple & Relationship Therapy* 15, no. 4 (2015): 1–26.

66. Roy F. Baumeister, Arlene Stillwell, and Sara R. Wotman, "Victim and Perpetrator Accounts of Interpersonal Conflict: Autobiographical Narratives about Anger," *Journal of Personality and Social Psychology* 59, no. 5 (1990): 994–1005.

67. Ibid., 1000.

68. Arlene M. Stillweli and Roy F. Baumeister, "The Construction of Victim and Perpetrator Memories: Accuracy and Distortion in Role-Based Accounts," *Personality and Social Psychology Bulletin* 23, no. 11 (1997): 1157–72.

69. Jill N. Kearns and Frank D. Fincham, "Victim and Perpetrator Accounts of Interpersonal Transgressions: Self-Serving or Relationship-Serving Biases?," *Personality and Social Psychology Bulletin* 31, no. 3 (2005): 321–33.

70. P. A. Fergusson and M. Ross, "Disclosure, Health and Well-Being," 1991. This is from unpublished data cited by Stillwell and Baumesiter in their review preceding their study.

71. Leonard Mlodinow, *Subliminal: How your Unconscious Mind Rules Your Behavior* (New York: Pantheon, 2012).

72. Jonathan Haidt, *The Happiness Hypothesis: Finding Modern Truth In Ancient Wisdom* (New York: Basic Books, 2006).

73. Ibid.

74. Eli J. Finkel, Erica B. Slotter, Laura B. Luchies, Gregory M. Walton, and James J. Gross, "A Brief Intervention to Promote Conflict Reappraisal Preserves Marital Quality Over Time," *Psychological Science* 24, no. 8 (2013): 1596–1601.

75. John M. Gottman, *The Science of Trust: Emotional Attunement For Couples* (New York: W. W. Norton & Company, 2011).

76. Jaclyn Cravens, Jason B. Whiting, and Rola O. Aamar, "Why I Stayed/Left: An Analysis of Voices of Intimate Partner Violence on Social Media," *Contemporary Family Therapy* 37, no. 4 (2015): 372–85.

77. Jason B. Whiting, Megan Oka, and Stephen T. Fife, "Appraisal Distortions and Intimate Partner Violence: Gender, Power, and Interaction," *Journal of Marital and Family Therapy* 38, supplement 1 (2012): 133–49.

78. Jason B. Whiting and Jaclyn D. Cravens, "Escalating, Accusing, and Rationalizing: A Model of Distortion and Interaction in Couple Conflict," *Journal of Couple & Relationship Therapy* 15, no. 4 (2015): 1–26.

Chapter 5

79. This story appeared in *The State*—a Columbia, South Carolina newspaper—on November 14, 2015. It was reprinted in the "News of the Weird" section of the *The Chicago Reader*, December 8, 2005, http://www.chicagoreader.com/chicago/news-of-the-weird /Content?oid=920742.

80. Charles Darwin, *The Expression of the Emotions in Man and Animals*, (Chicago: University of Chicago Press, 1965).

81. Jason B. Whiting, Megan Oka, and Stephen T. Fife. "Appraisal Distortions and Intimate Partner Violence: Gender, Power, and Interaction," *Journal of Marital and Family Therapy* 38, supplement 1 (2012): 133–49.

82. Ibid.

83. Ibid.

84. Renay P. Cleary Bradley and John M. Gottman, "Reducing Situational Violence in Low-Income Couples by Fostering Healthy Relationships," *Journal of Marital and Family Therapy* 38, supplement 1 (2012): 187–98.

85. Rui Fan, Jichang Zhao, Yan Chen, and Ke Xu. "Anger is More Influential than Joy: Sentiment Correlation," *Weibo PLOS One* 9, no. 10 (2014).

86. Daniel Goleman, *Social Intelligence* (New York: Bantam Books, 2006).

87. Ibid.

88. Haley Pettigrew, Jason B. Whiting, and Doug B. Smith, "Evaluation of an Intimate Partner Violence Intervention," (master's thesis, Texas Tech University, 2013).

89. Nick Haslam, Paul Bain, Lauren Douge, Max Lee, and Brock Bastian, "More Human Than You: Attributing Humanness to Self and Others," *Journal of Personality and Social Psychology* 89, no. 6 (2005): 937.

90. C. Terry Warner, *Bonds That Make Us Free: Healing Our Relationships, Coming To Ourselves* (Salt Lake City: Shadow Mountain, 2001).

91. Steven Pinker, *The Better Angels of Our Nature* (London: Penguin UK, 2011).

92. A. Gneezy and Dan Ariely, "Don't Get Mad, Get Even: On Consumers' Revenge," (manuscript, Duke University, 2010) 176.

93. Thomas Buckley, Soon Y Soo Hoo, Judith Fethney, Elizabeth Shaw, Peter S. Hanson, and Geoffrey H. Tofler, "Triggering of Acute Coronary Occlusion by Episodes of Anger," *European Heart Journal: Acute Cardiovascular Care* 24 (2015).

94. Jason B. Whiting, Timothy G. Parker, and Austin W. Houghtaling, "Explanations of a Violent Relationship: The Male Perpetrator's Perspective," *Journal of Family Violence* 29, no. 3 (2014): 277–86.

95. Daniel J. Siegel, *The Mindful Therapist: A Clinician's Guide to Mindsight and Neural Integration* (New York: W. W. Norton & Company, 2010).

96. Rick Hanson, "The Next Big Step: What's Ahead in Psychotherapy's Fascination with Brain Science?" *Psychotherapy Networker* 38, no. 1 (2014): 19.

97. Karen H. Rosen, Jennifer L. Matheson, Sandra M. Stith, Eric E. McCollum, and Lisa D. Locke, "Negotiated Time-Out: A De-Escalation Tool for Couples," *Journal of Marital and Family Therapy* 29, no. 3 (2003): 291.

98. John M. Gottman, *The Science of Trust: Emotional Attunement For Couples* (New York: W. W. Norton & Company, 2011) 112.

99. Lane Beckes, James A. Coan, and Karen Hasselmo, "Familiarity Promotes the Blurring of Self and Other in the Neural Representation of Threat," *Social Cognitive & Affective Neuroscience* 8, no. 6 (2013): 670–77.

100. Rollin McCraty, *The Energetic Heart: Bioelectromagnetic Interactions Within and Between People* (Boulder Creek, CA: HeartMath Research Center, 2003): 1. An adapted version of this paper is published as a chapter in *Clinical Applications of Bioelectromagnetic Medicine*, Paul Rosch and Marko Markov, eds., (New York: Marcel Dekker); Rollin McCraty, Mike Atkinson, and Dana Tomasino, "Impact of a Workplace Stress Reduction Program on Blood Pressure and Emotional Health in Hypertensive Employees," *The Journal of Alternative & Complementary Medicine* 9, no. 3 (2003): 355–69.

101. Sue Johnson, *Love Sense: the Revolutionary New Science of Romantic Relationships* (New York: Little, Brown and Company, 2013).

102. Sue Johnson, *Hold Me Tight: Seven Conversations for a Lifetime of Love* (New York: Little, Brown and Company, 2008): 49–50.

103. Stephen W Porges, *The Polyvagal Theory: Neurophysiological Foundations of Emotions, Attachment, Communication, and Self-Regulation (Norton Series on Interpersonal Neurobiology)* (New York: W. W. Norton & Company, 2011).

Chapter 6

104. Dana Ford, "Ariel Castro: Most Dramatic Moments from His Sentencing," *CNN*, August 2, 2013; J. Gordon Julien, "Kidnap Victim Michelle Knight: Ariel Castro Was 'Obsessed with Prostitutes,'" *TODAY*, November 5, 2013; Keith Ablow, "'I Am Not a Monster' — Inside the Mind of Ariel Castro," *Fox News*, August 1, 2013; Maggie Fox, "'Most of the Sex . . . Was Consensual': Castro's Blame-the-Victim Act All Too Familiar, Abuse Experts Say," *NBC News*, August 1, 2013; Michael Muskal, "Ariel Castro: Stages of Denial in Cleveland Sex and Torture Case," *Los Angeles Times*, August 2, 2013.

105. Virginia Goldner, "Morality and Multiplicity: Perspectives on the Treatment of Violence in Intimate Life," *Journal of Marital and Family Therapy* 25, no. 3 (1999): 325–36.

106. Phebe Cramer, *Protecting the Self: Defense Mechanisms in Action* (New York: Guilford Press, 2006), viii.

107. Daniel Goleman, *Vital Lies, Simple Truths: The Psychology of Self Deception* (New York: Simon & Schuster, 1996).

108. John M. Gottman, *The Science of Trust: Emotional Attunement for Couples* (New York: W. W. Norton & Company, 2011), 132.

109. Stephen W. Porges, *The Polyvagal Theory: Neurophysiological Foundations of Emotions, Attachment, Communication, and Self-Regulation (Norton Series on Interpersonal Neurobiology)* (New York: W. W. Norton & Company, 2011).

110. John M. Gottman, *The Science of Trust: Emotional Attunement for Couples* (New York: W. W. Norton & Company, 2011), 132.

111. Sue Johnson, *Hold Me Tight: Seven Conversations for a Lifetime of Love* (New York: Little, Brown and Company, 2008).

112. John M. Gottman, *The Science of Trust: Emotional Attunement for Couples* (New York: W. W. Norton & Company, 2011).

113. Christopher L. Heavey, Andrew Christensen, and Neil M. Malamuth, "The Longitudinal Impact of Demand and Withdrawal During Marital Conflict," *Journal of Consulting and Clinical Psychology* 63, no. 5 (1995): 797–801; Kathleen A. Eldridge, Mia Sevier, Janice Jones, David C. Atkins, and Andrew Christensen, "Demand-Withdraw Communication in Severely

Distressed, Moderately Distressed, and Nondistressed Couples: Rigidity and Polarity during Relationship and Personal Problem Discussions," *Journal of Family Psychology* 21, no. 2 (2007): 218–26.

114. Jacqui Gabb, Martina Klett-Davies, Janet Fink, and Manuela Thomae, "Enduring Love? Couple Relationships in the 21st Century," *Survey Findings Report* (Milton Keynes, United Kingdom: The Open University, 2013), 1–96.

115. Earl K. Miller and Jonathan D. Cohen, "An Integrative Theory of Prefrontal Cortex Function," *Annual Review of Neuroscience* 24, no. 1 (2001): 167–202.

116. Stephen W. Porges, *The Polyvagal Theory: Neurophysiological Foundations of Emotions, Attachment, Communication, and Self-Regulation (Norton Series on Interpersonal Neurobiology)* (New York: W. W. Norton & Company, 2011).

117. Janet Metcalfe and Walter Mischel, "A Hot/Cool-System Analysis of Delay of Gratification: Dynamics of Willpower," *Psychological Review* 106, no. 1 (1999): 3–19.

118. Jonathan Haidt and Selin Kesebir, "Morality," in Susan T. Fiske and Daniel T. Gilbert, eds., *Handbook of Social Psychology*, 5th Edition (Hoboken, NJ: Wiley, 2010).

Chapter 7

119. Matthieu Aikins, "The Surge," *Wired*, December 2013, http://www.wired.com/polio-vaccine.

120. Leonard Mlodinow, *Subliminal: How Your Unconscious Mind Rules Your Behavior* (New York: Pantheon, 2012).

121. Jacqui Gabb, Martina Klett-Davies, Janet Fink, and Manuela Thomae, "Enduring Love? Couple Relationships in the 21st Century," *Survey Findings Report* (Milton Keynes, United Kingdom: The Open University 2013) 1–96.

122. David Dunning, Kerri Johnson, Joyce Ehrlinger, and Justin Kruger, "Why People Fail To Recognize Their Own Incompetence," *Current Directions in Psychological Science* 12, no. 3 (2003): 83–87.

123. The original study on the couples' estimates was Michael Ross and Fiore Sicoly, "Egocentric Biases in Availability and Attribution," *Journal of Personality and Social Psychology* 37, no. 3 (1979): 322–36.

124. Daniel T. Gilbert, Matthew D. Lieberman, Carey K. Morewedge, and Timothy D. Wilson, "The Peculiar Longevity of Things Not So Bad," *Psychological Science* 15, no. 1 (2004): 14–19.

125. Milton Rokeach, *The Three Christs of Ypsilanti* (New York: Vintage Books, 1964).

126. Stephen King, *On Writing: A Memoir of the Craft* (New York: Scribner Books, 2000) 94.

127. Terry Trepper and Mary Jo Barrett, *Systemic Treatment of Incest: A Therapeutic Handbook* (London: Routledge, 1989).

128. Jason B. Whiting, Megan Oka, and Stephen T. Fife, "Appraisal Distortions and Intimate Partner Violence: Gender, Power, and Interaction," *Journal of Marital and Family Therapy* 38, no.s1 (2012): 133–49.

129. Albert H. Hastorf and Hadley Cantril, "They Saw A Game: A Case Study," *The Journal of Abnormal and Social Psychology* 49, no. 1 (1954): 129–34.

130. Silvia Knobloch-Westerwick and Jingbo Meng, "Looking the Other Way Selective Exposure to Attitude-Consistent and Counterattitudinal Political Information," *Communication Research* 36, no. 3 (2009): 426–48.

131. Elisha Babad and Yosi Katz, "Wishful Thinking—Against All Odds," *Journal of Applied Social Psychology* 21, no. 23 (1991): 1921–38.

132. Drew Westen, Pavel S. Blagov, Keith Harenski, Clint Kilts, and Stephan B. Hamann, "Neural Bases of Motivated Reasoning: An fMRI Study of Emotional Constraints on Partisan Political Judgment in the 2004 U.S. Presidential Election," *Journal of Cognitive Neuroscience* 18, no. 11 (2006): 1947–58.

133. Hart Blanton and Meg Gerrard, "Effect of Sexual Motivation on Men's Risk Perception for Sexually Transmitted Disease: There Must Be 50 Ways to Justify a Lover," *Health Psychology* 16, no. 4 (1997): 374–79; Ziva Kunda, "The Case For Motivated Reasoning," *Psychological Bulletin* 108, no. 3 (1990): 480–98.

134. Lars Hall, Petter Johansson, and Thomas Strandberg, "Lifting the Veil of Morality: Choice Blindness and Attitude Reversals on a Self-Transforming Survey," *PLOS One* 7, no. 9 (2012).

135. Daniel Goleman, *Vital Lies, Simple Truths: The Psychology of Self Deception* (New York: Simon & Schuster, 1996) 13.

136. Carol Tavris and Elliot Aronson, *Mistakes Were Made (But Not By Me): Why We Justify Foolish Beliefs, Bad Decisions, and Hurtful Acts* (New York: Mariner Books, 2007).

137. James Morrison, *Diagnosis Made Easier: Principles and Techniques for Mental Health Clinicians,* 2nd edition (New York: Guilford Press, 2014).

138. Virginia Goldner, "Morality and Multiplicity: Perspectives on the Treatment of Violence in Intimate Life," *Journal of Marital and Family Therapy* 25, no. 3 (1999): 325–36.

139. Christopher Peterson and Martin E. P. Seligman, *Character Strengths and Virtues: A Handbook and Classification* (New York: Oxford University Press, 2004).

140. C. Terry Warner, *Bonds That Make Us Free: Healing Our Relationships, Coming to Ourselves* (Salt Lake City: Shadow Mountain, 2001).

Chapter 8

141. Associated Press, "Sophomore's Project Makes People Think," *St. Louis Post-Dispatch,* November 2, 1997.

142. Alice M. Isen, Thomas E. Shalker, Margaret S. Clark, and Lynn Karp, "Affect, Accessibility of Material in Memory, and Behavior: A Cognitive Loop?," *Journal of Personality and Social Psychology* 36, no. 1 (1978): 1–12.

143. Carlos A. Estrada, Alice M. Isen, and Mark J. Young, "Positive Affect Facilitates Integration of Information and Decreases Anchoring in Reasoning Among Physicians," *Organizational Behavior and Human Decision Processes* 72, no. 1 (1997): 117–35; Norbert Schwarz and Fritz Strack, "Reports of Subjective Well-Being: Judgmental Processes and Their Methodological Implications," in Daniel Kahneman, Edward Diener, and Norbert Schwarz, eds., *Well-Being: The Foundations of Hedonic Psychology* 7 (New York: Russell Sage Foundation, 1999): 61–84.

144. Jennifer M. George and Arthur P. Brief, *Motivational Agendas in the Workplace: The Effects of Feelings on Focus of Attention and Work Motivation* (New Orleans: Tulane University, 1994); Mario Mikulincer, Phillip R. Shaver, Omri Gillath, and Rachel A. Nitzberg, "Attachment, Caregiving, and Altruism: Boosting Attachment Security Increases Compassion and Helping," *Journal of Personality and Social Psychology* 89, no. 5 (2005): 817.

145. Paula M. Niedenthal, Jamin B. Halberstadt, Jonathan Margolin, and Åse H. Innes-Ker, "Emotional State and the Detection of Change in Facial Expression of Emotion," *European Journal of Social Psychology* 30, no. 2 (2000): 211–22.

146. Steven R. H. Beach and Evelyn E. Sandeen, and K. Daniel O'Leary, *Depression in Marriage: A Model for Etiology and Treatment (Treatment Manuals for Practitioners)* (New York: Guilford Press, 1990).

147. Megan Oka, Jason B. Whiting, and Alan Reifman, "Observational Research of Negative Communication and Self-Reported Relationship Satisfaction," *The American Journal of Family Therapy* 43, no. 4 (2015): 378–91.

148. Bianca P. Acevedo, Arthur Aron, Helen E. Fisher, and Lucy L. Brown, "Neural Correlates of Marital Satisfaction and Well-Being: Reward, Empathy, and Affect," *Clinical Neuropsychiatry* 9, no. 1 (2012): 20–31.

149. Joseph P. Forgas and Rebekah East, "On Being Happy and Gullible: Mood Effects on Skepticism and the Detection of Deception," *Journal of Experimental Social Psychology* 44, no. 5 (2008): 1362–67.

150. Brad J. Bushman, C. Nathan DeWall, Richard S. Pond, and Michael D. Hanus, "Low Glucose Relates to Greater Aggression in Married Couples," *Proceedings of the National Academy of Sciences* 111, no. 17 (2014): 6254–57.

151. Shai Danziger, Jonathan Levav, and Liora Avnaim-Pesso, "Extraneous Factors in Judicial Decisions," *Proceedings of the National Academy of Sciences* 108, no. 17 (2011): 6889–92.

152. Emer J. Masicampo and Roy F. Baumeister, "Toward a Physiology of Dual-Process Reasoning and Judgment: Lemonade, Willpower, and Expensive Rule-Based Analysis," *Psychological Science* 19, no. 3 (2008): 255–60.

153. "'Hangry' People Get More Aggressive against Their Spouses," *English.news.cn*, April 15, 2014, http://news.xinhuanet.com/english/sci/2014-04/15/c_133261821.htm.

154. Amy F. T. Arnsten, "The Biology of Being Frazzled," *Science* 280, no. 5370 (1998): 1711–12.

155. Martin S. Hagger, Chantelle Wood, Chris Stiff, and Nikos L. D. Chatzisarantis, "Ego Depletion and the Strength Model of Self-Control: A Meta-Analysis," *Psychological Bulletin* 136, no. 4 (2010): 495–525.

156. Baba Shiv and Alexander Fedorikhin, "Heart and Mind In Conflict: The Interplay of Affect and Cognition in Consumer Decision Making," *Journal of Consumer Research* 26, no. 3 (1999): 278–92.

157. Mark Muraven, Dianne M. Tice, and Roy F. Baumeister, "Self-Control as a Limited Resource: Regulatory Depletion Patterns," *Journal of Personality and Social Psychology* 74, no. 3 (1998): 774–89.

158. Quoted in Sue Johnson, *Hold Me Tight: Seven Conversations for a Lifetime of Love* (New York: Little, Brown and Company, 2008), 91.

159. Margaret Wolan Sullivan and Michael Lewis, "Emotional Expressions of Young Infants and Children: A Practitioner's Primer," *Infants & Young Children* 16, no. 2 (2003): 120–42.

160. Mariana Vaillant-Molina, Lorraine E. Bahrick, and Ross Flom, "Young Infants Match Facial and Vocal Emotional Expressions of Other Infants," *Infancy* 18, no. s1 (2013): E97–E111.

161. Theodore F. Robles and Janice K. Kiecolt-Glaser, "The Physiology of Marriage: Pathways to Health," *Physiology & Behavior* 79, no. 3 (2003): 409–16; Theodore F. Robles, Richard B. Slatcher, Joseph M. Trombello, and Meghan M. McGinn, "Marital Quality and Health: A Meta-Analytic Review," *Psychological Bulletin* 140, no. 1 (2014): 140; Janice K. Kiecolt-Glaser and Tamara L. Newton, "Marriage and Health: His and Hers," *Psychological Bulletin* 127, no. 4 (2001): 472–503; Holly G. Prigerson, Paul K. Maciejewski, and Robert A. Rosenheck, "The Effects of Marital Dissolution and Marital Quality on Health and Health Service Use among Women," *Medical Care* 37, no. 9 (1999): 858–73.

162. Michael Pollan, *In Defense of Food: An Eater's Manifesto* (New York: Penguin Book, 2008).

163. Iris B. Mauss, Allison S. Troy, and Monique K. LeBourgeois, "Poorer Sleep Quality Is Associated with Lower Emotion-Regulation Ability in a Laboratory Paradigm," *Cognition & Emotion* 27, no. 3 (2013): 567–76; Sharon Zhang, Eve Leung, and Bailing Yang, *The Benefits of Sleep for Your Weight and Fitness (Yike MD Health Reports Book 5)* (Amazon Digital Services, 2011).

164. Erin C. Hanlon, Esra Tasali, Rachel Leproult, Kara L. Stuhr, Elizabeth Doncheck, Harriet de Wit, Cecilia J. Hillard, and Eve Van Cauter, "Sleep Restriction Enhances the Daily Rhythm of Circulating Levels of Endocannabinoid 2-Arachidonoylglycerol," *Sleep* 39, no. 3 (2015): 653–64.

165. Andrew Weil, *Spontaneous Happiness* (New York: Little, Brown and Company, 2011).

166. John J. Ratey and Eric Hagerman, *Spark: The Revolutionary New Science of Exercise and the Brain* (New York: Little, Brown and Company, 2013).

167. Johannes Michalak, Katharina Rohde, and Nikolaus F. Troje, "How We Walk Affects What We Remember: Gait Modifications through Biofeedback Change Negative Affective Memory Bias," *Journal of Behavior Therapy and Experimental Psychiatry* 46 (2015): 121–25.

168. Andréa Deslandes, Helena Moraes, Camila Ferreira-Vorkapic, Heloisa Veiga Dias Alves, Heitor Silveira, Raphael Mouta, Fernando A. M. S. Pompeu, Evandro Silva Freire Coutinho, and Jerson Laks, "Exercise and Mental Health: Many Reasons to Move," *Neuropsychobiology* 59, no. 4 (2009): 191–98; Timothy W. Smith, "Blood, Sweat, and Tears: Exercise in the Management of Mental and Physical Health Problems," *Clinical Psychology: Science and Practice* 13, no. 2 (2006): 198–202; Georgia Stathopoulou, Mark B. Powers, Angela C. Berry, Jasper A. J. Smits, and Michael W. Otto, "Exercise Interventions for Mental Health: A Quantitative and Qualitative Review," *Clinical Psychology: Science and Practice* 13, no. 2 (2006): 179–93.

169. John M. Gottman, *The Science of Trust: Emotional Attunement for Couples* (New York: W. W. Norton & Company, 2011).

155

170. Stephen W. Porges, "The Polyvagal Theory: New Insights into Adaptive Reactions of the Autonomic Nervous System," *Cleveland Clinic Journal of Medicine* 76, supplement 2 (2009): S86–S90.

171. Bryan E. Robinson, *Chained to the Desk: A Guidebook for Workaholics, Their Partners and Children, and the Clinicians Who Treat Them* (New York: New York University Press, 1998).

172. Timothy Ferriss discusses radical boundary setting in his book, *The 4-Hour Workweek: Escape 9–5, Live Anywhere, and Join the New Rich* (New York: Crown, 2009).

173. Steven C. Hayes, Kelly G. Wilson, Elizabeth V. Gifford, Victoria M. Follette, and Kirk Strosahl, "Experiential Avoidance and Behavioral Disorders: A Functional Dimensional Approach to Diagnosis and Treatment," *Journal of Consulting and Clinical Psychology* 64, no. 6 (1996): 1152–68.

174. Diane R. Gehart and Eric E. McCollum, "Engaging Suffering: Towards a Mindful Re-Visioning of Family Therapy Practice," *Journal of Marital and Family Therapy* 33, no. 2 (2007): 214–26.

175. John M. Gottman, *The Science of Trust: Emotional Attunement For Couples* (New York: W. W. Norton & Company, 2011).

176. Kristin Neff, *Self-Compassion: The Proven Power of Being Kind to Yourself* (New York: William Morrow, 2011).

Chapter 9

177. Robert Fulghum, *True Love* (New York: HarperTorch, 1998).

178. Mary Bowerman, "Couple Married 75 Years Died in Each Other's Arms," *USA TODAY*, July 3, 2015.

179. Vern Melvin Brown, unpublished memoir.

180. Martin Büber, *The Knowledge of Man: A Philosophy of the Inter-Human*, trans. M. S. Friedman & R. G. Smith, (New York: Harper & Row, 1965), 19.

181. W. Duane Boyce, "The Ecology of the Soul: Stewardship at Home and at Work," *National Forum* 75 no. 1, (1995): 29–32.

182. Jason B. Whiting, R. Scott Nebeker, and Stephen T. Fife, "Moral Responsiveness and Discontinuity in Therapy: A Qualitative Study," *Counseling and Values* 50, no. 1 (2005): 20–37.

183. Hannah Arendt, *Eichmann in Jerusalem: A Report on the Banality of Evil* (New York: Penguin Books, 1987).

184. Maria Popova, "John Steinbeck on Falling in Love: A 1958 Letter," *The Atlantic*, January 13, 2012, http://www.theatlantic.com/entertainment/archive/2012/01/john-steinbeck-on-falling-in-love-a-1958-letter/251375/.

185. Ontario Consultants on Religious Tolerance, "The 'Golden Rule' (a.k.a Ethics of Reciprocity) Part I: Passages in Religious Texts in 14 Faiths from the Bahá'í Faith to Satanism," *ReligiousTolerance*.org, http://www.religioustolerance.org/reciproc2.htm.

186. Blaine J. Fowers, *Beyond the Myth of Marital Happiness: How Embracing the Virtues of Loyalty, Generosity, Justice, and Courage Can Strengthen Your Relationship* (New York: Jossey-Bass, 2000).

187. Todd Goodsell and Jason B. Whiting (in press), "An Aristotelian View of the Family," *Journal of Family Theory and Review* (2016).

188. Aristotle, "Metaphysics" trans. W. D. Ross, in *The Basic Works of Aristotle*, ed. R. McKeon (New York: Modern Library, 2001) 681–926.

189. Brian Jory, Debra Anderson, and Cassandra Greer, "Intimate Justice: Confronting Issues of Accountability, Respect, and Freedom in Treatment for Abuse and Violence," *Journal of Marital and Family Therapy* 23, no. 4 (1997): 399–419.

190. Paul Bloom, "The Moral Life of Babies," *The New York Times Magazine*, May 5, 2010.

191. Rena Rasch and Mark Szypko, "Perception is Reality: The Importance of Pay Fairness to Employees and Organizations," *WorldatWork Journal Q* 3 (2013): 65–74.

192. William Doherty, *Take Back Your Marriage: Sticking Together in a World That Pulls Us Apart,* 2nd ed. (New York: Guilford Press, 2013).

193. "Louis CK Everything Is Amazing And Nobody Is Happy," YouTube video, 4:13, posted by "darrentyler," October 24, 2015, https://www.youtube.com/watch?v=q8LaT5Iiwo4.

194. Allen W. Barton, Ted G. Futris, and Robert B. Nielsen, "Linking Financial Distress to Marital Quality: The Intermediary Roles of Demand/Withdraw and Spousal Gratitude Expressions," *Personal Relationships* 22, no. 3 (2015): 536–49.

195. Suzanne Pileggi Pawelski, "The Happy Couple," in *Disarming Cupid: Love Sex and Science* (New York: Scientific American, 2013).

196. Christopher Peterson and Martin E. P. Seligman, *Character Strengths and Virtues: A Handbook and Classification* (New York: Oxford University Press, 2004).

197. Martin E. P. Seligman, *Flourish: A Visionary New Understanding of Happiness and Well-being* (New York: Atria Books, 2012) 33–34.

198. Laura E. Kurtz and Sara B. Algoe, "Putting Laughter in Context: Shared Laughter as Behavioral Indicator of Relationship Well-Being," *Personal Relationships* 22, no. 4 (2015): 573–90.

199. Robert R. Provine, *Laughter: A Scientific Investigation* (New York: Penguin Books, 2001).

200. Gregory A. Bryant and C. Athena Aktipis, "The Animal Nature of Spontaneous Human Laughter," *Evolution and Human Behavior* 35, no. 4 (2014): 327–35.

201. Alice Zhau, "How Text Messages Change from Dating to Marriage," *A Dash of Data,* October 14, 2014, http://adashofdata.com/2014/10/14/how-text-messages-change-from-dating-to-marriage/.

202. Arthur Aron, Christina C. Norman, Elaine N. Aron, Colin McKenna, and Richard E. Heyman, "Couples' Shared Participation in Novel and Arousing Activities and Experienced Relationship Quality," *Journal of Personality and Social Psychology* 78, no. 2 (2000): 273–84.

203. Terri Orbuch, *5 Simple Steps to Take Your Marriage from Good to Great* (New York: Delacorte Press, 2009) 122.

204. Ronald D. Rogge, Rebecca J. Cobb, Erika Lawrence, Matthew D. Johnson, and Thomas N. Bradbury, "Is Skills Training Necessary for the Primary Prevention of Marital Distress and Dissolution? A 3-Year Experimental Study of Three Interventions," *Journal of Consulting and Clinical Psychology* 81, no. 6 (2013): 949–61.

Chapter 10

205. This is a loose English adaptation of Aristotle's phrasing in *Nicomachean Ethics,* book 10.

206. The complete post and responses are found at http://ask.metafilter.com/281786/Did-my-boyfriend-just-get-married.

207. Daniel Kahneman, *Thinking, Fast and Slow* (New York: Farrar, Straus and Giroux, 2011), 26.

208. Larry Young and Brian Alexander, *The Chemistry Between Us: Love, Sex, and the Science of Attraction* (New York: Penguin, 2012).

209. Brent Atkinson, "The Great Deception—We're Less in Control Than We Think," *Psychotherapy Networker,* (January/February 2014).

210. Doug Boyd, "All Clear: ECU Lockdown Ends with No Arrest," *ECU News Services,* November 15, 2011, http://www.ecu.edu/cs-admin/news/eculockdown.cfm#.VcolmHFVhBc.

211. Doug B. Smith, Jason B. Whiting, Anne Prouty, and Jeff Crane, "Neural Responses to Conflict Stimuli in Female Victims of Intimate Partner Violence" (unpublished manuscript).

212. John M. Gottman, *The Marriage Clinic: A Scientifically Based Marital Therapy* (New York: W. W. Norton & Company, 1999).

213. Stephen W. Porges, *The Polyvagal Theory: Neurophysiological Foundations of Emotions, Attachment, Communication, and Self-Regulation (Norton Series on Interpersonal Neurobiology)* (New York: W. W. Norton & Company, 2011).

214. Stephen W. Porges, "The Polyvagal Perspective," *Biological Psychology* 74, no. 2 (2007): 116–43.

215. Elizabeth A. Robinson and M. Gail Price, "Pleasurable Behavior in Marital Interaction: An Observational Study," *Journal of Consulting and Clinical Psychology* 48, no. 1 (1980): 117–18.

216. H. Wallace Goddard and James P. Marshall, *The Marriage Garden: Cultivating Your Relationship So It Grows and Flourishes* (San Francisco: Jossey-Bass, 2010).

217. Daniel Kahneman, *Thinking, Fast and Slow* (New York: Farrar, Straus and Giroux, 2011) 35.

218. Janine Willis and Alexander Todorov, "First Impressions Making Up Your Mind after a 100-Ms Exposure to a Face," *Psychological Science* 17, no. 7 (2006): 592–98.

219. Leonard Mlodinow, *Subliminal: How Your Unconscious Mind Rules Your Behavior* (New York: Pantheon, 2012).

220. D. McRaney, *You Are Not So Smart: Why You Have Too Many Friends on Facebook, Why Your Memory Is Mostly Fiction, and 46 Other Ways You're Deluding Yourself* (New York: Penguin, 2012).

221. Daniel Kahneman, *Thinking, Fast and Slow* (New York: Farrar, Straus and Giroux, 2011) 32–38.

222. Marianne E. Lloyd, Deanne L. Westerman, and Jeremy K. Miller, "The Fluency Heuristic in Recognition Memory: The Effect of Repetition," *Journal of Memory and Language* 48, no. 3 (2003): 603–14.

223. Leonard Mlodinow, *Subliminal: How your Unconscious Mind Rules Your Behavior* (New York: Pantheon, 2012). See chart on p. 19.

224. Brett W. Pelham, Matthew C. Mirenberg, and John T. Jones, "Why Susie Sells Seashells by the Seashore: Implicit Egotism and Major Life Decisions," *Journal of Personality and Social Psychology* 82, no. 4 (2002): 469.

225. David J. Freedman, Maximilian Riesenhuber, Tomaso Poggio, and Earl K. Miller, "Categorical Representation of Visual Stimuli in the Primate Prefrontal Cortex," *Science* 291, no. 5502 (2001): 312–16.

226. Daniel Kahneman, *Thinking, Fast and Slow* (New York: Farrar, Straus and Giroux, 2011) 32–38.

227. Benjamin Franklin "1980/1733-1758," 3, quoted in Jonathan Haidt, *The Happiness Hypothesis: Finding Modern Truth In Ancient Wisdom* (New York: Basic Books, 2006).

228. Janet M. Cromer, "After Brain Injury: The Dark Side of Personality Change Part I," *Psychology Today,* March 9, 2012.

229. Ap Dijksterhuis, Henk Aarts, and Pamela K. Smith, "The Power of the Subliminal: On Subliminal Persuasion and Other Potential Applications," in *The New Unconscious*, eds. Ran R. Hassim, James S. Uleman, and John A Bzrgh (Oxford: Oxford University Press, 2006) 82.

230. James Daly, "Helen Fisher: In the Digital World, We're All Cavemen When It Comes to Love," *Wired*, https://www.wired.com/brandlab/2015/08/helen-fisher-in-the-digital-world-were-all-cavemen-when-it-comes-to-love/.

231. Gavin de Becker, *The Gift of Fear: Survival Signals That Protect Us from Violence* (New York: Bloomsbury, 2000).

232. Daniel J. Siegel, *The Mindful Therapist: A Clinician's Guide to Mindsight and Neural Integration* (New York: W. W. Norton & Company, 2010) 7.

233. Brent Atkinson, "The Great Deception—We're Less in Control Than We Think," *Psychotherapy Networker* January/February 2014, 30.

234. Kevin N. Ochsner, Silvia A. Bunge, James J. Gross, and John D. E. Gabrieli, "Rethinking Feelings: An fMRI Study of the Cognitive Regulation of Emotion," *Journal of Cognitive Neuroscience* 14, no. 8 (2002): 1215–29.

235. Daniel Goleman and Richard Boyatzis. "Social Intelligence and the Biology of Leadership," *Harvard Business Review* 86, no. 9 (2008): 74–81.

236. Peter Carruthers, "An Architecture for Dual Reasoning," in *In Two Minds: Dual Processes and Beyond*, eds. Johnathan Evans and Keith Frankish (Cambridge: Oxford University Press, 2008).

Chapter 11

237. Anne Morrow Lindberg, *Gift from the Sea* (New York: Vintage Books, 1991).

238. Shelly Gable, Gian C. Gonzaga, and Amy Strachman, "Will You Be There for Me When Things Go Right? Supportive Responses to Positive Event Disclosures," *Journal of Personality and Social Psychology* 91, no. 5 (2006): 904.

239. John M. Gottman and Nan Silver, *What Makes Love Last? How to Build Trust and Avoid Betrayal* (New York: Simon & Schuster, 2012).

240. Suzanne Pileggi Pawelski, "The Happy Couple," in *Disarming Cupid: Love Sex and Science*, from the Editors of Scientific American (New York: Scientific American, 2013).

241. Shelly Gable, Gian C. Gonzaga, and Amy Strachman, "Will You Be There for Me When Things Go Right? Supportive Responses to Positive Event Disclosures," *Journal of Personality and Social Psychology* 91, no. 5 (2006): 904.

242. Eldar Shafir, "Choosing Versus Rejecting: Why Some Options Are Both Better and Worse than Others," *Memory & Cognition* 21, no. 4 (1993): 546–56.

243. Martin E. P. Seligman, *Flourish: A Visionary New Understanding of Happiness and Well-being* (New York: Simon & Schuster, 2011).

244. Michael Ventura, "Appointments with Yourself," *Psychotherapy Networker* (January 4, 2015), https://www.psychotherapynetworker.org/blog/details/473/appointments-with-yourself.

245. Daniel Goleman, *Focus: The Hidden Driver of Excellence* (New York: Harper Collins, 2013).

246. James A. Roberts and Meredith E. David, "My Life Has Become a Major Distraction from My Cell Phone: Partner Phubbing and Relationship Satisfaction among Romantic Partners," *Computers in Human Behavior* 54 (2016): 134–41.

247. Brandon T. McDaniel and Sarah M. Coyne, "'Technoference': The Interference of Technology in Couple Relationships and Implications for Women's Personal and Relational Well-Being," *Psychology of Popular Media Culture* 5, no. 1 (2016), 85–98.

248. John M. Gottman, *The Marriage Clinic: A Scientifically Based Marital Therapy* (New York: W. W. Norton & Company, 1999) 109.

249. Russ Harris, *ACT with Love: Stop Struggling, Reconcile Differences, and Strengthen Your Relationship with Acceptance and Commitment Therapy* (Oakland, CA: New Harbinger Publications, 2009).

250. Douglas B. Smith, Jason B. Whiting, Jeff Crane, Kaitlyn Felderhoff, and Annie Stapp, "Couple Communication Patterns and Intimate Partner Violence" (Research poster presented at the AAMFT National Conference, Austin, TX, September 2015).

251. Tali Seger-Guttmann and Hana Medler-Liraz, "The Costs of Hiding and Faking Emotions: The Case of Extraverts and Introverts," *The Journal of Psychology* 150, no. 3 (2015): 342–57.

252. Brené Brown, *The Gifts of Imperfection: Let Go of Who You Think You're Supposed to Be and Embrace Who You Are* (Center City, MN: Hazelden, 2010), 52.

253. James V. Cordova, C. J. Fleming, Melinda Ippolito Morrill, Matt Hawrilenko, Julia W. Sollenberger, Amanda G. Harp, Tatiana D. Gray, Ellen V. Darling, Jonathan M. Blair, Amy E. Meade, and Karen Wachs, "The Marriage Checkup: A Randomized Controlled Trial of Annual Relationship Health Checkups," *Journal of Consulting and Clinical Psychology* 82, no. 4 (2014): 592–604.

254. Jason B. Whiting and Jaclyn D. Cravens, "Escalating, Accusing, and Rationalizing: A Model of Distortion and Interaction in Couple Conflict," *Journal of Couple & Relationship Therapy* 15, no. 4 (2015): 251–73.

255. Michael Fulwiler, "The 6 Things That Predict Divorce," *The Gottman Relationship Blog*, October 10, 2014, https://www.gottman.com/blog/the-6-things-that-predict-divorce/.

256. For a thorough discussion about communication skills and how to implement them, see Howard J. Markman, Scott M. Stanley, and Susan L. Blumberg, *Fighting for Your Marriage* (New York: Jossey-Bass, 2001).

257. Alan Baddeley, "The Magical Number Seven: Still Magic After All These Years?" *Psychological Review* 101, no. 2 (1994): 353–56.

258. Lola B. Walters, "The Grapefruit Syndrome," *Ensign*, April 1993, 13.

259. Ulric Neisser and Nicole Harsch, "Phantom Flashbulbs: False Recollections of Hearing the News about Challenger," in *Affect and Accuracy in Recall: Studies of 'Flashbulb' Memories*, eds. Eugene Winograd and Ulric Neisser (New York: Cambridge University Press, 1992) 9–31.

260. Oliver Sacks, *Hallucinations*, cited in Maria Popova, "Visionary Neurologist Oliver Sacks on What Hallucinations Reveal about How the Mind Works, *Brain Pickings*, https://www.brainpick ings.org/2014/07/09/oliver-sacks-hallucinations-ted/.

261. Oliver Sacks, "Speak, Memory," *The New York Review of Books*, February 21, 2013, http://www.nybooks.com/articles/2013/02/21/speak-memory/.

262. Leonard Mlodinow, *Subliminal: How your Unconscious Mind Rules Your Behavior* (New York: Pantheon, 2012).

263. Elizabeth F. Loftus and John C. Palmer, "Reconstruction of Automobile Destruction: An Example of the Interaction Between Language and Memory," *Journal of Verbal Learning and Verbal Behavior* 13, no. 5 (1974): 585–89.

264. Henry L. Roediger III, Erik T. Bergman, and Michelle L. Meade, "Repeated Reproduction from Memory," in *Bartlett, Culture and Cognition*, ed. A. Saito (London: Psychology Press, 2000), 115–34.

265. Jerry M. Burger and Rose M. Huntzinger, "Temporal Effects On Attributions for One's Own Behavior: The Role of Task Outcome," *Journal of Experimental Social Psychology* 21, no. 3 (1985): 247–61.

266. John M. Gottman, *The Science of Trust: Emotional Attunement for Couples* (New York: W. W. Norton & Company, 2011).

267. Lawrence J. Sanna and Edward C. Chang, "The Past Is Not What It Used to Be: Optimists' Use of Retroactive Pessimism to Diminish the Sting of Failure," *Journal of Research in Personality* 37, no. 5 (2003): 388–404.

268. Christopher Chabris and Daniel Simmons, *The Invisible Gorilla: How Our Intuitions Deceive Us* (New York: Harmony Books, 2011).

269. Craig A. Anderson, "Belief Perseverance," in *Encyclopedia of Social Psychology, eds.* Roy F. Baumeister and Kathleen D. Vohs (Los Angeles: Sage, 2007) 109–10.

270. Corey L. Guenther, and Mark D. Alicke, "Self-Enhancement and Belief Perseverance," *Journal of Experimental Social Psychology* 44, no. 3 (2008): 706–12.

271. Russ Harris, *ACT with Love: Stop Struggling, Reconcile Differences, and Strengthen Your Relationship with Acceptance and Commitment Therapy* (Oakland, CA: New Harbinger Publications, 2009).

272. Michael E. McCullough, Eric J. Pedersen, Benjamin A. Tabak, and Evan C. Carter, "Conciliatory Gestures Promote Forgiveness and Reduce Anger in Humans," *Proceedings of the National Academy of Sciences* 111, no. 30 (2014): 11211–16.

273. Sue Johnson, *Hold Me Tight: Seven Conversations for a Lifetime of Love* (New York: Little, Brown and Company, 2008).

Chapter 12

274. Humphrey Carpenter, *Tolkien: The Authorized Biography* (Boston: Houghton Mifflin, 1977).

275. Colin Duriez, *J. R. R. Tolkien: The Making of a Legend* (Oxford, UK: Lion, 2012).

276. "Letters," *The Letters of J. R. R. Tolkien*, eds. Humphrey Carpenter and Christopher Tolkien (London: George Allen & Unwin, 1981).

277. Alison Flood, "JRR Tolkien Advised by WH Auden to Drop Romance," *The Guardian*, February 11, 2014, https://www.theguardian.com/books/2014/feb/11/jrr-tolkien-advised-wh-auden-lord-of-the-rings.

278. Ivana Konvalinka, Dimitris Xygalatas, Joseph Bulbulia, Uffe Schjødt, Else-Marie Jegindø, Sebastian Wallot, Guy Van Orden, and Andreas Roepstorff, "Synchronized Arousal Between Performers and Related Spectators In a Fire-Walking Ritual," *Proceedings of the National Academy of Sciences of the United States of America* 108, no. 20 (2011): 8514–19.

279. Rollin McCraty, Mike Atkinson, Dana Tomasino, and Raymond Trevor Bradley, "The Coherent Heart: Heart-Brain Interactions, Psychophysiological Coherence, and the Emergence of System-Wide Order," *Integral Review* 5, no. 2 (2009): 10–115.

280. Steven P. Reidbord and Dana J. Redington, "Nonlinear Analysis of Autonomic Responses in a Therapist During Psychotherapy," *Journal of Nervous and Mental Disease* 181, no. 7 (1993): 428–35.

281. Rollin McCraty, *The Energetic Heart: Bioelectromagnetic Interactions Within and Between People* (HeartMath Research Center publication, 2003): 1-22.

282. Nataria T. Joseph, Thomas W. Kamarck, Matthew F. Muldoon, and Stephen B. Manuck, "Daily Marital Interaction Quality and Carotid Artery Intima-Medial Thickness in Healthy Middle-Aged Adults," *Psychosomatic Medicine* 76, no. 5 (2014): 347–54.

283. Ibid.

284. Paul J. Zak, *The Moral Molecule: How Trust Works* (London: Penguin, 2012).

285. Robert B. Zajonc, Pamela K. Adelmann, Sheila T. Murphy, and Paula M. Niedenthal, "Convergence in the Physical Appearance of Spouses," *Motivation and Emotion* 11, no. 4 (1987): 335–46.

286. Drake Baer, "Being Married for Decades Means That Your Bodies Become Biologically Alike," *Science of Us,* (May 26, 2016), http://nymag.com/scienceofus/2016/05/married-people -become-biologically-alike.html?mid=twitter_scienceofus.

287. Julianne Holt-Lunstad, Timothy B. Smith, Mark Baker, Tyler Harris, and David Stephenson, "Loneliness and Social Isolation as Risk Factors for Mortality: A Meta-Analytic Review," *Perspectives on Psychological Science* 10, no. 2 (2015): 227–37.

288. Naomi I. Eisenberger, Matthew D. Lieberman, and Kipling D. Williams, "Does Rejection Hurt? An fMRI Study of Social Exclusion," *Science* 302, no. 5643 (2003): 290–92.

289. Craig Eric Morris, Chris Reiber, and Emily Roman, "Quantitative Sex Differences in Response to the Dissolution of a Romantic Relationship," *Evolutionary Behavioral Sciences* 9, no. 4, (2015): 270–82.

290. Jeffrey C. Cooper, Simon Dunne, Teresa Furey, and John P. O'Doherty, "The Role of the Posterior Temporal and Medial Prefrontal Cortices in Mediating Learning from Romantic Interest and Rejection," *Cerebral Cortex* 24, no. 9 (2014): 2502–11.

291. Jerry Adler, "Smile, Frown, Grimace and Grin—Your Facial Expression Is the Next Frontier in Big Data," *Smithsonian.com* (December 2015) http://www.smithsonianmag.com/ innovation/rana-el-kaliouby-ingenuity-awards-technology-180957204/.

292. Kate Fox, "The Flirting Report: The Advanced Guide to Flirting," *Social Issues Research Centre,* 2004.

293. Ty Tashiro, *The Science of Happily Ever After: What Really Matters in the Quest for Enduring Love* (Ontario, Canada: Harlequin, 2014).

294. Ulf Dimberg and Monika Thunberg, "Rapid Facial Reactions to Emotional Facial Expressions," *Scandinavian Journal of Psychology* 39, no. 1 (1998): 39–45.

295. Jan Theeuwes and Stefan Van der Stigchel, "Faces Capture Attention: Evidence from Inhibition of Return," *Visual Cognition* 13, no. 6 (2006): 657–65.

296. Jennifer J. Heisz, Molly M. Pottruff, and David I. Shore, "Females Scan More Than Males: A Potential Mechanism for Sex Differences In Recognition Memory," *Psychological Science* 24, no. 7 (2013): 1157–63.

297. Robert Rosenthal and Lenore Jacobson, *Pygmalion in the Classroom: Teacher Expectations and Pupils' Intellectual Development* (New York: Holt, Rinehart, and Winston, 1968) 37–38.

298. Robert Rosenthal and Kermit L. Fode, "The Effect of Experimenter Bias on the Performance of the Albino Rat," *Behavioral Science* 8, no. 3 (1963): 183–89.

299. Andrew Newberg and Mark Robert Waldman, *Words Can Change Your Brain: 12 Conversation Strategies to Build Trust, Resolve Conflict, and Increase Intimacy* (New York: Penguin, 2012).

300. T. K. Logan, Robert Walker, Carol E. Jordan, and Carl G. Leukefeld, *Women and Victimization: Contributing Factors, Interventions, and Implications* (Washington, DC: American Psychological Association, 2006).

301. Jason B. Whiting, Megan Oka, and Stephen T. Fife, "Appraisal Distortions and Intimate Partner Violence: Gender, Power, and Interaction," *Journal of Marital and Family Therapy* 38, supplement 1 (2012): 133–49.

302. Joseph N. Cappella, "Controlling the Floor in Conversation," in *Multichannel Integrations of Nonverbal Behavior*, eds. Aron W. Siegman and Stanley Feldstien (Hillsdale, NJ: Erlbaum, 1985) 69–103.

303. Kate Fox, "The Flirting Report: The Advanced Guide to Flirting," *Social Issues Research Centre*, 2004.

304. Jeffrey A. Hall and Chong Xing, "The Verbal and Nonverbal Correlates of the Five Flirting Styles," *Journal of Nonverbal Behavior* 39, no. 1 (2015): 41–68.

305. Virginia Slaughter, Kana Imuta, Candida C. Peterson, and Julie D. Henry, "Meta-Analysis of Theory of Mind and Peer Popularity in the Preschool and Early School Years," *Child Development* 86, no. 4 (2015): 1159–74.

306. Oliver Sacks, *An Anthropologist On Mars: Seven Paradoxical Tales* (New York: Vintage, 1996).

307. Kamran Nazeer, *Send in the Idiots: Stories from the Other Side of Autism* (New York: Bloomsbury, 2006).

308. Marshall P. Duke and Stephen Nowicki, *Helping The Child Who Doesn't Fit In* (Atlanta: Peachtree, 1992).

309. Albert Mehrabian and Morton Wiener, "Decoding of Inconsistent Communications," *Journal of Personality and Social Psychology* 6, no. 1 (1967): 109.

310. Jared DeFife, "Reading Emotions," *Psychotherapy Networker* (March/April 2013).

311. Malcom Gladwell, *Blink: The Power of Thinking Without Thinking* (New York: Little, Brown and Company, 2005).

312. Sherlyn Jimenez, "Compassion," *The Encyclopedia of Positive Psychology*, ed. Shane Lopez, vol. 1 (Hoboken, NJ: Wiley-Blackwell, 2011).

313. Lane Beckes, James A. Coan, and Karen Hasselmo, "Familiarity Promotes the Blurring of Self and Other in the Neural Representation of Threat," *Social Cognition & Affective Neuroscience* 8, no. 6 (2013): 670–77.

314. John Walsh, "You Say Lateral Frontal Pole, I Say That Little Devil/Angel That Whispers in My Ear," *The Independent* (January 29, 2014), http://www.independent.co.uk/voices/comment/you-say-lateral-frontal-pole-i-say-that-little-devilangel-that-whispers-in-my-ear-9094043.html.

315. Steven Pinker, "The Moral Instinct," *The New York Times Magazine* (January 13, 2008), http://www.nytimes.com/2008/01/13/magazine/13Psychology-t.html.

316. Ted J. Kaptchuk, John M. Kelley, Lisa A. Conboy, Roger B. Davis, Catherine E. Kerr, Eric E. Jacobson, Irving Kirsch, Rosa N. Schyner, Bong Hyun Nam, Long T. Nguyen, Min Park, Andrea L. Rivers, Claire McManus, Efi Kokkotou, Douglas A. Drossman, Peter Goldman, and Anthony J. Lembo, "Components of Placebo Effect: Randomized Controlled Trial in Patients with Irritable Bowel Syndrome," *BMJ* 336, no. 7651 (2008): 999–1003.

317. Hui Liu and Corinne Reczek. "Cohabitation and US Adult Mortality: An Examination by Gender and Race," *Journal of Marriage and Family* 74, no. 4 (2012): 794–811.

318. Jarred Younger, Arthur Aron, Sara Parke, Neil Chatterjee, and Sean Mackey, "Viewing Pictures of a Romantic Partner Reduces Experimental Pain: Involvement of Neural Reward Systems," *PLOS One* 5, no. 10 (2010).

319. Don Wei, DaYeon Lee, Conor D. Cox, Carley A. Karsten, Olga Peñagarikano, Daniel H. Geschwind, Christine M. Gall, and Daniele Piomelli, "Endocannabinoid Signaling Mediates Oxytocin-Driven Social Reward," *Proceedings of the National Academy of Sciences* 112, no. 45 (2015): 14084–89.

320. Matthew D. Lieberman, *Social: Why Our Brains Are Wired to Connect* (Oxford, UK: Broadway Books, 2014).

321. Yahoo! Answers, retrieved from https://answers.yahoo.com/question/index?qid= 20120228145246AAepYWC .

322. Barbara Fredrickson, *Love 2.0: Finding Happiness and Health in Moments of Connection,* (New York: Plume, 2013).

323. Ibid.

324. Jennifer S. Mascaro, James K. Rilling, Lobsang Tenzin Negi, and Charles Raison, "Compassion Meditation Enhances Empathic Accuracy and Related Neural Activity," *Social Cognitive and Affective Neuroscience* (2012): 48–55.

325. Robert W. Levenson and John M. Gottman, "Physiological and Affective Predictors of Change in Relationship Satisfaction," *Journal of Personality and Social Psychology* 49, no. 1 (1985): 85–94.

326. Cited in Diana L. Tamir and Jason P. Mitchell, "Disclosing Information about the Self Is Intrinsically Rewarding," *Proceedings of the National Academy of Sciences* 109, no. 21 (2012): 8038–43.

327. Ibid.

328. James W. Pennebaker, "Writing about Emotional Experiences as a Therapeutic Process," *Psychological Science* 8, no. 3 (1997): 162–66.

329. Alan J. Hawkins, "What are they thinking? A national survey of married individuals who are thinking about divorce," *The National Divorce Decision-Making Project* (Provo, UT: Family Studies Center, Brigham Young University, 2015).

330. Gary D. Chapman, *The Five Love Languages: How to Express Heartfelt Commitment to Your Mate* (Chicago: Northfield, 2004).

331. Colin Duriez, *J. R. R. Tolkien: The Making of a Legend* (Oxford, UK: Lion, 2012).

332. Robert Epstein, "How Science Can Help You Fall In Love," *Scientific American Mind* (January/ February 2010): 26–33.

333. Sue Johnson, "The New Frontier of Sex & Intimacy," *TEDxUOttowa* (August 3, 2015), http:// tedxtalks.ted.com/video/The-New-Frontier-of-Sex-Intimac.

334. Sam Guzman, "Tolkien Speaks: The Secret to a Happy Marriage," *The Catholic Gentleman* (July 13, 2015), http://www.catholicgentleman.net/2015/07/tolkien-speaks-the -secret-to-a-happy-marriage/.

About the Author

Jason B. Whiting has spent the last twenty years studying the ups and downs of love. He has observed and interviewed hundreds of couples to understand how deception and distortion affect intimate relationships. This research has resulted in over sixty published articles and chapters, as well as awards from the *Journal of Marital and Family Therapy* and Texas Tech University.

In addition to studying the lives of couples, he enjoys teaching about relationships, supervising interns, and working with couples in a clinical practice. And as a husband and the father of six, he is swimming in family dynamics. In his free time, he reads books on a wide range of topics, plays racquetball and guitar, and folds huge piles of laundry.

SCAN to visit

0 26575 18618 5

drjasonwhiting.com